Get It Write!

Get It Write!

Creating Lifelong Writers, from Expository to Narrative

Kendall Haven

Teacher Ideas Press
Portsmouth, NH

Teacher Ideas Press
A division of Reed Elsevier Inc.
361 Hanover Street
Portsmouth, NH 03801–3912
www.teacherideaspress.com

Offices and agents throughout the world

Library of Congress Cataloging-in-Publication Data
Haven, Kendall F.
  Get it write! : creating lifelong writers, from expository to narrative / Kendall Haven.
     p. cm.
  Includes index.
  ISBN 1-59469-001-4 (alk. paper)
 1. English language—Composition and exercises—Study and teaching (Middle school)
2. English language—Composition and exercises—Study and teaching (Middle school)—
Activity programs. I. Title.
  LB1631.H294 2004
  428'.0071'2—dc22   2003027669

Editor: Suzanne Barchers
Production Coordinator: Angela Laughlin
Typesetter: Westchester Book Services
Cover design: Joni Doherty
Manufacturing: Steve Bernier

Printed in the United States of America on acid-free paper

08 07 06 05 04   VP   1 2 3 4 5

Contents

Acknowledgments

I owe great thanks to the people who helped me develop this book. *Get It Write!* is the result of many years of field development and testing with thousands of students from more than one hundred schools. To each of those schools, teachers, and students I owe a great thank you.

Fifteen schools and one group of homeschoolers field tested *Get It Write!* during the summer and early fall of 2003. For their collective thoughts, insights, and wisdom, I thank each and every one. I owe special thanks to two women: Suzanne Barchers, who shepherded and championed this project through the editorial and publishing process, and Roni Berg, the love of my life, who took the content I knew so well and made it both clear and understandable as well as visually appealing and comprehendible to readers. Finally, I owe a great mound of thanks to you, the reader, for using this material and for spreading the word: writing isn't complicated; it doesn't have to be dry and boring. Writing can be fun!

Introduction

This book will change the way your students write forever. After ten years as a research scientist, I shifted careers to become a touring storyteller and writer but brought the analytical and scientific approach I learned in science with me. I've spent two decades prying into the inner life of stories, dissecting stories, analyzing stories: What makes one story so successful and not another? What makes good stories so much more powerful than other narrative forms? What architectural elements do all successful narratives share?

I investigated the structure of stories like a detective studies a crime scene. I became a story sleuth, sifting every shred of evidence for clues that would reveal the inner workings of stories. That process ended with the discovery of the simple but revolutionary concepts presented in this book. I have now performed for twenty years as a master storyteller, and I am the author of twenty books with three hundred stories and more than one million words in print. Through those writings and performances, I have tested and verified each of my discoveries. The writing results of seventy thousand students who have been shown this system confirm that it works.

An example will help. You ask a student to create a story, and the student writes, "A boy went to the store." Is that a story? Of course not. To help this stuck student, you ask, "And *then* what happened?" "He went home."

"Yes, and *then* what?" "Then he played outside."

This story is going nowhere. Why? It was built on the wrong base, using the wrong approach and the wrong foundation. Notice the change in the way you view this story if we ask more productive questions. "*Why* did the boy go to the store?" "What was he *after* and why did he *want* it?" "Tell me about the boy. What was his name? His nickname? What do others call him? Why? Who are his friends? His enemies? What does he like to do? Dislike doing? What is he good at and bad at? What is he afraid of? Why? What is the worst thing he could run into on the way home? Why?"

Now your mind is roaring with ideas for this character and this story, isn't it? Why? Because we have shifted it from a plot-based story to a character-based story. We have begun to wield the intrigue and appeal of the approach presented in *Get It Write!*

Get It Write! contains detailed direction for, and extensive discussion about, seventy-seven carefully crafted activities and writing games designed to markedly improve the quality and consistency of *all* the narratives your students write. These activities walk students through the process of understanding, and then mastering, narrative architecture. Every activity and game in this book has been student tested. If my testers didn't think it was *fun* as well as *effective,* it isn't here. "Workbook" and "exercise" are too stuffy to describe *Get It Write!* Your students will enjoy the activities. Why? Because writing should be fun. These activities generate energy and enthusiasm. Writing should be energizing.

Get It Write! is my third book on story creation, following *Write Right!* (Teacher Ideas Press, 1999) and *Super Simple Storytelling* (Teacher Ideas Press, 2000). In this book you and your students will discover the profound importance and value of a few seemingly simple writing concepts. The first among these is: Create first; write second.

Sounds simple. But create *what* and write *what?* Also simple. Here is the complete concept:

CREATE FIRST; WRITE SECOND

- When you *create,* create the Eight Essential Elements (described below).
- When you *write,* write the details.

This one concept alone can revolutionize the way your students write. Let's see what those few powerful lines mean.

Create First; Write Second

Naturally, we humans get an idea and want to grab paper and pencil and start writing. Don't do it! First, pause to create eight specific narrative elements we'll call the Eight Essential Elements and only write them down once the story is fully formed in your mind.

The mechanical act of writing typically blocks students' creative processes. They can't create and write at the same time. Because student writers rush straight into writing, they typically make the following mistakes:

- They fail to take the necessary steps and time to make their characters interesting. Yet interesting characters, not interesting actions, are what pull readers into a story. Have students play with their characters and stories—talk about them, draw pictures of them, act like them—until they can see them in their mind as clearly as they see members of their own family.

- They fail to create specific goals and motives for their main characters. Every story is about the goal of the main character. That one bit of information tells readers where the story is going, how it will end, and the purpose and importance of every event and action.

- They fail to create enough details to allow readers to form vivid images of the story in their minds. They can't *write* details until they have *created* those details in their own internal imagery.

Must every writer plan (create) first and write second? No. Of course not. There are no mandatory rules about writing. However, creating first greatly reduces the amount of revision and editing after the first draft. Most students loathe revision and editing. If they develop the habit of pouring time and energy into the process of creating what they write, they will write a first draft that comes much closer to the story—or expository essay—they envisioned. The vast majority of students I have worked with find this a more satisfying and successful strategy.

Some professional writers do a lot of preplanning. Some don't. Those who don't love to pour their creative stream directly into words on paper. They know they will have more rewriting to do, that they must often throw out most of what they wrote in that first stream-of-consciousness burst of writing. They know that many—often dozens—of rewrites lie ahead. It is the way they have made writing work for them. However, it is not the approach that works best for most student writers.

When You Create, Create the Eight Essential Elements

In Chapter 1 of *Get It Write!,* students are introduced to eight simple, manageable, but powerful elements that define the structure of successful narratives (expository and creative), elements that will redefine the way students approach the process of creating what they write. Icons and definitions for these elements appear at right. The worksheets on the accompanying CD use the icons to identify which element is featured in each activity. In Chapter 2, students walk through the process of understanding, mastering, and

The *Get It Write!* Eight Essential Elements

 All stories are about characters. Story events happen to characters.

 Character traits are any information that makes a character seem clear, real, vivid, and interesting to readers.

 A goal is what the main character wants to *do* or *get* in this story. It's what the character is *after* in the story.

 A motive explains *why* that goal is important to the character.

 Conflicts and problems block a character from reaching a goal. Collectively they are called **obstacles**.

 Risk and danger represent the likelihood that something will go wrong and the consequences (what happens) to the main character when something goes wrong (the trouble the character gets into). Risk and danger create excitement.

 Struggles are what a character does (the action, the plot) to overcome obstacles and reach a goal.

 Details about the characters, settings, actions, and objects make a story seem real and vivid to readers.

applying these eight elements. They are characters, character traits, character goals, motives, conflicts and problems, risk and danger, struggles, and details.

Unfortunately, students usually omit several of these key elements from their writing and create the rest in the wrong order. Students typically begin their story planning by creating the action, the plot of the story. This is the greatest and most pervasive pitfall in student writing. The result is a story in which one thing happens, then another thing happens, then another, and another, and another—all seemingly with no purpose, no point.

Successful narratives are not about *what* happens. They are about the characters to whom it happens. But readers need more than just a character's identity. They need *interesting* characters. They need to know what those characters are trying to do or get in the story and why they are after those goals. They need to know what problems and conflicts stand in the character's way and how those obstacles create real risk and danger for the character. These are all elements that can and should be developed before plot.

When You Write, Write the Details

The first great secret of narrative writing is to create before writing begins. But, eventually, student writers will have to write their creation on paper.

What should they write? Which words and what information will cause readers to form the same vivid and intriguing images in their head that existed in the writer's head?

The answer is details—details about the characters, about the settings, about the action and events, and about the objects (things) that enter the story. Writers form vivid images in their own minds and write details on a page to convey those images to readers.

Student writers need to master two broad sets of writing skills—those that deal with the mechanics of writing (*how* they write) and those that deal with their narrative content (*what* they write). Mechanical skills include vocabulary (knowing the precise words to express an idea), spelling, punctuation, and grammar (the way to organize words into phrases, sentences, and paragraphs that will communicate the writer's thoughts and ideas to a reader). *Get It Write!* does not directly address the development of these skills.

Get It Write! focuses on narrative content—on *what* your students write—and arms students with vastly improved abilities to create, organize, and structure the narrative material they are going to write. It also improves their understanding and comprehension of, and appreciation for, literature they read.

Get It Write! is as applicable for expository writing as it is for creative, or story, writing. Both are forms of narrative writing. All narrative writings share common characteristics and structure. Those common traits are easiest to isolate and understand in stories. Don't be fooled into thinking that stories and expository writing must be approached differently or that their creation is driven by different principles and strategies. All narratives can be created and structured using the same simple, powerful concepts. But stories are the root structure of all narrative writing. If your students learn that architecture and master the Eight Essential Elements that make stories work, they'll master every other narrative form as well.

Far too often teachers and students struggle to memorize rubrics and rigid writing schemes. But rote schemes won't be particularly useful until your students understand narratives' core architecture—the foundation—that explains the logic of each specific rubric. The place to start is with stories, no matter what kind of writing your students want to master.

Consider this analogy: Writing is like building a house. We often focus too much on word choices, rubrics, transitions, paragraph organization, and spelling, which is like worrying about wallpaper, moldings, and decorations. They make a big difference in the final impact and success of the house, but they only have relevance after a solid foundation and structural framework are in place.

Want another analogy? Look at writing like cooking a great stew. Before you actually put a pot on the stove and begin to cook, you need to find a recipe to follow, you need to pick or buy fresh vegetables, potatoes, meat, flour, and spices. Once you have all the right ingredients lined up on the counter, *then* you start to cook. The Eight Essential Elements form the basic recipe—the creative habit—from which your students can build their individual masterpieces.

The elements I show your students and the approach I teach them are simply tools (like basic recipe ingredients) that—once learned and mastered—make it easier for students to let their individual creativity flow. I've worked with tens of thousands of students, and I have seen that the techniques and concepts I present in this book consistently helped them create narratives that more closely match what they envisioned, helped them develop themselves as writers, and helped them develop their writing talent.

Meeting Writing Standards with *Get It Write!*

State standards and writing assessments in virtually every state emphasize expository writing, not creative (story) writing. Yet *Get It Write!* devotes most of its space to story writing. Does this activity directly and efficiently support writing assessment prep and state language arts (writing) standards? The answer, of course, is yes!

Student narrative writings consistently fail to deliver the quality teachers and students hope for (and state standards mandate) for the same few reasons. No matter whether they're writing a story, a personal narrative, or an expository essay, everyone makes the same mistakes and falls into the same writing traps.

Standardized tests and writing assessments evaluate student writing on state-specific grading rubrics. The elements and scoring systems on those rubrics vary from state to state, but all focus on the same elements of student writing. Several elements measure the mechanics of writing—grammar, spelling, and punctuation. The rest score elements that deal with content—with *what* is written—voice, organization, logical flow and development, details, word choice, and so on. The skills associated with these aspects of writing are developed and vastly improved by the content and activities of *Get It Write!*

The Eight Essential Elements represent a map to creating effective expository essays and personal narratives. They form a virtual sentence-by-sentence outline for the presentation of these narrative forms. The story elements define effective alternate openings to better grab (impress) the reader. They create a dependable approach to expository writing that takes into account those elements most highly scored on most state assessment rubrics.

This book teaches your students a better, more successful way to approach and create *what* they write each time they write. *Get It Write!* material has consistently increased student's standardized test scores one grade level or more.

Get It Write! is designed to help your students easily and successfully meet state narrative-writing proficiency standards and writing assessments.

How to Use This Book

Get It Write! contains detailed directions for seventy-seven writing activities. The book integrates answers for every question into the text and presents practical discussion guides for each key concept. An accompanying CD-ROM contains a master copy of the student worksheets for each activity. Worksheets include all story segments and related questions, provide spaces for student work, but do not include any of the answers or discussion presented in the book.

Five types of information are included in each activity. They are differentiated as follows:

Directions are in normal type and describe the use and management of the activity.

Discussion paragraphs are screened and provide background information to explain key teaching points in the activity.

Story segments for use during the activity are indented, in a smaller typeface, and in italics.

Answers to student questions are also in italics and in a smaller typeface.

Sidebars reinforce key writing concepts and terms.

Print and copy the worksheets for each activity as you need them. The book contains all necessary directions and guides for administering, reviewing, and evaluating each activity.

Each activity lists the central concepts students should learn from the activity and provides a guide to the time the activity requires. The listed times should be treated as general estimates since they account for the typical amount of student discussion each question and activity generates when I conduct them. Discussions in your class with your students may vary considerably from this norm.

You have a critical role in your students' successful use of this book and in their mastery of these concepts. You don't have to be a skilled writer to teach students how to create and write effectively. You don't have to know this material ahead of time. *Get It Write!* leads and directs your every step. You will learn and master this material along with your students.

You will direct and lead class discussions, reviews, and sharing. It is important for your students to see and hear what their peers have created and written. This book contains extensive opportunities for students to share and discuss the key concepts as well as their answers and opinions. To support this discussion, a detailed explanation of each key concept is presented in each activity as well as explicit directions for the use of each activity. Even if you don't feel comfortable teaching creative and content writing, these steps and detailed explanations combined with the carefully designed activities successfully guide you in your effort to lead your students toward more effective narrative writing.

Help your students remember that what they learn in this book is not a set of writing rules, not requirements. Your students don't *have* to write a story this way any more than they *have* to write a story any other way. There are no "have to's." This book will show them truths about stories, will expose several common and usually destructive myths about writing, will show them the specific elements that fit together to make stories powerful and appealing, and will show them a very effective approach for creating and combining those elements.

Get It Write! is divided into four chapters.

Chapter 1, Eight Essential Elements, introduces the Eight Essential Elements developed and used throughout the book. Students get to see those elements in action in simple stories, to learn to recognize and identify each, and to get their feet wet with fun story activities as they wade into their job of sleuthing the true nature of stories.

Chapter 2, The Inside Story, looks individually at each of the eight *Get It Write!* elements in detail. Each separate element is closely examine to see how it is created, what it looks like, what it contributes to a story, and how it combines with other elements.

Chapter 3, Building Stories, allows students to view and assess story elements in combination and to manipulate groups of elements by working with short story segments. By evaluating and then creating story segments and whole stories, students learn to apply the knowledge they have gained in previous parts.

Chapter 4, Writing Assessment Preparation, applies the elements, concepts, and strategies learned in the first three chapters to expository writing to persuade or to inform and to personal narratives. Students learn a better approach to these important narrative pieces using the elements and concepts learned in the first three parts of this book.

Chapter 1

Eight Essential Elements

Activity 1: Is It a Story Yet?

What Students Will Learn:

The first seven activities of *Get It Write!* are designed to familiarize students with the *Get It Write!* Eight Essential Elements that shape all narratives, to make them feel comfortable with those eight elements, and to help them become used to the names, function, and look of each. Allow plenty of time to discuss students' answers after each activity and to ensure that they learn these eight elements before they begin to apply and use them.

In Activity 1, students will learn to identify the key elements that uniquely define a story and begin the process of learning the *Get It Write!* Eight Essential Elements.

Time Estimate: 15 minutes

Directions:

This exercise requires that you either read or tell a short story to your class. Included here is a story I often use because it is short, because it strongly accents the key story elements, because it is versatile and easy to mold to your personal style of story presentation, and because it works well. There is no student worksheet for this activity.

As you tell this story, you will stop periodically to ask your class if it is a story yet. Students must then defend their answers: *Why* is or *why* isn't it? The story is italicized here to separate it from the running exercise discussion. I provide the wording I use during this exercise. Feel free to use this wording or to paraphrase and improvise as you see fit.

Read this first part with a neutral, matter-of-fact tone:

El•e•ment *n*. One of the most basic, simplest, parts into which something can be divided. *Get It Write!* focuses on eight elements that are essential to your students' writing success.

> *Little Brian woke one morning after an all-night hard rain. He started the walk to school just as the rain ended. Clouds began to drift apart. Sunbeams filtered down, splashing light on the grass and sidewalk around him.*
>
> *That afternoon, Brian came home from school to find his mother waiting for him on the front porch.*

Stop here for discussion. Ask, "Is it a complete story yet, or is something critical still missing?" Make your students vote by show of hands. How many think it is? How many think it isn't? Typically, at this point, 85–90% will vote "no."

Ask them why they voted as they did. What critical bits of information are missing? What information do they still need to know?

Finally, ask the class what the story is about. Have them explain their answers. You will typically get a wide variety of answers at this point because the information defining what the story is about has not yet been included. We have locked onto a main character, Brian, but know neither his story goal nor the obstacles that keep him from reaching that goal.

Repeat or summarize the first part of the story before continuing. Read this new segment using an angry voice for the mother and an innocent but somewhat whiny voice for Brian:

> *Her fists were jammed onto her hips. Her foot angrily tapped on the wooden floorboards of the porch. Her eyes glared down the steps Brian would have to climb up if he was ever going to make it into the house for dinner that night.*
>
> *"Brian! What on earth happened to you today? The principal called!"*
>
> *"But Mooommm, I know she called. I was standing right beside her in the office when she did."*
>
> *"She was furious, Brian, and so am I. She said you were an hour and a half late for school. Why were you late?"*

Again, stop for discussion. Repeat the questions from the first break. "Is it a story yet?" Ask students why they voted as they did. Have students justify their answer. Why isn't it a story? What critical bits of information are still missing? What information do they still need to know? Ask them what important bits of information they learned during this story segment.

Ask the class what the story is about. Have them explain and justify their answers. You'll find that their answers now all revolve around the conflict and struggle the main character must face.

Finally, ask what your students still need to know in this story. They will demand two bits of information: why Brian is late and how his mother is going to punish him.

Point out to your students that both of these bits of information revolve around the story characters, their goals, motives, and conflicts. After all, characters—not plot—drive every story.

Repeat or summarize the story so far before continuing. Brian's final defense should also sound concerned and sincere:

> *"But Mooooommm. After all that rain, all the worms crawled out on the sidewalk. I was afraid the sun would dry them out and kill 'em, or that some of the mean kids would step on them and squish 'em. I had to put the worms back in the grass where they'd be safe. . . . There were a lot of worms, Mom."*

Again, stop here for discussion. Repeat the vote. You'll find that many students have shifted their vote to "yes."

Ask them what happened in that segment to change their vote. What did they hear that suddenly made it a story? The elements of this story are described in the Activity Review section.

Ask those who still vote "no" what they still need to know. Virtually all of these comments will involve wanting to know what the mother does next and whether Brian is going to be punished.

Saying that you'll add that part on, pour all the loving warmth and sweetness that you can into this last line:

> *And Brian's mother said, "Brian, I love you."*
> *That's the story of Brian.*

Discuss with your class which bits of information made them understand that story. You will find that when they understood who the main character was and what conflict he faced, they understood the story. Once they realized how that conflict would be resolved, they viewed it as a complete story.

Stories are all about characters and the trouble they get into. However, to make sense of conflict and trouble, readers need two other bits of information. Both were implied (rather than being directly stated) in Brian's story.

As we hear Brian's story, we assume that Brian wants to get out of being in trouble and that getting out of trouble is important to him. We assumed a goal and motive for the main character because none was specifically stated in the text. When no goal is stated, readers assume that what the main character wants is to resolve the conflicts he or she faces.

Every story is really about the main character's goal. The conflict between Brian and his mother is so important to listeners' understanding because it allows listeners to imply a goal for the main character—get out of trouble.

Characters (and what makes them interesting), goals (and why characters want them—their motives), and conflicts lie at the heart of every successful story.

Activity Review

This activity identifies two of the key elements readers need to understand a story: interesting characters and conflict. To think the story is complete, readers need to see how that conflict is resolved. While these two are key to understanding a story, all of the Eight Essential Elements are in every story, even a very short one:

Character and the **character traits** that make them interesting are two of the Eight Essential Elements developed in *Get It Write!*

Conflicts and problems form another of the Eight Essential Elements.

What a character is after in a story—the **goal**—and why the character wants that goal—**motive**—are two more of the Eight Essential Elements.

What the character does, how the character **struggles** to resolve conflicts and problems, is another.

The story **details**—about characters, settings, action, and objects—that make the story seem vivid and real comprise one of the elements.

Three of these elements are implied in the story of Brian, rather than being actually stated in the story's text. Goal and Motive are both implied and are discussed above.

Finally, listeners automatically understand that there is significant **risk and danger** (the last of the Eight Essential Elements) for Brian because it is his mother who's mad at him and the principal who called. The danger is greater than it would be if it were a neighbor or a stranger that was mad.

Those are the *Get It Write!* Eight Essential Elements. Beginning with Activity 2, your students learn and master each.

Activity 2: The Story Stew _____

What Students Will Learn:

Students will learn to recognize the Eight Essential Elements within the context of a provided story and will begin to learn the function and purpose of each element.

Time Estimate: 15 minutes

Directions:

This activity presents a brief discussion of, and an introduction to, the eight *Get It Write!* elements. You are encouraged to pull other passages and examples from books the class has recently read. They will help cement the meaning and nature of each element in students' minds.

Discuss the Eight Essential Elements with your students before asking them to complete the worksheet for this activity. Student worksheets include an abbreviated description of the Eight Essential Elements.

The place to start our exploration of a better way to write is by seeing the individual pieces (elements) that make simple stories work. Just as each ingredient in a story stew is an individual thing, separately grown and created and then blended together into an enticing whole, the individual elements of your students' stories can be shaped and created as individual pieces and then woven together seamlessly.

In *Get It Write!* students study those individual ingredients (called elements) to see how to use them to build consistently effective stories. With your support and reinforcement, these eight elements of *Get It Write!* will become a habit that directs how students view, approach, and create all narrative writing.

Cre•ate *vt.* To make or bring into being by applying the imagination. Successful writing requires the writer to create before turning to the mechanics of writing.

So what are these eight elements? The *Get It Write!* Eight Essential Elements are as follows (these are also summarized on the student worksheet):

1. Character	All stories are about characters. Story events happen to characters. Always start by identifying the main characters.
2. Character traits	Character traits are any information that makes a character seem clear, real, vivid, and interesting to readers. If readers think the story characters are interesting, they will like the story. An array of character traits is what writers use to make story characters interesting. These traits include the character's name, history, personality, fears, abilities, possessions, attitudes, actions, and voice among many others.
3. Goal	A goal is what the main character wants to *do* or *get* in this story. It's what the character is *after* in the story. The question to ask is: what does the main character want to—or need to—*do* or *get* in this story? The point and purpose of every story *is* the goal of the main character. Every story ends when the main character resolves this goal. Every story is *about* the goal of the main character.

4. Motive	A motive explains *why* a goal is important to a character. The more important the goal is, the more suspenseful and intriguing the story will be and the easier it will be to write.
5. Conflicts and problems	Conflicts and problems are the obstacles that block a character from reaching a goal. There must be some obstacles that block the character, or the character would already have reached the goal, and you wouldn't have a story. These obstacles are the root of every plot and every story event and action.
6. Risk and danger	Risk and danger represent the likelihood that something will go wrong and the consequences (what happens) to the main character when something goes wrong (the trouble the character gets into). Excitement does not come from *what* happens in a story (the action). It comes from the risk and danger created by the conflicts the main character must face.
7. Struggles	Struggles are what a character does (the action, the plot) to overcome obstacles and reach a goal. Characters must *struggle* in their attempts to get past obstacles and reach a goal. Readers don't want it to be easy for characters. The more they *struggle* (and suffer) through the actions your students plan, the better the story works.
8. Details	Details about the characters, settings, actions, and objects make a story seem real and vivid to readers. Once the story is created, it must be written. Create first; write second. Story details make it possible for readers to visualize a story in their minds.

In addition to defining each of these eight elements, the student worksheets include a table (reproduced here) that provides simple examples of each element. Pause to discuss these elements and allow students to offer additional examples. Critique and correct those who offer incorrect examples.

What is a . . .	Explanation	Examples
1. Character	Beings in stories that think and act on their own behalf	A person, a dog, a talking tree stump, and so on
2. Character trait	A trait, ability, fear, passion, history, relationship, or characteristic of a character that makes the character interesting to readers	A jagged scar across a cheek, six fingers on one hand, a fear of cats, the ability to high jump 8', a whiny voice, a collection of antique kites, and so on
3. Goal	What a character wants to do or get in a story	To get a million dollars, to become a star football player, to fly to the moon, to have pizza for dinner, to fly a kite, and so on
4. Motive	Why a character wants a specific goal; what makes that goal important to the character	To impress his or her classmates, to save his or her mother from becoming a slave, to feel good about her- or himself, to get revenge, and so on

What is a . . .	Explanation	Examples
5. **Conflicts and problems**	Obstacles that block a character from reaching a goal	The antagonist, a villain, a storm, prejudice, parents, and so on
6. **Risk and danger**	The bad things and the trouble a character could get into if things go wrong (worst-case scenario)	Embarrassment, being the laughing stock at school, being killed, being abandoned, and so on
7. **Struggle**	What a character does to try to get past conflicts and problems and reach a goal	Any action that is part of an attempt to reach a goal
8. **Detail**	Specific, unique information about the characters, settings, actions, and objects (things) in a story	Action verbs to describe actions, sensory details to describe objects and settings, and so on

Before students can successfully create and write each of these eight elements, they must learn to identify the eight elements and see how they function in a story and what each contributes to a story. The best way to do that is to peer inside simple stories.

Have your students read this simple, short story and answer the questions that follow. It is reproduced on the student worksheet.

> *Ten-year-old Violet Mudd went to Ike N. Write School with 637 other children. Every one of them had two legs and two eyes. They smiled at their teachers, talked with their mouths, and had hair on their heads. Violet hated being just like everyone else every day. She told her brother, "I'm going to paint my hair violet—because that's my name. That will make me different from all the other girls."*
>
> *The next day at school Violet was shocked to see nine other girls with violet hair. Oh, she was angry! Her nose twitched and itched. She felt embarrassed. She stomped and huffed. That night she told her brother, "I'm going to cover my hair in mud—because that's our name—so I will finally be different from the other girls."*
>
> *The next day at school thirteen girls and twenty-three boys wore great mountains of dried mud on their heads—just like Violet. She began to cry and almost ran home from school.*
>
> *That night she thought and thought, and then she smiled a mischievous smile. She told her brother she was going to shave her head and go to school bald. She told him, and then she shut the door to her room.*
>
> *The next morning every child in Violet's grade marched into school with a shaved head—except for Violet whose long, silky hair bounced in soft curls over her head and shoulders. "Finally," she smiled. Then she tapped her chin. "I wonder what I'll do to be different tomorrow . . ."*

That's a story. Let's see if each of the *Get It Write!* Eight Essential Elements are in even that short and simple a story. The biggest secret to learning to write well—for any kind of writing—is to learn what those eight elements are, how to use them, and how and when to create them.

It's easy! Tell your students to find each of these elements in the story of Violet and to complete their activity worksheet.

1. **Character.** Who is the story about? *The first line tells us who the main character is: Violet Mudd.*

2. **Character traits.** What information do you learn about Violet? *This is a very short story. Still, we learn several interesting things about Violet: her name, her age, the school she goes to, that she loves being different, that she is willing to try some pretty wild hairdos, that she gets mad (instead of flattered) when someone copies her, and that she's a clever girl. That's a lot to learn in such a short story.*

3. **Goal.** What is Violet after in this story? *The first line of the story tells us that she wants to be different. That is her goal in this story. (Notice that at the end of this story she resolves this goal. Stories end when the main character resolves the story goal.)*

4. **Motive.** Why does she want that? *The third line says that she hates looking like everyone else. That is her motive.*

5. **Conflicts and problems.** What keeps Violet from getting what she wants? *Two obstacles keep Violet from getting what she wants. First, everyone in her grade seems to want to look like her. Second, it appears that her brother secretly tells everyone what she is going to do with her hair.*

6. **Risk and danger.** What could happen to Violet if she doesn't get what she wants? *According to the story, Violet feels embarrassed and frustrated when other kids copy her. When she fails to make herself different, it makes her feel bad. That's not a lot of risk and danger, but it's enough to carry readers through a short story.*

7. **Struggles.** What does Violet do to try to reach her goal? *Notice that Violet doesn't get what she wants right away. She fails twice before she succeeds. Those failures and her efforts to figure out what is happening are her struggles. If she didn't have to struggle, it would be a boring story.*

8. **Details.** Can you find any details about characters, places, actions, or objects in this story? List four details you found. *There isn't much room for details in a very short story. Still, we find out a lot about Violet, about her school, about her wild hairdos, about the number of kids who copy her, and about her actions and reactions. Those details make the story seem vivid and real to readers.*

Review each answer with your class and see what your students found or omitted. These answers are not included in the student workbook. This activity is not a test. It is a chance for students to first meet, recognize, and identify the eight elements, a chance for them to begin to understand the purpose and look of each. Make sure you allow enough discussion time for every student to be clear on each answer before proceeding to other activities.

Activity Review

The *Get It Write!* Eight Essential Elements create the information readers need to become involved with a story. They define the information writers need to create to develop a successful narrative.

Those elements are numbered, and presented here, in the specific order that represents the natural progression for their creation. Even though this information may be *presented* in the story in any order, students should develop the habit of *creating* the elements in this order. Certainly, there will be some looping. New character traits will appear while the writer is working on conflicts, new motives will materialize while struggles are being defined, and so on. However, the order is important and will consistently help your students create consistently successful narratives.

Let's look at more stories and see how these Eight Essential Elements fit together, what each looks like, and what each contributes to a story. Then we can look more closely at each of the eight individual elements and see exactly how to create it. The secret to fun and successful writing is to take enough time to create these simple elements before beginning to write.

Activity 3: Story Steps

What Students Will Learn:

This demonstration activity is designed to walk students through the process of sequentially evaluating and selecting each of the elements. This activity will help them fix the nature, look, and purpose of each element in their minds.

Time Estimate: 30 minutes

Directions:

The order in which the Eight Essential Elements are created is almost as important as the identity of the elements themselves. In this activity, you and your students will walk through the process of sequentially creating the Eight Essential Elements. Use the paragraphs in this book to guide and shape your class discussion following each set of choices. Make sure that all students understand and agree with the correct choices at each step.

This activity is designed to be a group activity that you lead question by question. Pause to discuss and answer each individual question before allowing students to proceed to the next question. Stop signs appear throughout the student worksheets to 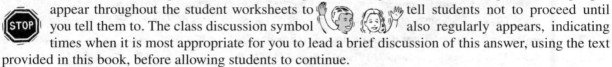 tell students not to proceed until you tell them to. The class discussion symbol also regularly appears, indicating times when it is most appropriate for you to lead a brief discussion of this answer, using the text provided in this book, before allowing students to continue.

The odd-numbered questions in this activity always ask, "What should we do next?" Don't give students more than 10 to 15 seconds to consider their answers before asking them to declare their answers and engaging them in discussion based on the paragraphs in this guide that follow each question. These questions establish the order of progression from element to element that will be used in *Get It Write!*

Even-numbered questions ask students to select substantive story information. Allow students more time (45 to 60 seconds) to consider their answer. For even-numbered questions, it is acceptable for the class to augment the provided choices with their own creative ideas for each story element. A virtually infinite number of possible correct answers exist for each element. A select few of those are included in the provided answers.

We are going to create new thinking processes and new writing habits in *Get It Write!* It is essential that students see clearly and correctly both what the Eight Essential Elements are and the order in which they are created as they begin the process of rebuilding their thinking about, and approach to, stories and other narrative writing. These discussions also give students a chance to express and explore their natural creativity and to be energized by the creative ideas of others. There are fifteen questions to walk through and talk about with your class. All appear on the student worksheet.

Create first; write second
- When you *create,* create the Eight Essential Elements.
- When you *write,* write the details.

1. How should we start? What should we do first?

    A. Decide on an exciting ending

    B. Just start writing

    C. Take a nap

    D. Create a main character

E. Write an "About the Author" page

F. Dream up some action

Ans: D

A and F are part of the story's plot line, the action. We'll plan that last, not first. Planning action first is the most common reason student stories fail.

B is tempting, but it is the other of the two great misconceptions that sabotage student writing. Create first; write second.

D is the correct answer. Once you have an initial idea to create a story, the place to start is always by identifying and creating the **main character,** *who* the story will be about (Element #1). Many may be tempted to choose action—the plot. Action alone is always boring. Excitement comes from the risk and danger conflicts create. Each of these elements depends on character. Create character first, action last, and the stories will work better and be easier to write.

2. So let's create a character. Pick one of these four choices that you think would make the best main character for a story.

A. A place in the woods where no one has ever been

B. An orange balloon

C. A tiny female spider

D. Running away from a bear

Ans: C

Let's look at the four choices. Remember to allow your students a chance to tell why they picked their answer and to debate alternative answers before you provide the following information.

A could be a character, but, really, it's a place, a setting. It will be easier on you to find a character who could do something in that place.

D is an action, not a character, and can't be *who* the story is about.

Both B and C are possible choices. However, a spider can already think, move, and act on its own accord and in its own best interest. It will be an easier character to work with than a balloon. Let's choose C, the spider, and go on.

3. What should we do next?

A. Invent an exciting ending

B. Create the book title for this story

C. Create character traits for the spider

D. Create action! action! action!

E. Just start writing

Ans: C

A is wrong, both since a story's end is defined by the main character's goal (which we haven't yet created) and since it is part of the plot (the last thing we will plan). It's too early to think about the ending.

Story titles (B) are not really part of a story. Titles are advertisements for the story. The best time to write an ad is after the product has been created. Save titles for the very last thing you create after you have finished the final draft.

D refers to plot, or action. Often writers are tempted to jump straight to the action and imagine wonderful plot events for the character to do (like run away from a bear). But that is the surest way to bore readers. Readers won't understand your story's action until they understand the elements.

E is wrong. It's way too early to write this story. Create first; write second.

C is the correct answer. Next you must develop a set of **character traits** that will make the main character interesting to readers. Since many of the story's other elements depend on these traits, writers should develop characters before they develop stories.

4. Let's pick some character traits for this female spider. Which of the following eleven items could you use as character traits for this spider?

A. A giant, mutant, radioactive hornet gets mad at her and attacks.

B. She steps on flypaper and is trapped.

C. She has only seven legs.

D. She wears dark glasses as a disguise.

E. Her favorite food is blue cornmeal mush.

F. Her parents live far away, on the other side of the spooky woods.

G. She has painted yellow racing stripes on her sides to make her look faster.

H. She is afraid of flies.

I. Her name is Cecelia Sue.

J. She loves the moon because it was the first thing she saw when she emerged from her mother's sack.

K. She likes juice and cookies.

Ans: C, D, E, G, H, I, J, K

Let's look at the choices.

A isn't about the spider. It's about another character (a hornet). This idea would do better as a conflict for the main character that creates risk and danger. Let's save it for later or for another story.

B is about the character, but it is an action, an event. It's part of *what* might happen in the story (the struggles and plot). It's not a trait of the main character.

F isn't a trait of the main character. It is about her parents. The other eight choices are all character traits. They each give us information directly about the character that could make her interesting. Let's use them all.

If you were really going to write this story, you'd want to identify dozens more character traits—we'll talk about all the kinds of character information you might create later. But, for now, let's go on with just these seven.

5. What should we do next?

   A. Create action! action! action!

   B. Create a goal for the main character

   C. Design the book cover

   D. Invent an exciting ending

   E. Just start writing

   Ans: B

A and D are part of the plot, the last thing we will create. It is still far too early to successfully create either A or D. Create plot last, not first.

E will still be wrong for another nine questions. Create first; write second.

B is the correct answer. We know *who* the story is going to be about. Next we need to know *what* this story is going to be about. We need to identify what the main character wants to do or get in this story—her **goal.** That's Element #3.

6. Here are five items. Which ones do you think make the best goal for Cecelia Sue, the spider?

   A. She is chased by a hungry lizard and eaten.

   B. She likes to swim.

   C. She wants to find her parents, who live on the other side of the spooky woods.

   D. A tarantula tries to block her from entering the spooky woods.

   E. She wants to get an eighth leg.

   F. Cecelia Sue meets a lizard-eating snake.

   Ans: C or E

Let's look at the possible choices.

A is an action. It is just something that happens to her, not something she wants to do or get. A could become an element of struggle during the story, but it can't be a goal.

B is a character trait, something that she likes. We could create a story where she wants something that has to do with swimming, but, as worded, B can't be what our spider wants or what this story is about.

D is what someone else in the story wants. This could become a conflict and problem for our spider. It certainly has plenty of danger. But D doesn't say what the main character wants to do or get. D is not a goal.

F is an action, something Cecelia Sue does. F is not a goal.

C and E are both good goals for our main character. Either would tell readers exactly what this story is about. Either would tell readers exactly what the main character is after. Yes, you could use both C and E and have Cecelia Sue want two things. But multiple goals will make the story longer and more complicated. Let's pick C. Cecelia Sue wants to find her parents. That will be her goal in this story.

7. What should we do next?

   A. Take a photo for the book cover

   B. Create problems for Cecelia Sue

   C. Create action! action! action!

   D. Create a motive to explain Cecelia Sue's goal

   E. Decide on a great opening hook

   F. Just start writing

Ans: D

B is a possible answer. Once a goal has been established, problems that block a character from that goal can be created. However, it will be far easier to create effective problems and conflicts if we wait until a motive for the goal has also been created. B is possible but not the best choice.

C is still wrong. We have three elements to create before we are ready for action. (Remember, create action last, not first.)

E, the story's opening scene, is important. But that scene is part of the plot and is best created after the plot has been laid out and the ending (resolution) has been defined. It's too early to worry about first scenes now.

F is still wrong. We won't forget our good story ideas as we continue to develop the story, and our story will be difficult to write and will never engage our readers unless all eight *Get It Write!* elements are created first.

D, motive, is the correct answer. We know *what* Cecelia Sue wants in this story. But we don't know *why* she wants that goal, why finding her parents is so important to her (and to readers). Next, we need to invent her **motive** (Element #4), why she needs to find her parents.

8. Here are six items. Which one do you think makes the best motive for Cecelia Sue's goal?

    A. She is chased by a hungry lizard and eaten.

    B. She wants to save her parents from the hungry lizard that plans to eat every spider in the spooky woods.

    C. She is hungry.

    D. She wants to be famous.

    E. She wants to get an eighth leg.

    F. She is bored.

    Ans: B

Let's look at the possible choices.

A is an action. It is something that happens. It can't be the reason she wants to find her parents. A is not a motive.

E is actually a possible goal for Cecelia Sue. We could make up a story about her search for an eighth leg. But that want, alone, does not explain why she wants to find her parents. A motive has to explain why a character wants a particular goal. A good motive makes that goal very important to the character.

B, C, D, and F are all possible reasons why she wants to find her parents. We could even use all four. However, C, D, and F don't make her goal seem very important, do they? They are all selfish motives. Saving her parents might make her famous, but it won't make readers enthusiastically support Cecelia Sue and want to read her story.

B is the best answer. The lizard will be useful later in making the story exciting, and saving her parents from being killed makes her goal seem much more important. B is the best answer for a motive. We could include D as a secondary motive. Increasing a character's motives always increases reader interest in a story.

9. What should we do next?

    A. Create problems and conflicts that block Cecelia Sue

    B. Create more motives

    C. Create action! action! action!

    D. Just start writing

    E. Plan a book signing tour

    Ans: A

Let's look at the possible answers.

Additional motives (B) are always welcome and helpful. If they come to you as you create other elements, consider their usefulness for this story. However, we have already created a strong motive and won't plan to revisit that element.

We discussed C and D before. We're not to either one yet.

A is the correct answer. We're ready to create some **problems and conflicts** (Element #5) that block Cecelia Sue from reaching her goal. These obstacles will help us later decide what events to plan in the plot line of this story.

10. Here are eight items. Which ones do you think make good obstacles for Cecelia Sue?

   A. A hungry lizard wants to eat all the spiders in the spooky woods.

   B. A friendly fly will carry a message to her parents.

   C. She gets lost.

   D. A mean tarantula won't let her enter the spooky woods.

   E. She doesn't know where her parents are.

   F. She doesn't have a map of the spooky woods.

   G. She doesn't have enough money to rent a car and drive.

   H. Cecelia Sue is afraid of the dark.

   Ans: A, D, E, F, G, and H

Let's look at the possible choices.

C is an action. It is something that happens, not a conflict or problem.

F is a problem that could lead to the action described in C.

B sounds like someone who will help Cecelia solve problems, not a problem itself.

A, D, E, F, G, and H are all problems or conflicts. Each one blocks Cecelia Sue from finding her parents. We could use them all but, if you had to pick three, which would you pick?

   Ans: A, D, and H

Students are also asked to write why they picked the three they picked. Let's look at the choices and reasons for picking them.

E, F, and G are *problems*. They keep Cecelia from her goal. But they don't create much excitement, do they?

A, D, and H are *conflicts*. They put Cecelia in conflict with another character. (For H she is in conflict with herself. She has to face her own fear.) Notice that conflicts—rather than problems—more easily make a story exciting because they make it easier to create risk and danger. Conflicts are better choices for the central obstacles we create for our stories. H is also a character trait that makes Cecelia Sue more interesting. As you develop any other part of a story, you are always also developing your main character. A, D, and H are the best answers.

11. What should we do next?

   A. Create more motives

   B. Create action! action! action!

C. Create suspense

D. Define the risk and danger for each conflict and problem

E. Just start writing

Ans: D

Let's look at the possible answers.

It never hurts to consider additional motives at any time during a story's development (answer A). However, we do not want to consider a new goal. That would change the whole story and cause us to start over in our planning. A is not the right answer.

C calls for suspense. Suspense is a powerful, easy-to-use writing tool and will be covered later. In short stories, suspense comes primarily from the goal and motive of the main character. If we effectively chose those two elements, then we laid the groundwork to make readers wonder about this story's outcome. (That's suspense.) We do not need to dwell on suspense now.

We're inching closer to B and E. But we're not there yet.

The correct answer is D. Now we need to make sure the story is going to be exciting. Pause here to discuss the word exciting, or excitement. What students I talk to desire the most is to write exciting stories. Most fail.

Does every story have to be exciting? No. But excitement is one of the most powerful ways to make readers like and keep reading your story.

What *is* excitement? Excitement is a feeling in readers that makes them need to keep reading to see what happens next. We have all felt that rush of excitement while reading or watching a good story. The feeling of excitement makes readers speed to the next sentence and to the next page. Every writer can create this feeling in readers with a little bit of planning and practice.

Writers create excitement by making sure that the problems and conflicts they choose create real **risk and danger** for the main character (Element #6).

12. Here are seven items. Which ones do you think represent the most exciting risk and danger for Cecelia Sue that can be created by our three chosen conflicts (A, D, and H in Question 10)?

    A. The spooky woods are as dark as a moonless night.

    B. The tarantula is a hundred times as big as Cecelia and is in a terrible rage because a spider cheated it at cards.

    C. With only seven legs, Cecelia Sue limps and the lizard can feel the vibrations of a limp two miles away.

    D. Cecelia Sue's mother loves to bake fly pie, and the lizard can smell fly pie from clear across the woods.

    E. The tarantula is a soldier tarantula armed with an electric bug zapper guarding the entrance to the spooky woods and won't let anyone pass who can't multiply fractions. Cecelia Sue has always been terrible at math.

    F. An owl lives in the tallest tree in the woods.

    G. The river is wide and fast.

    Ans: A, B, C, D, and E

Lets look at the possible choices.

F and G don't directly relate to the conflicts we have already chosen, so these would not be good choices.

The other five make the story more exciting, don't they? They'll make our character have to struggle harder to keep her parents from being eaten by the lizard. We make stories more exciting by making it harder for the main character to overcome the conflicts and problems we have created and by making the consequences of failure more dangerous.

Let's pick all five, A, B, C, D, and E.

Ask your students if they can now see the story starting to form in their minds. Do they sense what must happen during the story? That's good. We have created six of the eight *Get It Write!* elements and should have a sense of how this story is going to go.

13. What should we do next?

A. Create action! action! action!

B. Invent details

C. Create a plot

D. Create struggles for Cecelia Sue

E. Just start writing

Ans: D

Let's look at the possible answers.

It's too early to develop story details (B). We still don't know what's going to happen in the story—what we'll have to create details for.

A, C, and D call for the creation of plot. Finally, it is time to plan what is going to happen in this story. All three answers are correct.

However, the key word to help students understand and develop effective plot and action is **struggle** (Element #7). D is the best answer. The action and events in a plot must create opportunities for a character to struggle.

Here are some quick definitions:

Action: Anything that a character does is an action. Lifting a glass, sighing, and raising a hand are all actions.

Event: Event and scene may be used interchangeably. An event is an occurrence that could contain a great number of separate actions. Two people meeting for a chess match is an event, so is a dragon chasing someone over a cliff, and so is a person staying home to curl up on the couch with a good book.

Plot: A plot is the sequence of events that tells a story. Actions build into events that string together to create a plot.

Not every event will make sense to readers. Not all actions will excite them. To be excited, readers must understand that these actions are a character's struggling attempts to overcome obstacles (at great risk and danger) to reach an important goal. That's why we had to create the other elements first and create the action last.

14. Here are ten possible events. Which ones do you think will make good plotting events for our story?

    A. Cecelia Sue tries to say the password to the tarantula but can't get the required multiplication right on three tries.

    B. A friendly fly promises to take a message to Cecelia Sue's mother, telling her not to bake a fly pie.

    C. The lizard feels the vibrations of Cecelia Sue's limp and races hungrily toward her through the spooky woods.

    D. Cecelia Sue stops at a gas station to get a map of the spooky woods.

    E. Cecelia Sue goes for a swim in a neighbor's pool.

    F. Cecelia Sue becomes so frightened by the pitch-black dark of the spooky woods that she panics and climbs the tallest tree.

    G. A giant, mutant, radioactive hornet gets mad at her and attacks.

    H. Cecelia Sue's map leads her into a flypaper trap. All seven of her legs stick to the paper, and she is unable to move.

    I. Her dangling blue earrings catch the moonlight, giving away her location.

    J. The hungry lizard jumps out of a tree right in front of Cecelia Sue just when she is close enough to see the chimney on her parents' house.

    Ans: A, B, C, D, F, G, H, I, and J

Let's look at the possible choices.

Any of these events could happen in Cecelia Sue's story, but E doesn't seem to fit with any of the information we have created so far. It would be harder to fit that action in with the goal and obstacles we have created for our character. E should be rejected.

G is a potentially exciting action, but it doesn't relate to any of the problems and conflicts we have already picked. We could use this event in the story, but we would have to add the hornet as a conflict. We would also have to make sure readers understand why the hornet wants to attack Cecelia Sue and that the reason relates to Cecelia Sue's attempt to save her parents. Let's also reject G.

The other seven could all easily become part of this story. Let's take all eight (A, B, C, D, F, G, H, I, and J) as events that will happen in this story. We still need to order these events, fill in exactly what will happen during each event, and create one of them into a climax for the story. We also need to decide if and how Cecelia Sue will eventually find her parents and reach her goal (story resolution and ending). Those decisions are all part of plot development.

15. What should we do next?

    A. Create details

    B. Write an award acceptance speech

    C. Just start writing

    D. Invent a great opening hook

    E. Create more characters

Ans: A

Let's look at the possible answers.

D is part of the plot. As we lay out the plot line we create the scene where Cecelia Sue confronts the last and greatest obstacle that stands between her and saving her parents. (Most likely, that scene will be event J in Question 14). That scene will be our climax scene. We *do* need to identify the climax scene, but would have done it while organizing the events during the previous question.

Writers never create characters (answer E) for no reason. If, as we created goals, motives, obstacles, and struggles for Cecelia Sue, we had identified needed supporting characters, then we would have paused and developed them. That work, however, would have already been completed by this point in the story development.

A is the correct answer. Now we know the story. We know who and what it is about. We know what will make it interesting and exciting. We know what will happen. Now you are ready to write the story. To do that you must create the details about the characters, the settings, the events and actions, and the things in the story that will make it seem real and vivid to readers. Details are the eighth of the *Get It Write!* elements.

The student worksheet asks them to list five details that the class has already created for this story. Certainly, more than enough details exist in the choices that we have made so far in the development of this story. Additional details could come from additional information the class has created to augment the listed choices.

Once a student writer has created each story element, laid out the plot line from opening scene to final resolution, and can visualize each event and action in detail in their minds, *then* they are finally ready to write!

Activity Review

It is always best to create the *Get It Write!* Eight Essential Elements sequentially, in order, from one through eight. As students create information for each new step, they will find that they want to jump back and revise information they created for previous elements. That's good. Effective writers do that all the time while they create and write. Encourage students to feel free to revisit each element and add to it or revise it as new ideas jump into their mind. However, it is *not* as successful to jump ahead and invent ideas for any elements until they have worked their way sequentially up to that element.

This approach and these concepts are probably new to your students. As they become more comfortable and familiar with the Eight Essential Elements, that confusion will melt away.

It is a good writing habit to create the Eight Essential Elements in order. But the writer need not present them to the reader in that same order. Once created, the information that forms the eight elements may be written in whatever order will be most interesting, pleasing, and understandable to the writer and readers.

Activity 4: Story Stew Two

What Students Will Learn:

This is another activity to help students learn to recognize each of the Eight Essential Elements and to understand their contribution and their most common order of presentation in a story.

Time Estimate: 15 minutes

Directions:

It is important to give students a number of opportunities to experience the Eight Essential Elements and to see them in action before turning to the process of creating each individual element. In this activity, students will be given the elements one at a time and out of order. Students will have to recognize each element and decide both what they have and what they still need.

The questions following each new story piece are designed to force students to ponder what each element contributes to the story and to decide which elements need to precede and to follow the new piece for the emerging story to make sense.

> **Es·sen·tial** *adj.* Necessary, such that one cannot do without it. The eight elements we will study are essential to your writing success.

The student worksheets do not include any discussion or answers for this exercise. Both are shown here. Let students complete the entire activity. Then discuss it as a class piece by piece.

1. Let's build another story, element by element. Have students read this paragraph and answer the questions that follow.

   > *Once there was a frog, a frog named Fred—Fred du Frog—sitting on a lily pad in the mud. Three little frogs sat in a circle around him. In the lake (to Fred's left) lived a frog-eating crocodile. In the woods (to Fred's right) lived frog-eating bears. If the frogs hopped into either the lake or the woods, they would be eaten!*

   Which of the Eight Essential Elements are present in this segment? *Ans: (3) A main character is identified (Fred), risk and danger are identified (being eaten), and (potentially) problems and conflicts are identified (crocodiles and bears). "Potentially" is included because, without knowing the goal, we cannot be sure crocodiles and bears will be conflicts.*

   Which are missing? *Ans: The other five.*

2. Let's add one of the missing elements.

   > *Finally Fred said, "Weeeell, boys. I guess—somehow—I'm going to have to get across to the other side of the lake."*

   What element did we just add?
   A. Goal
   B. Conflict
   C. Details
   D. Action

   Ans: A. A Goal for the main character (get across the lake)

   What does this added element do for the story? How does it affect you, the reader? *Ans: The main character's goal defines what the story is about. It is the purpose for all the events of the story. Also notice that the goal allows the crocodile and bears to become important conflicts since it is now clear that they block Fred from reaching his goal.*

Where would you add this new information in our story segment? *Ans: It is normally best to introduce the main character before telling readers what that character's goal is. Add the goal at the end of the originally provided paragraph.*

What elements are still missing? What do you still need to know? *Ans: Now that we have a goal, we most need to know motive, why Fred needs to cross the lake. We still need to make this character interesting (character traits), we need to know what Fred does (struggles), and we need the details that will make the story vivid and real.*

3. Let's add another missing element.

> *One of the little frogs said, "Big Fred, we have nothing to eat. All the frog food is way over on the other side of the lake."*
>
> *Fred answered, "Weeeell, boys. I know it is. I've been thinkin' 'bout that."*
>
> *"But, Big Fred, if you swim across the lake to get the food, the crocodile is going to eat you. If you hop around the lake through the woods, the bears will eat you."*
>
> *Fred answered, "Weeeell, boys. I know they will. I've been thinkin' 'bout that, too."*
>
> *"But, Big Fred, if you don't get us food real soon, we're going to starve."*
>
> *Fred answered, "Weeeell, boys. I know we will. I've been thinkin' 'bout that."*

What element did we add?

A. An ending

B. Action

C. Character traits

D. Motive

Ans: D. We created a motive for the main character (to keep the frogs from starving) that explains why he wants to achieve his goal (go across the lake). But we have also revealed the way our main character talks and some of how he thinks. These are character traits, which help make the main character more interesting. Giving Fred the hiccups or having him always confuse left and right would also be interesting character traits.

What do these newly added elements do for the story? How do they affect you, the reader? *Ans: Motive explains why characters want what they want and do what they do. Without knowing motive, readers will never appreciate your character's struggles.*

Where would you add this information into our story segment? *Ans: A good place to add these lines is just in front of the main character's goal. Readers most often need this information before they can appreciate and understand that goal.*

4. Let's add more.

> *Fred du Frog was a big frog—a B-I-G frog. He spread out to cover his entire lily pad. Fred called himself Big Fred. The other frogs called him Big Fred. The birds at the lake called him Big Fred.*
>
> *Fred had a job at the lake: he sang the sun up each morning. Fred said that the sun wouldn't come up until he sang it up.*
>
> *And the other frogs believed him. And the birds at the lake believed him.*
>
> *Every morning Big Fred sat on his lily pad watching the sky grow light over the eastern hills across the far side of the lake. Then he'd begin to croak until the birds called, "Hey, Big Fred! You did it! Here comes the sun!"*

What element did we add?

A. An ending

B. Conflict

C. Character traits

D. Motive

Ans: C. We added character traits (Fred's size, his job, his relationship with the birds)—information about the main character—to make the main character more interesting. Nicknames make a character interesting. Jobs, relationships, and attitudes make a character interesting.

What does this newly added element do for the story? How does it affect you, the reader? *Ans: Character traits make a character interesting and memorable. They also help readers anticipate how a character will act and react in a story situation.*

Where would you add this information in our story segment? *Ans: It is important to make readers care about your main characters right away. A good place to add this information is at the beginning, after the opening paragraph, before introducing goal and motive. Those elements focus the reader on the subsequent problems and action.*

What elements are still missing? *Ans: We still need two of the Eight Essential Elements. First, we need to create struggles—what Fred is going to do, how he is going to try to get across the lake and not be eaten. He might try a disguise. He might talk the birds into carrying him. He might build a catapult (frogapult). There are dozens of schemes Fred could use to try to get across the lake. Second, we still need many more details. While we have included some details about our main character (Fred), we need more details about setting, actions, objects, and other characters to make our story vibrant and real.*

Still we have a good beginning. Here is what we've created so far, sequenced in the order we decided to use:

> *Once there was a frog, a frog named Fred—Fred du Frog—sitting on a lily pad in the mud. Three little frogs sat in a circle around him. In the lake (to Fred's left) lived a frog-eating crocodile. In the woods (to Fred's right) lived frog-eating bears. If the frogs hopped into either the lake or the woods, they would be eaten!*
>
> *Fred du Frog was a big frog—a B-I-G frog. He spread out to cover his entire lily pad. Fred called himself Big Fred. The other frogs called him Big Fred. The birds at the lake called him Big Fred.*
>
> *Fred had a job at the lake: he sang the sun up each morning. Fred said that the sun wouldn't come up until he sang it up.*
>
> *And the other frogs believed him. And the birds at the lake believed him.*
>
> *Every morning Big Fred sat on his lily pad watching the sky grow light over the eastern hills across the far side of the lake. Then he'd begin to croak until the birds called, "Hey, Big Fred! You did it! Here comes the sun!"*
>
> *One of the little frogs said, "Big Fred, we have nothing to eat. All the frog food is way over on the other side of the lake."*
>
> *Fred answered, "Weeeell, boys. I know it is. I've been thinkin' 'bout that."*
>
> *"But, Big Fred, if you swim across the lake to get the food, the crocodile is going to eat you. If you hop around the lake through the woods, the bears will eat you."*
>
> *Fred answered, "Weeeell, boys. I know they will. I've been thinkin' 'bout that, too."*
>
> *"But, Big Fred, if you don't get us food real soon, we're going to starve."*
>
> *Fred answered, "Weeeell, boys. I know we will. I've been thinkin' 'bout that."*
>
> *Finally Fred said, "Weeeell, boys. I guess—somehow—I'm going to have to get across to the other side of the lake."*

Notice the effect of adding a specific goal for the main character. It tells readers what the story is going to be about. It will make readers sift through every line of the story searching for clues as to how the goal will be accomplished.

Notice also that we have not yet added smooth transitions between the individual elements. For example, you might add the words "One day" as a transition in front of the line: *One of the little frogs said, "Big Fred, there's no food . . ."*

Activity Review

The first six of the *Get It Write!* Eight Essential Elements define the story and create story structure. The seventh element, struggles, which we create after these first six have been determined, defines what will happen (scene by scene) in our story. That is, struggles lay out the story's sequence of events and actions. We call that sequence the plot. Rich, multisensory details (Element #8) come last and make each character, action, place (setting), and thing seem real and alive to readers. Each element has a separate and specific job to do. The writer creates each one separately, but they blend together seamlessly in an effective story.

Activity 5: Mix and Match

What Students Will Learn:

Increase student understanding of the Eight Essential Elements and refine their sense of the look and function of each element.

Time Estimate: 10 minutes

Directions:

Through matching the elements in two story segments, this simple activity ensures that your students can successfully recognize the different elements and reinforce their understanding of each element's purpose in and contribution to a story. The student worksheet does not include the answers shown here. It should take only two to three minutes for students to complete this worksheet and another four or five for the follow-on questions.

Check each student's work to ensure that they have successfully learned to identify each element and to understand what plausible plotting events look like.

First Story Segment

Here is the story segment to analyze:

> *In the checkerboard countryside in the far-off Land of Oz, a young girl named Dorothy, who was clothed in a blue-and-white checked pinafore and sparkling ruby slippers, desperately wanted to go home to Kansas. She missed her Auntie Em terribly and was frightened by almost everyone she met in this emerald-green land.*
>
> *However, Dorothy did not know how to get to Kansas—or even how to get out of Oz. Even worse, a wicked witch chased her. She might wander alone here forever or the witch might kill her and all her friends to get those ruby slippers.*

Seg•ment *n.* A part divided from the whole by a natural junction. Story segments are shorter and easier to deal with than whole stories.

Tell your students to match each line of the story on the left with the appropriate story element on the right and draw a line connecting each line and its element name.

(*Hint:* One of the lines does not match any element, and one element does not match any of the lines.)

Story Lines

1. *In the checkerboard countryside in the far-off Land of Oz,*

2. *a young girl named Dorothy*

3. *who was clothed in a blue-and-white checked pinafore and sparkling ruby slippers*

4. *desperately wanted to go home to Kansas.*

5. *She missed her Auntie Em terribly and was frightened by almost everyone she met in this emerald-green land.*

Story Elements

A. Goal (what the character wants)

B. Struggle (what the character does)

C. Main character (who the story is about)

D. Conflict/Problem (what keeps the character from reaching her goal)

E. Character traits (information about the character)

6. *However, Dorothy did not know how to get to Kansas—or even how to get out of Oz. Even worse, a wicked witch chased her.*

7. *She might wander alone here forever or the witch might kill her and all her friends to get those ruby slippers.*

    Ans: 2-C, 3-E, 4-A, 5-G, 6-D, 7-F

F. Risk and danger (what could happen if the character does not get past problems and conflicts)

G. Motive (why the character wants to reach her goal

1. Which element does not match any of the lines in the story?

   Ans: Struggle

2. Which line does not include one of the Eight Essential Elements?

   Ans: Line 1

3. Which one of the Eight Essential Elements is not listed in the matching game?

   Ans: Details

4. Which of the following five items could be plausible ideas for part of this story's plot (struggle)? Circle all correct answers.

   A. Dorothy loves to play hopscotch.

   B. Dorothy challenges the witch's flying monkeys to a checkers duel and wins.

   C. Dorothy learns of the power of the slippers from a friendly witch.

   D. Dorothy has lost her dog, Toto.

   E. Dorothy learns that the witch loves country music.

   Ans: B, C, and E. A is a character trait that could be used in some story event (struggle). D is a problem that could add risk and danger to the story.

5. What information is given in the first line of this story (*In the checkerboard countryside in the far-off Land of Oz*)? Ans: Details about the setting

Second Story Segment

Let's try matching the elements in another story segment. Have your students match each line of the story on the left with the appropriate story element on the right and draw a line connecting each line and its element name. Here is the story segment they'll be analyzing this time:

> *On a crisp October day in the park, a plump caterpillar who loved to sing and dance and kick his hundred legs high in the air wanted to crawl all the way across the park to find Mother Nature, herself. The caterpillar was afraid to change into a butterfly and knew that Mother Nature was the only one who could save him.*
>
> *But hundreds of children ran and stomped in the park, and hungry birds circled high overhead. If the caterpillar wasn't crushed by a foot or eaten by a bird, it would surely be dried out and killed by the burning sun.*

(*Hint:* One of the lines does not match any story element, one element does not match any of the lines, and one element matches two lines.)

Story Lines

1. *On a crisp October day in the park,*

2. *a plump caterpillar*

Story Elements

A. Goal (what the character wants)

B. Struggle (what the character does)

3. *who loved to sing and dance and kick his hundred legs high in the air*

4. *wanted to crawl all the way across the park to find Mother Nature, herself.*

5. *The caterpillar was afraid to change into a butterfly and knew that Mother Nature was the only one who could save him.*

6. *But hundreds of children ran and stomped in the park, and hungry birds circled high overhead.*

7. *If it wasn't crushed by a foot or eaten by a bird, it would surely be dried out and killed by the burning sun.*

C. Main character (who the story is about)

D. Conflict/Problem (what keeps the character from reaching his goal)

E. Character traits (information about the character)

F. Risk and danger (what could happen if the character does not get past problems and conflicts)

G. Motive (why the character wants to reach his goal)

Ans: 2-C, 3-E, 4-A, 5-G, 6-D, 7-F.

1. Which element does not match any of the lines in the story? *Ans: B. Struggle*

2. Which line does not include one of the listed story elements? *Ans: Line 1*

3. Which of the following five items would make sense as part of this story's plot (struggle)? Circle all correct answers.

   A. The caterpillar is afraid of bees.

   B. The caterpillar rides across the grass on the backs of a dozen ants.

   C. The caterpillar carries a leaf over its head, so the birds won't see it.

   D. The caterpillar is thirsty.

   E. The caterpillar sings a song that the birds like.

   Ans: B, C, and E. A is a character trait. D is a problem. Neither is an action (event) that could become part of the plot.

4. What information is given in the first line of this story (*On a crisp October day in the park*)?

   Ans: Scenic detail

Finally, the worksheet asks students to describe the difference between risk and danger and struggles. Many students initially confuse these two elements. This segment is a good opportunity to demonstrate that difference.

Allow several students to read their answers and have the class discuss and debate this difference. Use the following paragraph as a guide for that discussion.

Risk and danger depict what *could* happen. Struggles present what actually *does* happen. Risk and danger represent the worst case, the trouble the main character could get into, everything bad that could logically happen if nothing works for the character. Struggles tell readers what the character actually does to try to get to the goal and what actually happens to them as a result.

In this story segment, we never learn what the caterpillar does. Thus, the segment does not include any mention of struggles. However, the last sentence clearly lays out what could happen as the caterpillar tries to cross the park and, thus, represents risk and danger.

Activity Review

Notice how much you know about this story from three simple sentences. You know what it's about, where it's going, and what's probably going to happen. Those sentences created suspense, curiosity, and excitement. It's fun and easy to do—just create the Eight Essential Elements first.

Sometimes the elements (especially the first six) are spread apart in a story; sometimes they are bunched together (as in this story segment). But they are always there. Take the time to create them first. Writing the story will be much easier and far more successful.

Activity 6: Recognizing the Eight Essential Elements _____

What Students Will Learn:

Students should be able to quickly and correctly identify the elements in this short story segment. This story also introduces the concept of implied information.

Time Estimate: 10 minutes

Directions:

Let your students complete their worksheet before reviewing and discussing the answers. Read this short story and answer the questions that follow.

> *Itsy Bitsy the spider climbed leg over leg over leg over leg over leg over leg up the waterspout. No spider had ever climbed all the way to the top, and she wanted to be the first.*
>
> *"Oh, Itsy," wailed her mother. "Why can't you be like your brother, Teensy Weensy, and be content to climb in the bushes where it's safe?"*
>
> *Itsy wiped two hairy legs across her tiny spider nose and answered, "A spide's gotta do what a spide's gotta do! And I gotta do it first to see what I can see from the top."*
>
> *Down came the rain and washed the spider out. Out came the sun and dried up all the rain, and Itsy Bitsy spider climbed up the spout again.*

The Eight Essential Elements

- Character
- Character traits
- Goal
- Motive
- Conflicts and Problems
- Risk and danger
- Struggles
- Details

Have your students find each of the elements in this story segment and list them as directed.

1. Who is the main character? *Ans: Itsy Bitsy, the spider*

2. What character traits do you learn about this character? *Ans: Her goal, her determination and bravery (personality), her dialogue (voice)*

3. What is the goal of this character? *Ans: To climb to the top of the waterspout*

4. Why is that goal important to the main character (what's her motive)? *Ans: She wants to be the first to see what she can see from the top.*

5. What conflicts and problems block this character? *Ans: Three. Rain, her mother's objections, and—apparently—the height or the difficulty of the climb. (No other spider has been able to do it.)*

6. What risk and danger do these problems create for the main character? (It could be implied, not actually stated.) *Ans: The climb is dangerous. Rainwater could kill Itsy. Mom is worried and might become angry. Often "getting washed out" is deadly.* Create and list two things that could go wrong or two ways Itsy could get in trouble implied in the story. *Ans: Itsy could drown in another burst of rain. Itsy could get in trouble with her mother. Whatever killed the other spiders who tried to climb to the top could get Itsy. Allow students to read their original answers.*

7. How does the character struggle? What does she do to try to reach her goal? *Ans: First, by her slow, steady leg climb to the top. Second, she starts all over again after the rain.*

8. Name something that happens in the story segment that is *not* part of the main character's struggle to reach a goal. *Ans: "Wipe two legs across her spider nose" is an action that is not part of her attempt to reach the top. Answering her mother is part of her attempt since her mother could order Itsy to climb down.*

9. What details are included about the characters, settings, and actions? *Ans: There are few modifiers in this story. All details are provided in the form of specific nouns and verbs that define (describe) the characters, settings, and actions of the story.*

Activity Review

Review with students how much you know from these simple sentences. You know so much about the story because they include the *Get It Write!* Eight Essential Elements.

Some of the elements were not overtly stated in this story segment but were, instead, strongly implied by what the characters said and did. The conflict between Itsy and her mother is not overtly stated; it is implied by what they say. Readers assume that there must be some tension and conflict between them because they did not agree in their one line of dialogue.

Writers often imply, rather than state, important information through characters' words and actions. This is particularly true for goals and motives (Elements #2 and 3). It is important to show the specific actions and words of a character, which make the character more interesting to readers. Also, showing what characters say and do allows readers to draw general conclusions from specific evidence and draws readers into the story. Readers like to see what a character says and does and then conclude, "Ahhh! I get it! I know what she's really after."

Have your students watch for implied goals and motives when they read and note exactly how the author led them to the correct conclusions. Your students can do the same thing as writers. It is important to note, however, that the author had to know exactly what the character's goals and motives were. Writers don't imply this information to themselves, only to readers. Actually, to imply goals and motives, a writer needs to understand them better than if the writer were to directly state them.

Activity 7: Building Group Stories _____

What Students Will Learn:

This activity is a good review and refresher activity, a fun one to use anytime you want to review and refresh your student's mastery of the Eight Essential Elements.

Time Estimate: 10 to 15 minutes

Directions:

There is no student worksheet for this activity. It is a verbal game that depends on you to actively direct and manage the contributions of each group of students. This group game is fun, energizing, and powerfully instructional. Your students will get to see the elements in action, being built and shaped as the class proceeds.

In this game, your class will use the *Get It Write!* Eight Essential Elements to create a story as a class. To do this, the class must be divided into six teams (or tables). You will direct your students to improvisationally create a story—one element at a time, with each element being created by a different table.

You begin the activity by having the students at Table #1 create a main character and simple first impression (see Activities 9 and 10). This should take less than one minute. Table #2 then creates at least four interesting traits for this character, all from different categories of character information (see Activity 12). Table #3 then creates a goal for this character. Table #4 then creates a motive for that goal, and so on.

After each table creates their part, you may refer the story back to a previous table if more information about that element is needed. For example, if Table #4 creates a motive that mentions the parents of the main character, the teacher may ask Tables #1, 2, and 3 to create appropriate information about these new characters. Each table must use the information already created to guide their process of creating their particular story element.

You should make the following table designations:

Table #1. The Character Table. This table will create each character used in the story beginning with the main character by creating a first impression for that character (what the character is, relative age, name, a job or hobby, one personality trait, and current emotional state). They will do the same for any other characters identified during story development. They are responsible for creating characters that work well in the story.

Table #2. The Character Trait Table. This table will create at least four significant traits about the main character. Nothing this table invents may contradict what Table #1 has already created. This table will also provide any additional traits as required based on the ideas of any other table, including appropriate traits for the antagonist and any supporting characters. This table is responsible for creating character traits that make the story easy to develop for other tables and make the characters (and story) interesting.

Table #3. The Goal Table. This table will create goals for every character created during story development. They will also revise or adjust the goals as needed based on ideas created by other tables. This table is responsible for making the story seem important to listeners and easy for other tables to develop.

Table #4. The Motive Table. This table will decide why each character wants and needs to reach their particular goal, that is, why that goal is so important to the character. They will also create new motives as needed based on story development by other tables. This table is responsible for making each goal vitally important to its character and for creating motives that make the job of subsequent tables easier.

Table #5. The Conflict and Problems, Risk and Danger Table. This table will create at least two worthy conflicts or problems that block the main character and will also make clear exactly how they create risk and danger for the main character. This table is responsible for making the story exciting by providing strong conflicts and enough risk and danger so that it will be easy for the struggle table to make up their part.

Table #6. The Struggle Table. This table will identify the major events that let the main character encounter the risk and danger created by Table #5. Table #6 decides what the main character is going to do to try to overcome conflicts and reach the stated goal. This table must make the story exciting by having the main character confront the created risks and dangers along the way. This table must also decide on the ending and climax of the story, and, finally, identify the opening scene and how the story will start.

You will act as activity moderator and narrator and have the following jobs:

1. Regularly summarize the story and direct the creation process at each table.
2. Keep each table moving at a fast clip so that the story builds and flows without delays. Better that they create something quickly than take the time to ponder and debate their portion of the story.
3. Ensure that each table creates only their specific element. When a table begins to create more than their assigned element, point it out and refer that new information to the correct table.

The class as a whole must make sure that each table accomplishes their assigned mission and successfully creates their part of the story. You should regularly have the class debate or discuss whether a particular table created information for their element that is both consistent with other story information and helps make it easy for other tables to create their parts. You may decide whether or not to have the class intervene and improve the contribution of any table.

Often one table's creation requires previous tables to adjust their original ideas. As an example, imagine that the Conflict and Problems Table creates an antagonist or a friend of the main character. The Character Table must create a first impression for that character, the Character Trait Table must create significant character traits, the Goal Table must create a goal, and the Motive Table must come up with motives for this new character. Those new bits of information may cause the Conflict and Problems Table to amend their version of the conflict and risk and danger created by this new character.

If the Conflict and Problems Table said that the main character was shy and hence risked embarrassment (to create internal conflict), then being shy, which is a character trait, must be passed back to the Character Trait Table and okayed before it can be used.

Students from one table may not change or contradict the ideas created by a previous table. Only the students at the designated table may alter what has been created for their element.

At the end of this fifteen-minute game, summarize the final story outline and review the process the class used to create the story. In particular, review how the tables interacted and how the elements created at one table directed what other tables could and had to create.

Activity Review

The story your class developed has not yet been written. Still, every student in the room will have a clear vision of exactly how the story will go and what will make it both exciting and enjoyable. Few details have been created and many more would need to be written before the story could be written successfully. Still, the *Get It Write!* Eight Essential Elements have—as they always will—created a solid structure for this story. By dividing the elements among tables, each student gets a clear picture of the purpose, sequencing, contribution, and look of each element and of how all the elements interact to form a story.

Chapter 2

The Inside Story

We have seen through the first seven activities that there are Eight Essential Elements that define a story and that student writers should develop the habit of creating before they begin to write. Now we're ready to focus more closely on each individual story element. We'll play some writing games and exercises to understand each of the Eight Essential Elements. We'll see exactly where they come from, how they are created, and what they look like. It's amazing how easy they are to work with and master once your students see exactly what they are.

A musical analogy: In Chapter 1, we listened to an orchestra play simple melodies and tried to pick out, or identify, the sound of each instrument (element). In Chapter 2, we will study each instrument in isolation, discovering which kind of music it makes and how it works. In Chapter 3, we will recombine the instruments to build new melodies.

It's not at all hard to do. Once internalized, the Eight Essential Elements make both story creation and story writing more fun and successful.

The chart shows each of the Eight Essential Elements and the corresponding activities and chapter discussion.

Where to Find Each Element in Chapter 2 of *Get It Write!*

Element Number	Name	Found in Activities . . .	On Pages . . .
1	Character	8–10	34–40
2	Character Traits	11–19	41–66
3	Goal	20–22	67–75
4	Motive	23–25	76–82
5	Conflicts and Problems	26–29	83–93
6	Risk and Danger	30–32	94–101
7	Struggles	33–38	102–119
8	Details	39–52	120–147

ELEMENT #1: CHARACTER

Who is the story going to be about? Who is the main character?
This material should be discussed with your students before they proceed to Activity 8.

A story—every story—is all about characters. Stories are not about *what* happens (plot and action) but rather about the characters who must do those actions. If readers enjoy the characters, they will enjoy the story.

But what is a character? A tree in the woods is just a tree—part of the setting—not a character. What would turn that tree into a character? The ability to walk? To talk? To think?

Have your students discuss and debate this question. A character is a central figure who consciously acts during the course of a story. A tree is just a tree, a part of the setting, unless the writer gives that tree the ability to think, plan, and act. Then the tree becomes a character—one readers will want to learn about and follow through the story.

A character could be a person, a dragon, a worm, or a shoelace. It could be a tree, a leprechaun, a snake, or a storm. A character can be any being or object in a story, as long as it can think, plan, and act in its own interests.

Activity 8: Who Is It? _____

What Students Will Learn:

This is an introductory activity. It is designed to help students recognize an effective story character and to separate characters from their actions.

Time Estimate: 10 minutes

Directions:

This activity may be completed individually, or it may be conducted as a group activity. Student worksheets do not include follow-up discussion of each answer. Use the following paragraphs to guide that discussion. Ensure that students see *why* each possible character either is, or is not, a good choice for a main character. A good main character is one who will be easy for the writer to develop and write about and one who fits easily with the subject, goals, and conflicts of the story.

The main character of a story is the character the story is mostly about. It is the goal of the main character that is resolved at the end of the story.

Have your students circle each item in the list that could be the main character of a story.

1. An army ant
2. A crumpled piece of paper
3. Chasing a butterfly
4. A lost boy
5. A city
6. Being afraid of a snarling tiger
7. An evil doctor who wants to outlaw peanut butter and chocolate
8. A pixie who can't fly
9. A thundering waterfall
10. Trying to win a million dollars
11. A TV show
12. The moon
13. Climbing a castle wall while a dragon belches fire from above

Ans: 1, 2, 4, 7, 8, 9, and 12

Now let's look each item on the list: choices 3, 10, and 13 are actions, things that happen, not characters; 6 is a character trait (something about a character), but not a character; the other nine could all be circled; however, 5 and 11 would be very difficult to make into good characters. A city is not a single character. It is made up of many individual characters, as is a TV show. While it is not impossible to turn a city into a story character, it would be difficult and inadvisable.

1, 2, 4, 7, 8, 9, and 12 (the other seven) would be good choices for a story character. You could use any of these to create a wonderful story. Notice that 7 and 9 might also make excellent antagonists (conflicts the main character must overcome). Remember, antagonists are also characters.

Activity Review

Characters are thinking, feeling agents in a story. Characters act in their own interest. Stories are always about characters. To make the writing easy, start by picking a main character that will be easy and fun to develop and write about, one for whom you can easily develop and refine the other story elements. Don't hesitate to change main characters if the process of creating the other elements turns into a developmental struggle. Every story can be told from more than one point of view. If the character and viewpoint a student has chosen doesn't work well for the story the writer wants to tell, it's often best to change the characters.

Activity 9: A Good First Impression _____

What Students Will Learn:

Students will understand the content, use, and importance of characters' first impressions.

Time Estimate: 10 to 15 minutes

Directions:

How does a writer first introduce a character to readers so that readers instantly begin to care about and remember that character? Writers must give some but certainly not all of the information that has been developed for that character. What should the writer include? What should be left out?

Writers need to begin by creating a few essential bits of information about that character, or a **first impression.** A first impression is a way to introduce a character to your readers, so they will remember, and become interested in, that character. First impressions are given when introducing a character into the story. This impression consists of a few key bits of character information designed to fix that character in readers' minds.

The saying "a good first impression is important" is as true for story writing as it is for life. But writers can't pause the story to give a complete bio of a character. That would kill the energy and pace of the story. Let's see if we can uncover the kinds of information that make for effective first impressions.

> **Char·ac·ter** *n.* A being in a book, play, or other narrative capable of thought and action. Characters must think and act on their own behalf, which is what differentiates characters from objects.

Tell your students to pretend they are going to meet someone for the first time. What would they want to know about this new person right away?

Have students make a list of eight things they would first want to know on the lines provided on their activity worksheet. Do not allow them to collaborate on these lists. They should work individually.

Lead a class discussion about what they included in their lists. Build a class list on the board, using the items mentioned most often.

Most writers agree that the following bits of character information are the most effective to use for a first impression:

- Species (what the character is)
- Name
- Age (relative age is okay—a baby, a teenager, an old man, etc.)
- Primary job, activity, or function
- Current emotional state (how the character feels right now—particularly if that feeling is extreme)
- One unique quirk, habit, or characteristic (something the character likes or hates, is good at or particularly bad at, something the character is afraid of or needs to have, something the character has done or wants to do, etc.)

• One thing this character strongly reminds the reader of

• One action or activity the character is doing right now

Compare the class list and the individual student lists to this composite list. Discuss the items on this list with your students and search for examples in stories they have recently read. Have them invent examples for each of these categories of information.

The worksheet then asks students to identify the items on their list—or on those read by other students—that seemed boring. Which items were interesting? Students are asked to list the three most interesting and three most boring items.

It is not necessary to have students actually read these lists. Rather, have students discuss why some were boring and some interesting. What is it about the way they were worded and written that made them either boring or interesting? This discussion acts as a preliminary introduction to the material beginning in Activity 11: what makes description and detail effective and interesting. Allow several students to read the one bit of character information they found most interesting and explain why it interested them.

Any information included in a first impression is really part of the character traits (Element #2) the author invents for each character. First impressions are both an important part of story writing and a good way to ease into the important topic of describing a character. We expand to consider all the character traits beginning with Activity 11.

Activity Review

Certainly, student writers don't have to use every one of those bits of information each time they introduce a character. Writers will use the ones that make the most sense for the character and the story. But these bits of information seem to be most effective in getting readers to initially understand and remember a character. Of course, each writer will have to create much more information than these few bits about the characters that are central and important to the story. However, a strong first impression is the best way to introduce a character to readers.

Writers do not begin the process of character development by creating a first impression. They begin by creating a wide range of character traits that make the character interesting. This is Element #2, character traits. This process of creating character traits is best done through verbal games and exercises. Several are introduced in *Get It Write!* After a complete and interesting character is created, it is easier to select the few, specific bits of information that form a powerful first impression. See *Write Right!* and *Super Simple Storytelling* for complete directions to a wide variety of verbal character-development activities.

Activity 10: A Lasting Impression _____

What Students Will Learn:

Students will learn to recognize effective first impressions and to understand how these impressions draw the interest of readers.

Time Estimate: 25 to 30 minutes in class plus one out-of-class assignment

Directions:

This activity is divided into two parts. The first is a quick classroom activity. The second is a longer homework assignment that can be modeled first in class.

Part 1. The student worksheet lists five possible first impressions. Students are directed to circle the ones they think work well and are effective. Their worksheet does not include any discussion of the answers but does have space for them to write what they would add to correct each of the ineffective first impressions.

Im·pres·sion *n*. An effect produced on the feelings and senses. A first impression is the initial impression of a character provided by the writer.

1. The rock sat on a high hill that overlooked a long valley.
2. Old Uncle Quigley, a thin man who stood bent over like a human question mark, hid under the basement stairs every time a thunderstorm rumbled into town.
3. Jamaica Boom Boom was a happy caterpillar who loved to sing and dance, kicking fifty of his legs at a time high into the air.
4. There was once a nervous pine tree on the edge of a dark forest whose job was to protect a large family of mushrooms that lived around its trunk from the glare of the sun. It seemed like an easy job, but the pine tree worried and fretted over every tiny thing.
5. Running uphill was harder work than running downhill for the residents of Glosterboch.

Ans: 2, 3, 4

Now let's look at each of the five.

Number 1 presents a rock, but gives us very little information about the rock—not even any evidence that the rock is anything more than just part of the setting. Number 1 should not be circled.

Number 5 is interesting, but it doesn't tell us anything about a specific character.

The other three are good character first impressions. None of them gives readers all of the possible bits of information that could be used in a first impression. But each includes enough to make readers remember and care about the character.

With your class, compare the information included in each of the three effective first impressions with the complete list presented in Activity 9. Which first impression did your students like best? Why?

Review the information students wanted to add to impressions they thought were inadequate. Compare the added information to the Activity 9 list.

Part 2. Have your students search through three stories they have recently read to find which character traits the authors used in the first impressions. Have the students assess first impressions of six (two in each story) main characters. Have students fill in this table on their worksheets with their results. Their worksheet also asks them to identify the stories and characters they used.

Type of Information	**Number of Times Used in the First Impressions for My Six Characters**
• Species	_____
• Name	_____
• Age	_____
• Function	_____
• Emotion	_____
• Quirk or habit	_____
• What it reminds me of	_____
• Other bits of information used by the authors	_____

Lead a class discussion to compare students' findings. What kinds of character information were used most often in creating good first impressions? Were there any that students particularly liked and remember? Share those with the class. Which kinds of character information did the authors use that students enjoyed?

Activity Review

First impressions come from fully developed character traits (Element #2). Create first; write second. A first impression, however, is the first thing readers will see and learn about a character. Successful first impressions hook readers into the story and make them want to read more about that character.

It is important for readers to remember a new character as soon as that character is mentioned. A strong first impression is the best way to cement a new character in the minds of readers and to make readers curious about, and interested in, that character. Nothing in a story is more important than the story's central characters. A strong first impression helps start the process of making readers care deeply about the struggles and fate of the characters.

First impressions are easier to create after student writers have gotten used to recognizing them in stories they read.

ELEMENT #2: CHARACTER TRAITS

What character traits make this character interesting?

The first of the *Get It Write!* elements is to identify the main character. The second element is to create the character traits that make a character interesting to readers. Making characters interesting to readers is the most important job for a writer. If readers enjoy the characters, they will enjoy the story. Writers should ask the following questions: What makes a character interesting? What kinds of character information should a writer use? How does a writer present this information to make readers interested in those characters? In the next few exercises, we'll explore characters and character traits to find the answers to each of those questions.

Activity 11: Getting to Know You _____

What Students Will Learn:

Students will begin to explore the vast field of character information. They will also learn what makes a bit of character information interesting to readers.

Time Estimate: 15 to 20 minutes

Directions:

Creating interesting characters is a critically important task for each writer; however, it is also a confusing and difficult task. We begin our exploration of character with the characters students know best.

In the blank spaces on the student worksheet, have your students write three things that they think makes themselves, another family member, and someone who is neither a family member nor a classmate interesting. That is, they should write which traits they think someone else would find interesting when first meeting these people.

In•ter•est•ing *adj.* Sparking curiosity about, or attraction to, something. Characters must interest readers to make readers willing to read the narrative.

This is typically a confusing and difficult task for many students, who will claim that there is nothing interesting about them. The counter to that argument is that there are hundreds of bits of interesting information about everybody: what they've done, where they've been, what they're good at, what they're bad at, what they love, what they hate, and so on. However, I recommend you minimize the amount of guidance and suggestions you offer. Let the students struggle with the concept of what makes a character interesting.

Give students enough time to write something in each of the nine blank spaces on the worksheet. Tell them that they should not discuss or share what they write with anyone until told to do so and that they should not reveal anyone's personal secrets during this activity.

After students have written nine interesting characteristics (three about each of the three different people), have each student pick their favorite three characteristics—the three they think are most interesting. They need not be about the same person. For example, they might choose one characteristic about each character or two about one person and one about another.

Tell each student to write the three best, most interesting statements on their worksheets. First, give them these instructions: we don't want to know which person you are writing about; we only want to know the interesting part. So, if you are a boy, you will write "he" in each of the three statements (no matter which person the statement is about). If you are a girl, you will write "she" for each. If, for example, you are a boy, and you wrote that your mother makes the biggest and best cakes in the world, you would now write "He makes the biggest and best cakes in the world."

Lead a brief class discussion focusing on why this activity is so hard. Point out to students that, if they knew which kinds of information to use and the characteristics of effective character details, then it would be easy to make any character interesting.

Allow four students to read their three best to other students. If a boy reads, he will always say "he" instead of naming the person he is really talking about. A girl will always say "she." This way, other students won't focus on the person being described but on the character description.

Don't allow any discussion between readers. After all four have read, have students fill out the next part of their activity worksheet. Their directions are as follows: "Twelve bits of character information have now been read. Which ones did you find most interesting? Which ones made you laugh? Which ones got your attention? On the lines below write the three you thought were most interesting and that you remember the best and can picture most vividly in your mind."

Allow several students to share their top choices. Discuss why those particular character traits are more interesting than the others. Search for common characteristics of these students descriptions. Good character descriptions share the following characteristics:

Accuracy   The description you write should tell readers the truth about your characters, or the readers will get both confused and angry. You shouldn't say the character has a blue shirt on and then, one page later, change it to red. You shouldn't say that he's tall and then tell readers he's only four feet tall. Readers need to believe the description the writers provide.

Some will say, "But my character is fictional. There is no truth." Yes, there is. You must stay consistent with the truth—the reality—you create within the story.

Specificity   It is critically important that character descriptions be as specific as possible. This makes it easier for readers to picture the character. If a woman is tall, that is of little interest because it's not specific. *How* tall? Say that she is so tall she can rest her chin on her husband's head, or that she is tall enough to bang her head on door frames and has a line of bumps across her forehead as reminders of the times she forgot to duck. Don't say he is good at sports. That's too general and ordinary. Be specific. Say he is the best high jumper in the county. Don't say that a character is weird. That means something different to every reader. Tell readers specifically what the character does and let readers conclude on the own that he is weird.

Uniqueness   The things that make characters different and unique make them interesting. If a boy has two arms, that's not very interesting. Almost everyone has two arms. But if that boy had three arms or no arms, that's interesting. Being a good swimmer isn't interesting. Lots of people are. But if this character won two Olympic gold medals for the back stroke, that's interesting because it is both specific and unique.

Unusualness   Besides finding aspects of characters that make them different, look for aspects and traits that are unusual. Also search for unexpected or unusual ways to describe and compare them. It's not very interesting if a child is afraid of the dark. That's common. But if a grown man is afraid of sunlight, that's interesting because the very idea is unusual as well as unique.

Vividness   Good character descriptions create vivid pictures in readers' imaginations. Readers want to be able to vividly see in their minds the characters the writer describes. Think of ways to describe characters that will create more vivid pictures.

List these on the board and offer examples of each from the descriptions offered by different students. These five characteristics are important guides to making any character description more effective and interesting.

Pick several individual statements of character information read by your four volunteer readers and have the class improve these descriptions to make the character being described more interesting. They will, of course, have to fictionalize the character to be free to change the description to make it more interesting. That's fine for this activity.

What did they do to create greater interest? They had to make the character descriptions more specific, unique, unusual, and vivid. If you want, you may model the use of one or more of the five criteria of good character details to make a vague and general description far more interesting.

Activity Review

Student character descriptions are often vague and general: "She is nice. He is good at sports." Help students develop the habit of writing specific events and actions that show what the character does and says. From these specifics, readers will successfully and happily draw the general conclusions.

Vivid, interesting character descriptions are essential to successful story writing. As we will see later, it is details about the character that create strong, effective descriptions. Characters are one of the four aspects of a story that must be described in detail (we will discuss the other three later). Characters came first because they are the single most important element in any story. Stories are all about characters.

Moreover, we will find that the character traits created as writers begin story planning will act like a story map, suggesting, directing, and shaping later development of story plotting events. Creating strong character traits always helps create plot.

Activity 12: What a Character! _____

What Students Will Learn:

This activity will arm students with the available informational tools to create interesting characters.

Time Estimate: Part 1, 15 minutes; Part 2, about 20 minutes for follow-up discussion and about 30 minutes to complete the form, which may be assigned as homework

Directions:

Part 1. We have already seen that good character descriptions are accurate, unique, unusual, specific, and vivid. But what kinds of information can be used to describe characters? Should you talk about their eyes? Their fears? Their feet? Their abilities? Their voice? Their hair? Their history? All of these?

Discuss the following chart with your students. Their worksheet includes the chart but none of the following discussion. Either copy the chart onto an overhead transparency or write it on the board as an easy group reference.

Start by having your students pick one character they all know well (one from a recently read class book or someone like Harry Potter, Dorothy of Oz, Superman, etc.). Their job will be to identify everything they can think of that makes that character interesting. Each time a student offers some new information, the student must also say which one of the fifteen categories of character information (listed on the chart) they think the specific bit of information they are offering belongs to.

The class's job is to make sure that each bit of offered character information is categorized correctly. They may challenge and debate any proposed category. Use the category descriptions listed below the chart to settle any uncertainty.

Keep track of which categories students have and have not used in offering information on this chosen character. Make sure that the class identifies at least one bit of information from each category for this character.

As students offer characteristics that they think make this character interesting, remind them that all effective character descriptions must be accurate, specific, unique, and unusual.

Let's see which kinds of information about a character your students can use to make the character interesting.

Categories of Character Information

Physical	Internal	Situational
1. Name	7. Personality	13. Actions/Reactions
2. Sensory information	8. Voice	14. Feelings
3. Job/Activity	9. Abilities/Talents	15. Story information
4. History	10. Weakness/Flaws	
5. Comparisons (reminds you of . . .)	11. Passions	
6. Relationships	12. Fears	

These categories need some explanation.

Physical. These are categories you can see and know as an outside observer. They are physical traits.

1. **Name.** A character's formal name, nickname, what he or she calls him- or herself, what others call the character

2. **Sensory information.** Information you would gather with your own senses if you were with this character, what the character looks like, sounds like, smells like, and so on

3. **Job/Activity.** A character's job, hobbies, activities, quirks, patterns, daily patterns, possessions, and so on

4. **History.** What the character has done, where he or she has been, what has happened to the character in the past

5. **Comparisons.** One thing or person this character most reminds you of, how you would **compare** the character with some other well-known being or thing

6. **Relationships.** The character's good friends, casual friends, enemies, and so on

Internal. These categories relate to a character's internal thinking and non-physical qualities of the character.

7. **Personality.** How this character deals with others, the character's dominant emotional state, as well as the character's beliefs, attitudes, traits, tendencies, and so on

8. **Voice.** The character's speech patterns, vocabulary, phraseology, accent, unique repeated lines (tag lines), the sound of his or her voice, and so on

9. **Abilities/Talents.** What the character is particularly good at, including anything that this character is significantly better at than others in his or her species

10. **Weaknesses/Flaws.** What the character is particularly bad at, including physical abilities as well as character flaws—anything that is a shortcoming for this character

11. **Passions.** What the character loves or hates, any strong emotional attachment or obsession

12. **Fears.** What the character is afraid of

Situational. These categories relate to the changing events of a particular story.

13. **Actions/Reactions.** How the character acts and reacts in different situations that arise during the story

14. **Feelings.** What the character is feeling at different moments and situations throughout the story

15. **Story Information.** The goals, motives, conflicts, dangers, and struggles the character must face during the story

Make sure your students understand each of these categories before proceeding.

That's a lot of information to invent for each major character in a story! Three things will make it easier for your students.

First, tell them to take their time. There is no need to fully develop a character in one quick burst of creativity. Students should play with their characters. Pretend to have conversations with them. Pretend to be their characters. Get their friends and family to help create ideas about their characters. Don't let the main character get away with being dull and ordinary—make the character interesting. They are your students' characters. They'll do what the student writers make them do—but only what the writers make them do.

Second, student writers don't have to invent all of this information for every character. For the story's main character, the more information they create the better. For other characters, students might create little more than a good first impression. Notice that a first impression pulls information from about one-third of the fifteen categories of possible character information. First impressions are a start toward creating complete and interesting characters.

Third, several of these categories usually make characters the most interesting. These include voice, fears, reactions, weaknesses, story information, and one unique trait or characteristic *plus* how the *character* feels about that unique aspect. Remind students to spend extra time developing these traits for their main characters.

Create first; write second

- When you *create,* create the Eight Essential Elements.
- When you *write,* write the details.

Part 2. This part may be conducted in class or assigned as homework once the class has agreed on the first three bits of information about the character. Working with so many categories of character information will seem easier if we begin with a fun example of how they can be used.

This activity, as well as Activities 14, 15, and 16, deals with the process of developing a story character. Students may either create a new character specifically for these activities using the following directions, or you may have them use a character they are developing for another writing project. If you opt for the latter, skip the directions, asking the class to create a common character first impression. Students will fill in the requested information for the character they are already developing.

Let's use the fifteen categories of character information to create a new character. To make it interesting, have everyone in the class develop a version of the same character.

As a class, agree on the following first impression elements:

- What is this character? _____
- Name of character: _____
- Age of character: _____

Now students complete the following Character Profile Sheet, creating their own unique character from these three common bits of information. They may be as inventive and creative as they like. There are no right or wrong answers—only ones that successfully make the character more interesting and ones that don't.

The questions on the student worksheet are reproduced here.

Character Profile Sheet

Remind students to search for traits that are unique, unusual, and specific.

My character is a _____ named _____

Age: _____

Physical description (include two things that make this character unique—different from the other characters): _____

If you were to see this character, what would he or she remind you of? _____

Character's job or function (how does the character spend time?): _____

Two quirks or habits of this character: _____

Two important moments from this character's past: _____

Describe the character's voice and typical things the character says: _____

Name two talents or abilities of this character: _____

Name two weaknesses or flaws of this character: _____

List two things this character likes: _____

List two things this character dislikes: _____

Name one thing this character loves the most: _____

Name one thing this character hates: _____

Name two things that terrify this character: _____

Find four or five words that describe how this character deals with others (the character's personality): _____

If you met this character, what would you **like** about him or her? _____

What would you **dislike**? _____

Additional traits that make this character interesting: _____

Have several students read aloud the character traits they created. Watch the class's reactions to each listed trait to see which they found interesting. Discuss why each mentioned trait either is, or is not, interesting. Focus this discussion on the five criteria for effective character details: accurate, specific, unique, unusual, vivid (see Activity 11).

Following this sharing and discussion, give students a chance to revise their list of traits to make them more effective and interesting. The more they practice creating and then improving these character traits, the easier it will be for them to smoothly incorporate effective character development into their writing habits.

Point out that it would have been easier to create interesting characters in groups. Students should, when possible, use groups—friends, classmates, family, and so on—to generate a wide variety of ideas when creating their characters.

Interesting characters create energy and enthusiasm for a story—both in readers and in writers. Don't rush the process of inventing interesting characters. It is the best place for student writers to unleash their natural story energy.

Activity Review

Interesting character traits are critically important to the success of every story. However, it takes practice to create successful sets of traits. The more your students practice and the more they watch how published authors create and present interesting character traits, the easier the process becomes, and the easier it becomes to develop powerful, effective stories around those characters.

Here are three thoughts to reinforce with your students:

1. Writers and their stories always benefit from more character information. Most student writers don't create nearly enough character traits. They may not use all of the information they create. Still, the character and story will be better and stronger the more they create and the better they can see the characters in their mind's eye. Tell them to think of all they know about their own

family members. They should try to develop story characters to that same level of detail so that they can see them in their mind's eye as well as they can see their family.

2. Characters are best developed through verbal exercises and games. Have students be (act like) their characters. Talk about, and to, their characters. Have others ask questions about their characters. Spending time working on characters always pays off when students finally write the story.

3. The more character information student writers create, the easier it will be to create the story's plot. Successful plot and struggle flow from characters.

Activity 13: Building Character

What Students Will Learn:

Students will practice creating interesting bits of character information using different informational categories. They will begin to understand how to use these categories to build interesting, easy-to-write-about characters.

Time Estimate: 30 minutes plus an out-of-class assignment

Directions:

It will be easier for your students to create interesting character information in the varied categories after they have seen how successful authors do it. Before we turn back to creating characters, it is time to turn to literature and see how others present the character information they have created.

Direct each student to pick two story characters from well-known published stories and identify one trait, or interesting bit of information, in each of the fifteen categories for each character. A chart on the student worksheet can be used to record this information. If one of the characters students select appears in more than one story, tell students to use information from only one story. They may imply (create) any information they cannot specifically find in a story. This activity may be assigned as homework.

Des·crip·tion *n.* A portrayal in words of a person, a scene, an event, and so on.

Trait *n.* A distinguishing characteristic, quality, or feature.

Writers use character traits to describe their characters to readers.

Have students set their lists aside for several days before sharing with other students. Before sharing with the class, students should try to make each listed trait stronger and more interesting by making the trait more specific, by changing the trait to something more unusual or unique, or by changing it to something that creates a stronger visual image in the mind of readers.

Have students read both versions of their lists of character traits for class comment. Which were more interesting? Why?

Activity Review

Creating interesting character traits takes practice. It is a learned skill. Effectively writing those traits as strong, interesting story details also takes practice. However, it does not require any skills or abilities beyond the reach of any of your students.

It will help students become better character writers if they focus on character information when they read. What information did the author provide? How did the author weave that information into the story? Why did it make the characters interesting?

Students should concentrate most on creating character information that is specific. They tend to create vague and general character traits. As they learn to be specific and visual in their descriptions, their characters will automatically become more interesting.

Verbal games and exercises will help students develop their characters. *Write Right!* and *Super Simple Storytelling* contain many verbal character games. Two, Activities 14 and 15, are included in *Get It Write!*

Activity 14: One-on-One-on-One-on-One _____

What Students Will Learn:

Students will use this verbal game to learn more powerful and interesting ways to describe their characters and to learn to recognize which character information is most effective.

Time Estimate: 15 minutes

Directions:

You may use this game as a demonstration of character development techniques, as part of student story development using students' own story characters, or as a continuation of the development of the characters in Activity 13. During a One-on-One-on-One-on-One, students explore what makes a character interesting to readers.

Offer these directions to your students before beginning a One-on-One-on-One-on-One. After completing the One-on-One-on-One-on-One, students may fill in the worksheet with any insights and new ideas they have gotten.

There are many more traits your students could create for the character they developed during Part 2 of Activity 12. Let's play two games to help them further develop this character. Each student's goal will be to make this character more complete and easier to write about and to present to readers as an interesting character when they write a story. The description of this game was taken from the book *Write Right!*

In this exercise students will describe the character they created in the previous activity. Students may talk about any aspect of the character and about any category of character information to present an interesting character to listeners. Students may talk about what a character has done; what the character likes; the character's hopes and fears, voice, habits, quirks, likes, and dislikes; and so on. Students should feel free to invent new character information as they go.

Per·son·al·i·ty *adj.* The total of the psychological, intellectual, and emotional characteristics that make up an individual. The group of character traits that make up a character's personality represent one of the fifteen kinds of information writers use to make characters interesting.

Have students pair off. All telling will be done one on one. Pairs sit facing each other, knee to knee and eye to eye, with no desks or tables between them. They quickly agree on who is #1 and who is #2. As soon as they are settled, the teacher calls, "Student number 1, begin your character description." Student #1 talks about his or her character to Student #2 for one minute. Based on the character profile the student wrote for the previous activity, Student #1's goal is to make the character sound as intriguing and interesting as possible to Student #2. Student #2 listens. There should be no interruptions, questions, or comments from listeners.

The teacher times the telling, shouting, "Stop!" after one minute. Immediately the teacher directs Student #2 to begin a one-minute description of his or her character, while Student #1 listens. There should be no discussion time between tellers. Make these transitions as rapid as possible. Student #2's goal is the same as Student #1's—describe the character and make the description as interesting as possible.

After Student #2 finishes the minute of telling, have everyone switch partners, again allowing for no discussion or comment time. As soon as students are settled with new partners and agree on who will be #1 and #2, they repeat the exercise. Finally, they switch partners again and both tell about their character for a third and final time.

Many teachers vary the times for each telling in two ways. First, there is nothing magical about 60 seconds for the duration of each telling. Some teachers for lower grades shorten the time to 30 or 40 seconds, slowly increasing that time toward one minute over the course of the school year.

Second, many teachers trim a few seconds off the first round of telling and add a few to the third round without announcing it to the class. Tell students each round will last one minute. Then, stop them at 50 or 55 seconds the first time and at 70 seconds the third. Descriptions will grow more elaborate and detailed with each telling. They'll need more time to tell the same character description during the third round.

Students should finish this activity by jotting down notes on their worksheets, describing the new ideas and insights they gained during the exercise. The four questions students are asked are:

Character traits (descriptions) I used that I think were effective: _____

New ideas I got for my character: _____

Things I heard from other students that I could incorporate into my character: _____

Traits I still need to work on for this character: _____

Many teachers follow these notes with an additional evaluation period. Have students make journal entries answering these questions.

Of the three descriptions I heard from other students:

• Which did I enjoy the most, and why?
• Which character can I most vividly remember and why?
• What did the teller do to make me remember it?
• When did I laugh? What did the teller say to make me laugh?
• When was I most bored and why?
• What did the teller say to make me so bored?

These evaluations help students fix what they have learned about their character, and about effective character description in general, in their mind. They also become a good source of information for how to make a character a successful main character in future stories.

Activity Review

In less than the fifteen minutes required for a One-on-One-on-One-on-One, the students both work continuously on their story and assist others in their work. All students described their characters; saw in the face of their listener whether their description effectively created an interesting character image; twice restructured, reworded, and revised that description; and tested the effectiveness of each of these revised versions through their second and third tellings.

While students are listening, they accomplish three important tasks. First, they provide instant, explicit, nonverbal feedback for the teller. Because they sit directly in front of tellers, the tellers can't avoid recording and interpreting this nonverbal feedback. Second, they review and restructure their own story for the next telling. Third, they sift through the structure, phraseology, and wording of the other tellers' stories for anything they want to borrow and incorporate into their own work.

Activity 15: The Character Game _____

What Students Will Learn:

Students will learn to use peer ideas and questions to develop new aspects of their characters.

Time Estimate: 15 to 20 minutes for each part

Directions:

In this verbal game, use either a character students are developing for their own writing assignments or use the character created in Activity 12 and further developed in Activity 14. Following the group game, students may fill out the activity worksheet with any new character ideas.

Often, using outside help—the thoughts and ideas of others—is the best way to develop story characters and make them interesting to readers. One excellent way to incorporate others' thoughts and ideas is with the Character Game. The description of this game was taken from the book *Write Right!*

The Character Game is most effective during the initial stages of story planning when the major story elements have been created but not yet fully developed.

Part 1 of the Character Game is a more analytical, intellectual exercise. Part 2 is a right-brained physical exercise. Doing both parts better ensures a consistent, complete character image in the mind of each student writer.

Part 1. Divide the class into groups of four (ideal) or five (acceptable). The groups sit in chairs in a circle. One student at a time is chosen to be "it." The student who is "it" begins by telling the group about his or her main character (about 45 seconds). The goal is to paint as interesting and complete an image of this character as possible in the allotted time. Have students include answers to the following six questions in their introduction. These questions both help students decide what to say about their characters and stimulate better questions from the group.

> **Flaw** *n.* A blemish, weakness, or defect.
>
> **Fear** *n.* The emotion aroused by impending or seeming danger, pain, or evil.
>
> A character's flaws (in general) and fears (in particular) often make a character most interesting to readers.

1. What are the goals, flaws, problems, risks, and dangers this character faces in this story?
2. What are the unique and interesting aspects of this character's physical being and personality? What are the character's hopes and fears?
3. How does this character want the story to end, and why?
4. How does this character feel about the story's antagonist, and why?
5. Why does the writer like this character?
6. Why does the writer think we should care about this character? What will make the character interesting and unique to readers?

The group now has 2.5 minutes to ask questions about any aspect of this character—about any of the fifteen categories of character information or about any of the statements the student made during the introduction. The group's goal is twofold. First, group members should demand clarification of anything that isn't clear about this character. If it isn't clear to them, it probably isn't clear to the writer and won't be clear to a reader. Second, they should probe for any undefined or ambiguous aspects of this character in the writer's mind. The group should try to stump the student who is "it" buy asking questions the student hasn't thought about or for which they don't have a ready and easy answer:

"Where was this character born?"

"What are this character's favorite and least favorite foods?"

"What color are his eyes?"

"What was this character's favorite thing to do when she was half her present age?"

"Name three things this character is afraid of."

"What sports is this character good at and bad at?"

"Does he like to comb his hair?"

"How many friends does this character have, and why?"

All character questions are fair game.

The student who is "it" must answer all questions, even if they have to make up an answer on the spot. But the student should be encouraged to ask the group for ideas and opinions on any aspect of the character the "it" student is uncertain about. This is an opportunity for writers to seek peer ideas and help in developing and defining their characters.

After a 2.5-minute question-and-discussion period, the group selects the next student to be "it."

Part 2. Students stay in the same groups and in seated circles for Part 2 of the Character Game. One student is again chosen to be "it." This student steps outside the circle, becomes the main character (adopts full physical and vocal characterization), and reenters the group as the character. The student walks as the character would walk, sits as the character would sit, introduces him- or herself as the character in the way the character would, and tells about his or her characteristics and the story for 30 to 45 seconds. For this exercise, all characters (whether a snail, a tree, a dog, or a shoe) may speak English.

This is not an acting exercise. Students should not be judged or criticized based on their ability to physically and vocally portray their characters. It is a writing exercise that uses character acting to develop a clearer image of the character in the mind of student writers.

Emphasis should be placed on first presenting the character's personality, attitudes, and manner through characterization and, second, on revealing the character's goals, fears, problems, desires, and personality through what the student chooses to say—or not say. To do this, let students use the following six questions as a guide in their introductions:

1. What do you want, why do you want it, and why don't you already have it?

2. What are your favorite things to do? Your least favorite?

3. Which of the other characters in this story do you like? Which do you respect? Are there any you loathe or despise?

4. Why should this story be about you?

5. What do you want to happen to the antagonist at the end of the story?

6. Name one thing you have done that you are proud of and one that you regret.

The group now has one minute to pepper this character with questions. All questions must be directed to the character in second person as if it were the character and not the student sitting in front of them. The questions may be about the character's history, attitudes, fears, desires, likes, and dislikes; clarification on any statements made by the character; the story; or the character's feelings toward other story characters. The goal of the group is to probe for inconsistencies in the character presentation and for undefined aspects of the character. In other words, their goal is to stump the character with their questions. The "it" person must stay in character the entire time they are "it."

Again, the goal of this exercise is not to act well but, rather, to use acting as a vehicle to help the writers develop a stronger mental image of their characters and to develop those characters in more detail.

It should also be emphasized that the focus is not on anatomical correctness of the characterizations. Students don't have to *be* a duck, a tree, or a bear. Rather, they should personify nonhuman characters and represent the personality, attitude, and manner—the essence—of that duck, tree, or bear.

After the one-minute question period is over, the character leaves the circle still in character. Once outside the circle, the student drops the characterization and returns to the group, as the next person leaves to become his or her character.

You may have students finish this exercise by taking a moment to jot down notes on their worksheet concerning the new ideas and insights they gained during the exercise. The following areas are listed for notes on their worksheet:

Character traits (descriptions) I used that I think were effective: _____

New ideas I got for my character: _____

Things I heard from other students that I could incorporate into my character: _____

Traits I still need to work on for this character: _____

Activity Review

Successful story writing depends on creating more complete, expansive, multifaceted, and detailed images of each major story character. Strong images include not only the physical look and circumstances of a character but also the character's history, memories, attitudes, beliefs, and mannerisms. Groups help us expand our creative processes and produce stronger, richer, more interesting characters.

Notice that we haven't talked at all about a story yet, just about a character. If we spend time developing characters before we use them in stories, we will always be paid off with stories that are easier to write and far more interesting to readers.

Activity 16: Voice Choice _____

What Students Will Learn:

Students will understand what is meant by, and what influences, a character's voice and will practice creating a unique voice for their character.

Time Estimate: Part 1, 10 minutes; Part 2, 15 to 25 minutes

Directions:

For this activity students will need a character to use and develop. Use either the character they created and developed in Activities 12, 14, and 15 or a character your students are developing for their own stories. This activity is divided into two parts. Begin with a general class discussion about dialogue and voice before you proceed to Part 1. Student workbooks do not include any narrative discussion about voice. Use the following paragraphs as a guide for this discussion.

Let's look more closely at one specific category of character information: voice. Voice refers to *what* characters say (dialogue) and *how* they say it.

Why should your students pay particular attention to a character's dialogue? Because readers feel that they learn more about a character from what the character says and the way the character says it than from any other category of character information. From dialogue, readers feel they learn about the personality, beliefs, attitudes, and feelings of a character. Dialogue, more than any other kind of information reveals a character to readers effectively. Through dialogue, readers feel closer to, and more interested in, story characters. Dialogue draws readers into a scene and inside the character. Voice and dialogue are powerful character traits that your students, as writers, should learn to use effectively.

Voice *n.* The sound uttered from a mouth. A character's voice includes both *what* the character says and *how* the character says it.

However, there is a problem: effective dialogue is tricky to write. Why?

1. Dialogue is its own language. Effective dialogue lies between formal narrative writing and casual conversation. Listen to ordinary conversation. It's slow, repetitive, crammed with interruptions and back tracking, jumps from subject to subject, is horribly imprecise, is peppered with dangling fragments and phrases, and is loaded with "um's," "ya know's," and "like's." Real conversation is hard for an outsider to follow and is boring.

   Formal narrative writing is stiff, overly structured, and doesn't sound like the talk of real people. Dialogue has to blend formal narrative writing and casual conversation. It must sound like conversation but be as efficient, organized, and understandable as formal narrative writing. That's already asking a lot!

2. Dialogue has three jobs. It must reveal the inner workings of the character, it must advance the story by providing important story information, and it must be consistent throughout the story by holding to the voice of each character.

   That's why learning to write effective dialogue takes practice. It has so much to do in a story!

Part 1. To make dialogue easier to write, first create a specific voice for each character. What is a voice? Voice is a combination of two things: what a character says and the way the character says it. Voice is the unique and recognizable way each character talks during a story.

You recognize many voices by the *sound* of the voice. If you hear a person talk or laugh, you instantly know who is talking. For some people, you recognize certain phrases they often use or the way they put sentences together. (Yoda in the *Star Wars* movies has a unique way of structuring his sentences.) Some people you know talk a lot; some talk very little. You have learned to recognize them by their voice: what they say and the way they say it.

On the lines on the student worksheet, have your students list as many factors as they can think of that could determine, or affect, the voice of a character. This should be completed as an individual activity. There will be time for discussion later. First, have each student struggle with his or her list.

Have students read the factors they wrote. Build a composite master list on the board of the factors they mentioned most often. There are many they could have mentioned. Here are seven factors that are commonly recognized as being important in determining each character's voice:

• Age

• Region and regional accent

• Education

• Physical factors (size, vocal characteristics, etc.)

• Personality

• Feelings or current emotional state

• Personal quirks, habits, or speech patterns, and flaws

How many of those did your students include in their master list? Did they think of others that could be used to create a specific character voice?

Each character's voice determines *what* the character will say (the words the character uses, what the character chooses to talk about, and how the character organizes those words into sentences) and *how* the character sounds when he or she talks (tone, volume, pace, etc.).

Part 2. How do students create a voice for their characters? First, create a character and decide on those traits and factors that could help determine the character's voice. Then, experiment and play with the character's voice. Students should play with their own voice and see all the ways in which they can change it. Listen to other people and try to describe their voices. Listen to cartoon characters and describe their voices. Read stories and study how authors create and describe their characters' voices.

Now your students will create a voice for their character. Decide whether they are to use the character they have developed over the past few activities or one they are developing for some other writing project. They should already have some sense of how this character talks. Now it's time to be more specific.

On these lines on the student worksheet, have your students fill in the information that defines their character's voice:

Name and species: _____

Age: _____ Region: _____

What is the physical sound of this character's voice (loud, soft, clear, mumbled, nasal, childlike, whiny, gruff, sinister, soft, singsong, breathy, deep, resonant, etc.)? _____
_____

If you heard the character, how would you describe the way he or she talks to others? _____

_____

Is there anything interesting or unusual about how the character uses words and sentences? Does the character use long, run-on sentences? Short, one-word answers? Does the character repeat words a lot? Does the character jump around from thought to thought or stay with one thought until through? Does the character use a big vocabulary? _____

_____

Is there anything that makes this character's voice unique (different from the voices of other characters)? _____

Are there phrases or words the character typically (characteristically) says? _____

What does this character's voice remind you of? _____

_____

Have students share the character voice they created. First, they can describe the voice, but then they should try to imitate the character's voice and talk to the class as their character would talk. After several students have described their character's voice and have tried to talk like their character, allow students time to jot down notes to revise or refine their character's voice. The more they practice creating a specific voice for each character, the easier it will become for them to develop voice.

No, it is not necessary that every voice be unique. But it will be much easier for each student writer if the students know clearly and specifically what each character's voice is like.

Discuss students' character voices as a class. Which were most interesting? Why? Were they presented with information that was more specific, unique, unusual, and vivid?

Activity Review

What a character says (and doesn't say) combined with the way the character says it creates a character's voice. Voice is an important category of character information and a powerful tool for making characters interesting. Being able to clearly hear a character's voice is essential to weaving character dialogue into the action events of a story.

What makes writing effective dialogue hard to write is that dialogue is its own language. It requires practice to master. We will continue work on dialogue through the next three activities.

Taking the time to create a definite voice for each character makes it much easier for your students to write dialogue that will bring their stories to life. Two cautions follow:

1. Be sure that each character's voice is consistent with the character's age, personality, region of origin, and so forth.

2. Make sure that each character's voice remains consistent throughout the story.

Activity 17: One-Sided Conversation _____

What Students Will Learn:

Students will practice creating an effective character voice and will use that voice to communicate important story information.

Time Estimate: 20 minutes

Directions:

This is a fun activity to use anytime to refresh your students' skills in creating effective character voice and dialogue.

Once your students have created a voice for their characters, the dialogue they write for that voice should both zip the story forward and still sound like real conversation. Here is a good exercise to help your students practice writing better dialogue.

Describe the following situation for your students and be sure they are clear on the concept before proceeding to the actual activity.

Imagine sitting in a room with someone who is talking on the telephone. You hear only one side of the conversation— only what the person you are listening to says. You never hear what the person on the other end of the line says. Your students are going to create and write that one side of a conversation as if they actually heard what this person said during a telephone conversation.

Con·ver·sa·tion *n.* Informal and friendly talk.

Di·a·logue *n.* Conversation in a book, movie, play, and so on.

The dialogue of characters is mostly made up of conversation—informal, casual talk.

First, as a class agree on the following:

1. The fictional human character (the **main character**) whose words (dialogue) students will write (create just a name, sex, and age for this character, for example, *Max is a fifteen-year-old boy*)
2. Who this character is talking to (the antagonist) on the telephone (for example, *Max's mother*)
3. What the main character wants or needs (**goal**) from the other person during this conversation (for example, *Max wants permission to stay out until 1:30 A.M. on a school night*)

Students will then individually create the following items for their own version of this conversation:

1. A specific voice for the main character
2. Two reasons why the person on the other end of the phone line doesn't want to give the main character what he or she wants (**conflict**)
3. Why the main character wants that goal (**motive**)

An example of the format they should use is shown in the following dialogue. ("————" is used to show when the person on the other end of the telephone is talking.)

Example of a One-Sided Conversation

Background Information

Character:_____ *Steve, a sixteen-year-old boy (S)*_____

Other person he or she is talking to:_____ *his grandmother (G)*_____

Goal:_____ *talk Granny into buying Steve a new car*_____

Motive:___ *He thinks he'll look cool, and he's tired of his parents driving him on dates.*_____

Key traits of this character's voice:____ *Steve is hesitant and "ummm's" and "uuuuh's" a lot.*____

Other person's two reasons for not giving the main character what he or she wants:

1.___ *Steve has already had two accidents while driving with his learner's permit.*_____

2.___ *Steve's grades are way below the "C" average he was supposed to maintain to get his license.*___

One-Sided Conversation

S: *Ummm, hi, Granny. Whatcha doin'?*

G: ——

S: *Your poker club? Sure hope you, ahhh, win lots of money.*

G: ——

S: *Well, see, ummm. It's almost my brithday—my sixteenth birthday.*

G: ——

S: *No, next week, Granny. Cathy's birthday is in January.*

G: ——

S: *Well, anyway, uuuum, I know what I, ahhh, want you to get for my present this year. See, I, ummmmm, need some wheels.*

G: ——

S: *Not a bicycle, Granny. A car.*

G: ——

S: *I don't want you to give me a ride. You have to . . . well, ummm, buy me a new car.*

G: ——

S: *Granny? . . . Ummmm, Granny! Stop laughing like that. I'm serious.*

G: ——

S: *I only had two accidents. And they weren't my fault. And, ahhhh, besides they don't count cause it wasn't my car.*

G: ——

S: *I know that's what we said. But, ahhh, my grades are almost a "C" average.*

G: ——

S: *Well, that's only one-and-a-half grades below a C average . . .*

G: ——

And so on.

Have students use the worksheet to write their one-sided conversation. They may only write the actual words their main character says. They may continue the conversation on the back of the page if they need more room. Their goals as they write are to:

- Make their character interesting
- Present a clear and consistent voice for this character that will give readers a good sense of the character's personality and emotions
- Reveal the conflict between the main character and the other person as well as that other person's reasons for not wanting to give in to the main character
- Show exactly how the conversation (conflict) ends (resolution)

After the students have written their conversations, allow volunteers to read what they have written to the class. The reader should not read the antagonist's reasons for not wanting to do as the main character wants. The class should be able to identify them from the dialogue.

Each student should read the dialogue in character voice, pausing during those times when the antagonist is speaking. Briefly discuss the voice they created for this character and how their dialogue revealed the key information they were assigned to include.

Have your students save this dialogue to use during the next activity.

Activity Review

Dialogue carries great energy and reveals character. With practice, every student can create consistently effective dialogue. Dialogue is worth practicing because it is such a valuable way to create interest in a character. The key to creating dialogue is to first create a clear voice for every character. How do they talk? What do they say? How do they say it?

Effective dialogue must also convey important story information, moving the story forward while it reveals character. The more students study dialogue when they read and the more they practice writing it, the better theirs will become.

Activity 18: Compression

What Students Will Learn:

Students will learn to edit their dialogue to focus on the key elements of effective dialogue.

Time Estimate: 30 to 40 minutes

Directions:

Lead a class discussion on effective dialogue, on real conversation, and on compression, using the following paragraphs as a guide. The student worksheet does not include any of this discussion.

Beginning writers often allow their characters to talk in long, flowing sentences and in complete paragraphs before someone else says anything. First, that is not typical of real conversations—especially under stressful conditions (and story events most commonly are stressful). Even worse, rambling complete sentences often hide the emotional impact and energy that the dialogue was intended to convey.

Com•pres•sion *n.* Being reduced in volume or length to express more concisely. Compressed dialogue more concisely expresses the emotions and intent of each character unblocked by any unessential words.

Humans converse in short bursts, in phrases. They interrupt each other. They repeat, or echo, previous statements. They use nonspecific pronouns when they should use nouns. They hem and haw, struggling through long pauses to find the right words. They stop midthought. They jump from thought to thought. Real conversation is almost impossible for an outsider to follow. However, if a writer takes all that inefficiency out, the resultant written dialogue sounds too stiff and formal.

Written dialogue is also often bloated with more words than necessary. This slows the story and hides the power of the necessary words. The Compression Game is designed to help students find the greatest power from their characters' words and to make each word of dialogue as effective as possible.

The Compression Game is very simple. This description was taken from the book *Write Right!* Students will convert the one-sided conversation dialogue they wrote into compressed dialogue, which means that no character is allowed to say more than a maximum number of words before being interrupted by another character's speech. The writer must compress their character's speech each time they talk to stay within that word limit.

In this exercise let's use a seven word limit. (You can set almost any number you want, but five, seven, and nine words are the most popular limits.) Your students will now rewrite their one-sided conversation, but their character may never say more than seven words before the person on the other end of the phone interrupts and says something. Students must still convey all of the key information that appeared in the original dialogue.

Tell them to focus on three things to make compression work:

1. The key elements of their character's voice
2. The conflict and struggles their character faces in the conversation
3. The emotional state of their character

Then they should get rid of all the words they don't absolutely need.

A form (in the same format as was used for the one-sided conversation) is provided on the student worksheet for this activity. Students may use the back of that page if they need more room.

Have several students share their compressed dialogue with the class and compare the energy, emotion, and excitement of the compressed versions with the original versions. As before, they should read the dialogue in their character's voice and pause whenever the person on the other end speaks. The emotions of the characters and the conflict of a scene usually come across more strongly when dialogue is compressed and all unneeded words are removed.

Activity Review

All good writing presents the minimum number of words necessary to paint the desired mood, scene, tone, action, and characters. Dialogue is a tempting place to splurge and stuff in extra words that do little except weigh down the interaction of two or more characters. Paring down each character's statement to a few powerful, revealing words improves the story. The tools writers have to make dialogue sound real include interruption, repetition, pauses, echoes, jumps from topic to topic, tension (or disagreement), reversals, and changes in tone and mood. These tools also make dialogue more powerful and effective.

Activity 19: Narrative to Dialogue _____

What Students Will Learn:

Students will learn to include important story information in their dialogue while maintaining a consistent voice for their characters.

Time Estimate: 40 to 60 minutes

Directions:

Here is another useful exercise to help students hone their skills at writing dialogue. It is called Narrative to Dialogue. This description is taken from the book, *Write Right!*

For this activity, you will need to locate half a page of narrative information in a story the students have recently read. Students will know the characters and the sound of their voices. They know the flow of the story and the history behind, and the significance of, the information in the chosen scene. They also know the relationships between the characters. This knowledge will make the job of writing dialogue much easier. The chosen section of text should include little or (preferably) no dialogue and should include strong action and events as well as description.

> **Nar·ra·tive** *n.* An orderly description of events. All prose writing forms narratives. Stories, essays, letters, journal entries, and so on are all narratives.

Introduce the activity with the following discussion. There is no student worksheet for this activity.

A very common dialogue problem for beginning writers is an inability to include essential story information in their dialogue. Beginning writers are much more comfortable placing important information in narrative exposition. However, good dialogue both reveals character and propels the story forward. This exercise will help students develop the ability to make dialogue serve as a meaningful, effective element of their stories.

The idea of this game is simple. Each student will convert the chosen section of narrative into script form. In a script, all story information is provided through what the various characters say. Students must include all story information appearing in the original passage in the characters' dialogue and must make the dialogue seem like real, plausible conversation between the various story characters.

Agree as a class on the identity of the characters who may be used in this script. Not all of the characters your students will need to use may be mentioned in the chosen story section. Use any characters the class agrees they will need to use.

Students should follow three rules:

1. No one may use a character that does not appear anywhere in the story.

2. No one may use a character that the class has not agreed to use. Students may not use a narrator.

3. All information must come from the story characters and be logically said to other characters.

The students' challenge will be to convert story information into dialogue and keep the story moving, without making the dialogue seem stiff and unrealistic.

After all of the students have completed their scripts, have several read their efforts aloud. In particular, let the class discuss the following questions:

What story elements and kinds of information were easy to shift into dialogue? Which were hard?

(Typically action and detailed scenic description are hard. Character feeling, reaction, and interaction are easy.)

Which dialogue lines sounded natural and real? Which sounded forced and phony? Why?

Were students able to maintain the voice of each character throughout their scripts? If not, what made it hard?

Activity Review

Good dialogue reveals character, establishes (or increases) story tension, and moves the story forward. Not all story information can go naturally and easily into dialogue. We *do* rather than *talk* in the midst of action. We don't normally describe either actions or things that others can see. We don't describe events everyone already knows. In conversation we don't talk in long exposition. All of these human tendencies make it more difficult to use dialogue to describe all aspects of a story. Still, dialogue must move the story forward. It must give us important information: character motive, intent, reaction, and interpretation and information that sets up future action.

Have students listen to good radio drama tapes to study techniques others have successfully used to convert all story information into character dialogue. Finally, have students practice writing dialogue. Practice is the key to successful story writing.

ELEMENT #3: GOAL

What does the main character want to do or get in this story?

Lead the following discussion with your class about the meaning, purpose, and power of a story **goal** before proceeding to Activity 20.

Element #3, the **goal** of the main character, seems so obvious and simple but is really the one element most commonly overlooked by student writers. Failure to create a specific goal for the main character is the second most common reason student stories fail. A goal is what the main character wants to do or get in the story. The same character might want to do or get many different things. Each goal could form its own story.

The goal of the main character tells readers the following information:

• What the story is about
• How the story will end
• How to understand and interpret every action and event in the story

The following is an example:

Fuffle, the dog, wanted some ice cream.

This sentence contains a character and a goal. What is this story about? A dog who wants ice cream. Every story is about the goal of the main character.

How will the story end? Fuffle will either get his ice cream or he will not get his ice cream. Every story ends when the main character resolves his or her goal. When students speak of a solution, they commonly (and erroneously) refer to solving the conflicts and problems (problem and solution). Solving problems does not end a story or satisfy readers. Successfully ending a story and satisfying readers does not require solving all (or even any) of the story's problems. What students really mean is how the story ends. That is determined by when and how the main character resolves the story goal.

Readers will understand and interpret each event in the story by determining whether it helps Fuffle get ice cream or makes it harder for him. The goal tells readers the point and purpose of every scene and event in a story.

What will happen in this story? Fuffle will try (probably in a number of ways) to overcome whatever obstacles block him from getting the ice cream he wants. Plot comes from obstacles that arise to block a character from a goal.

Here is another character and goal.

Little Maysie wanted to be the best baseball player in her school.

Notice that you already have a feel for what is likely to happen in this story. You know where you are going and what the story will be about. That is the power of a goal.

That's a lot of story information from just one simple idea! The goal of the main character is the most important single bit of information your students will ever create for their stories.

Does every main character have to want to do or get something in every story? Yes, they do. Without a goal you don't have a story. Without a goal, there is no point to the story and its individual events. We all want and need many different things. Some are big; some are small. Some are noble; some are selfish and petty. The writer's choice of a story goal tells both reader and writer what the story will be about and what to focus on while they read—or write.

Does a writer always have to directly state their main character's goal in the text of the story? No. Goals can be implied through the actions, thoughts, and words of the main character, but the writer must know exactly what this goal is and must make it clear to readers or the story will never make any sense and will never be interesting.

Im•plied *adj.* Suggested without being stated. Goals and motives are the elements most often implied in narrative writing.

Having completed this discussion and having impressed your students with how important a goal is, proceed to Activity 20.

Activity 20: Is It a Goal? _____

What Students Will Learn:

Students will learn the look of a story goal and how the goal relates to character.

Time Estimate: 10 to 15 minutes

Directions:

Allow students to individually complete this simple exercise. Use the paragraphs below as a guide for the follow-up discussion for this activity.

Let's learn to recognize character goals. Here are six statements. Have students circle either "Yes" or "No" after each to say that it either does or does not present a character and goal.

Goal *n.* An aim or objective. All characters have many goals. Often a character's goals conflict with each other. Some will be more important to the character than others. Successful stories focus on one central goal for the main character.

1. Jorge wanted to climb to the very tipity-top of the elm tree. But he was afraid.

   Yes or No?

2. Little Fernley loved to peek under fallen leaves to see what treasures he would find.

   Yes or No?

3. Carlos sprinted down the hill when he heard the roar of a bear.

   Yes or No?

4. George picked himself up out of the mud, wiped the blood off his split lip, and vowed, someday, to beat up Max for a change.

   Yes or No?

5. Donya wanted to win the cookie-eating contest at the county fair, but so did Mongo the Huge.

   Yes or No?

6. Margaret swam four miles every morning before dawn, in summer and freezing winter, slowly becoming stronger and faster.

   Yes or No?

   Ans: Yes: 1, 4, 5; No: 2, 3, 6

Let's look at each statement.

Number 1 clearly includes a goal: climb to the top of a tree.

Number 2 tells us a character trait, something this character loves, but it doesn't say that he wants to do it in this story.

Number 3 tells us something Carlos did. We don't have any idea of what Carlos wants to do or get. We don't even know if he is running toward or away from the bear.

In Number 4, George's vow is something he wants desperately to do. That is a goal.

Number 5 clearly includes a goal for Donya and one for Mongo. They both want the same goal.

Number 6, again, tells us only something that Margaret did. It would be easy to imagine things she might want to do: to make the swim team, to set a school swim record, and so on. But no goal is included or directly implied in the information we are given.

Activity Review

The goal of the main character is the most important single bit of information in a story. It defines what the story is about and where it will end. The writer must clearly and specifically know this goal before beginning to create a story. However, goals are not always clearly stated in the text of a story. Often they are implied—hinted at by the actions, words, and thoughts of a character. Readers figure out what characters are after by interpreting what they say and do.

In Sentences 1, 4, and 5, a goal is clearly stated. In Sentences 2 and 6, a goal is not stated but is hinted at. If little Fernly loves to look under leaves, we might assume that, on any given day, he might want to do exactly that. That would be a goal. But we are not told that he wants to. We have to guess.

Similarly, Margaret must have some reason (goal) for doing all that swimming. Readers would need more information to see exactly what that goal is, but they already have a general sense of what it might be.

Activity 21: The End _____

What Students Will Learn:

Students will clearly see the link between story goal and story ending.

Time Estimate: 10 to 15 minutes

Directions:

Story goals tell readers what a story is about. A goal creates the basic structure of a story.

Now let's look at how a goal always points readers toward a story ending. Stories end when the main character's goal is resolved. Readers will not know *how* it will be resolved or *how* the writer will get them to that ending point, but they know where the story has to go.

Writing is also much easier and requires far less rewriting when the writer knows exactly where the story is going before beginning to write. Have students complete the worksheet for this activity. Then review and discuss their answers.

Res•o•lu•tion *n.* The act of bringing to a close, the statement of final solution. Stories end when the main character resolves (one way or another) the central goal.

Shown in the following list and on the student worksheet are three statements printed in *italics*. Each statement includes a character and a goal. Following each statement are three choices for how that story will end. In each case, students should pick the one that makes the most sense for this story and state why they chose that answer.

1. *A bent pine tree standing at the edge of the forest watched Christmas after Christmas as the townsfolk brought a pine tree into town and decorated it with lights and tinsel until it shone like a dazzling star. And, oh, that bent and twisted pine tree wanted to be this year's Christmas tree!*

   A. A lumber company cuts much of the forest and leaves ugly bare hillsides that turn into oozing mud with the November rains.

   B. The bent tree is never chosen by the town, but a family of birds builds a shiny nest out of tinsel in its branches and lives there through the winter, protected from bitter winter storms by the bent tree's branches.

   C. A boy from town digs a play fort next to the bent tree and uses it as a clubhouse with other boys.

   Ans: B. It is the only answer that resolves the goal of the tree.

2. *Carmen sat in the stands cheering for her brother. But Carmen dreamed of being on the football team herself, and having a thousand people cheer for her.*

   A. Carmen goes to tryouts and turns out to be a great passer and makes the team.

   B. Carmen gets an "A" in both science and English on her report card.

   C. Carmen's brother makes the state all-star team.

   Ans: A. It is the only answer that resolves Carmen's goal.

3. *While a cat fiddled "Hey, Diddle, Diddle," a cow stood in the pasture munching grass and stared at the full moon riding high in the sky. And that cow longed to jump clear over the moon.*

   A. The cow learns how to fiddle as well as the cat.

   B. The cow tries to jump over the moon but never makes it and has to give up when her knees give out from all that jumping.

C. The cat is hired by a band and plays in a big theater every Saturday night.

Ans: B. It is the only answer that resolves the goal of the cow.

Now let's look at each of your students' choices.

For statement #1, B is the best answer. Choice C might happen, but it has nothing to do with the goal. If the story ended there, we'd still be wondering about the Christmas tree. Choice A could happen during the story but doesn't tell us anything about becoming the town's Christmas tree. As you read Choice A, you were probably thinking that that would *help* the bent tree become the Christmas tree because most of the straight and tall ones were being cut down. **Goal** tells us how to interpret every story action and event.

For statement #2, A is the best answer. It makes sense. Carmen wants something and by the end of the story we find out whether or not she got it. Choices B and C talk about different things. They might happen during the story, but they could never be where the story ends.

For statement #3, B is the best answer. Again, Choices A and C could happen during the story, but they don't make any sense as ending points for the story. Notice that a character doesn't automatically get what he or she is after. In two of these examples, the story ends when the character realizes that he or she will never achieve the goal and has to settle for something else. Still, each story ends when the main character resolves the goal.

Activity Review

The goal of the main character defines what the story is about. It defines how the story will end. It defines the point and purpose of every scene and event in a story. There is no single bit of story information that is more important than the main character's goal.

Student writers should pick goals that will make it easy for them to write the story. Motives must explain why a character wants a certain goal. Obstacles will block a character from this goal. The plot (struggles) will be a character's attempts to reach this goal. Not all goals lend themselves to the easy creation of effective motive, obstacles, and struggles. Remind your students to play with possible goals—to shop around for a good goal—before they settle on one for their story.

Activity 22: Getting Goals

What Students Will Learn:

Students will learn to recognize stated and implied goals within the context of a story segment.

Time Estimate: 30 to 40 minutes

Directions:

If students learn to recognize the goals in stories they read, they'll be better able to create and word the goals in their own stories. Additionally, they will develop the habit of creating strong, specific goals in the stories they write.

Have students read the three story segments shown on their worksheet (also shown here) and complete the questions following each. They must decide if a goal is included in each segment and whether it is stated or implied.

The student worksheet instructs students to stop after the first segment's questions for a class discussion. Make sure your students understand which writing elements are, and are not, included and allow several students to read the goal and motive they have created. Have the class ensure that each goal and motive are both plausible and appropriate.

Create first; write second

- When you *create*, create the Eight Essential Elements.
- When you *write*, write the details.

Segment #1

> *Little Red Riding Hood shuffled through billowing dust, buzzing flies, and smelly flowers along the winding meadow path. She felt embarrassed that she had to wear this stupid red cape—just because her grandmother made it. It was itchy, didn't fit, and had zero style points. Thank goodness none of her friends would be caught dead in this horrid, woodsy meadow and wouldn't see her. And Granny didn't like croissants or lattes. No! Granny loved to grin and smack her gums together while she gnawed on bean sprout and tofu cookies—that Little Red had to carry in her basket. Disgusting!*
>
> *Cool grannies lived in condos in town and took their granddaughters to fancy restaurants. Not her granny. She had to live in the woods in a cottage with no electricity or running water. She didn't even own a car! Oh, if something exciting would happen along the way and sweep her away from this embarrassment. . . . Then Little Red came to a crossroads in the woods where a wolf stood, leering at her.*

Does this segment include a goal for the main character? *Ans: Yes*

If so, what is it? *Ans: Have something exciting happen and sweep her away*

If there isn't a stated goal here, what do you think would be the best goal for this character to have in this story? Why? *Ans: There is a stated goal.*

Using either the goal stated in the segment or one you invented, create motive to make that goal more interesting and important *Ans: This calls for students to create their own motives. There is no one correct answer. Any answer they can justify using known story information is correct.*

Which other story elements can you find in this segment? *Ans: Character, character traits, motive, potential risk and danger (the wolf), and implied conflict (with whomever makes Little Red visit her grandmother and wear the red cape).*

Segment #2

> *Jack's mother got Jack a job working for a farmer.*
> *"But, mother, I'm already pretty busy lounging in the hammock all day."*
> *"We need the money to buy food."*
> *Jack nodded. "Eating's okay—so long as I don't have to set the table or clean up . . . or cook . . . or shop . . . or do dishes . . . or cut anything up . . ."*
> *Next day the farmer ordered Jack to paint his fence.*
> *"All of it?"*
> *"Every fence post," smiled the farmer.*
> *"Both sides?"*
> *"All four sides, top to bottom. All 4,276 of them. Starting now!"*
> *"Uh-oh. I don't think working's nearly as much fun as the hammock . . ."*

Does this segment include a goal for the main character? *Ans: Not specifically*

If so, what is it? *Ans: While there is no stated goal, a general goal is implied: avoid work and lounge in the hammock.*

If there isn't a stated goal here, what do you think would be the best goal for this character to have in this story? Why? *Ans: This calls for students to create their own goals. There is no one correct answer. Any answer they can justify using known story information is correct.*

Using either the goal stated in the segment or one you invented, create motive to make that goal more interesting and important. *Ans: This calls for students to create their own motives. There is no one correct answer. Any answer they can justify using known story information is correct.*

Which other story elements can you find in this segment? *Ans: Character, some character traits, three potential conflicts (Jack versus his mother, Jack versus the farmer, and one internal conflict—work versus being lazy).*

Segment #3

> *Henny Penny marched into the center of the barnyard. "Listen up! Who is going to help me plant my seeds?"*
> *All the other animals shuffled from foot to foot and stared at the ground. "Very well, I'll do it myself!" And she stomped off in a huff as the other animals muttered, "Probably for the best. She'll do a better job than we would."*
> *Two weeks later Henny again sternly cleared her throat in the center of the yard. "Who will help me hoe my rows of corn?"*
> *All the other animals shuffled from foot to foot and stared at the ground. "Very well, I'll do it myself!" And she stomped off in a huff as the other animals muttered, "Probably for the best. She'll do a better job than we would."*

Does this segment include a goal for the main character? *Ans: Yes*

If so, what is it? *Ans: Get help with her work*

If there isn't a stated goal here, what do you think would be the best goal for this character to have in this story? Why? *Ans: There is a stated goal.*

Using either the goal stated in the segment or one you invented, create motive to make that goal more interesting and important. *Ans: This calls for students to create their own motives. There is no one correct answer. Any answer they can justify using known story information is correct.*

Which other story elements can you find in this segment: *Ans: Character, some character traits, conflict (resistance of other animals), struggles*

Activity Review

Goals and character lie at the heart of every successful story. The main character's goal defines the structure and purpose of the story. It defines the ending point. It tells readers how to interpret and view every event in the story.

To successfully structure a story, the writer must first decide on exactly what their character is after in the story. The more specific the goal is, the easier it will be to write the story.

ELEMENT #4: MOTIVE

Why does the character want the goal? What is the character's *motive*?

Every character is after something. They all have goals. Each individual story focuses on a character's struggles to reach one specific goal. But readers will decide how to view that character and that goal by learning *why* the character wants that particular goal. A character's reasons for wanting a particular goal are called the character's motive. The job of a motive is to make a goal seem important to the character. The more important the goal becomes, the more interested readers will be in the story and in that character.

Activity 23: Motive a Must _____

What Students Will Learn:

Students will learn the importance of, and the role of, character motive in a story.

Time Estimate: 15 to 20 minutes

Directions:

This is an introductory activity to begin students thinking about, and recognizing, the importance of motive to readers' enjoyment of a story.

Each of the following four story versions presents the same character and goal. Each, however, presents a different motive. Have students complete their worksheets before discussing the role of motive.

Mo•tive *n.* The sense of need, desire, fear, and so on that prompts an individual to act. Motive explains why characters do what they do and why they want (or need) what they want.

Version #1: *A great white shark, named Sharky, wanted a puppy. Sharky was bored with just swimming and eating, and he didn't want to do any of his chores around the reef where he lived. Sharky thought that a puppy could entertain him. Maybe he'd even be able to teach the puppy to do tricks—or even to do Sharky's chores so Sharky could just float around all day.*

Version #2: *A great white shark, named Sharky, wanted a puppy. Sharky was hungry and tired of fish, fish, fish every day. He wanted some juicy puppy for dinner—maybe barbecued . . . maybe stuffed and roasted . . .*

Version #3: *A great white shark, named Sharky, wanted a puppy. Sharky felt desperately lonely. Every creature in the ocean hated him because he was a great white shark. If he couldn't find a friend—someone to talk to and laugh with—he would go insane. Puppies were friendly and cute. Maybe a puppy would be his friend since no one else would.*

Version #4: *A great white shark, named Sharky, wanted a puppy. Sharky has pledged his life to maintaining world peace. But an angry feud between land and sea animals was about to boil into all-out war. Sharkey had to stop that war from starting. He believed that his only hope was to show that land and sea animals could live in harmony, and he would do this by adopting and raising a puppy. So he wanted—he needed—to get a puppy.*

In the spaces provided on the worksheet, students are asked to describe how the different motives in each version make them feel about the character and goal. They are also asked to identify the version that presents their favorite motive and to explain (justify) why that one is their favorite.

Discuss each version with your class and note how changing Sharky's motive changes reader reaction to character and goal. Let students debate their favorite version, but force them to justify their pick with concrete story material and with story concepts presented in *Get It Write!*

There is no one correct response to each new motive, nor is there a single best motive they should pick as their favorite. Writers must learn that different readers will respond differently to what they write. However, most students in the class, like most readers, will have common reactions to various motives.

Finally, summarize the activity by leading the following discussion with your students:

Notice that you react differently to the character (Sharky) and to his goal (get a puppy) depending on his motive (*why* he wants the puppy). As a character's motive makes his goal more important, as the motive shows why the character desperately needs to achieve his goal, the story automatically becomes more interesting to readers.

When Sharky's motive makes his goal seem noble, readers root harder for Sharky to reach his goal. When his motive reveals his passion, he becomes much more interesting to readers. In writing terms, motive increases suspense by making the goal more important to the character and to society in general (more noble). Just as is true with character details, motives that are unexpected (unusual), unique, and specific are more interesting to readers.

Because Sharky in Versions # 1 and 2 is first lazy and then cruel, you probably don't want him to get his puppy unless he changes his attitude. In Versions #3 and 4, you are probably more sympathetic toward Sharky and want him to succeed because he is first in desperate need and then more noble.

Pas•sion *n*. An intense or violent emotion. A character's passions (loves, hates, etc.) are one of the fifteen categories of information writers can use to make their characters interesting.

Activity Review

Goal determines where the story will end (character resolves goal—either gets it or doesn't). **Motive** determines which possible ending readers want and expect.

Strong motives increase story suspense, make the story and character more important to readers, and dictate the attitude of readers toward characters and their goal. Take time to play with, search for, and develop strong motives for your characters. It will make the story much easier to create and write.

Besides making the story more interesting, notice also that a character's motive provides more information to make the character interesting. Motive gives readers a glimpse into the personality and thinking of a character. Motive is one of the situational character traits you can use to make your characters more appealing to readers.

Activity 24: Connecting Goals and Motives _____

What Students Will Learn:

Students will learn to link goal and motive and will understand how these two must fit closely together.

Time Estimate: 10 to 15 minutes

Directions:

Have students complete the activity worksheet. Then review the answers (listed in this section) to ensure that they have successfully learned to link motive to character and goal.

Motives explain why a character wants or needs a particular goal. Motives give meaning to a goal. On the left of the following list are six characters and goals. On the right are six motives. Connect each goal with the motive that best explains why the character would want that goal. There is a motive for each character and goal, and each motive goes with only one character and goal.

Notice that some characters are "he's," some "she's," and others are "it's." To keep from giving away which motive goes with each goal, every pronoun on the motive side is written for a female character and placed in parentheses to show that it might not be the right gender for that motive. Tell students to feel free to change these pronouns to make the gender in the motive fit with the gender of the character and goal to which they connect it.

Character and Goal	**Motive**
1. Once a moth wanted to fly all the way to the sun.	A. (She) loved (her) family and had a baby daughter (she) had never seen.
2. A school wall clock wanted to lie and tell the wrong time.	B. (Her) family would be soooo proud and (her) parents would buy (her) a big gift.
3. A fourth-grade girl wanted to get straight As.	C. (She) was dazzlingly brilliant and glorious and no one had ever gone that high before.
4. A young earthworm wanted to find his parents.	D. Everyone (she) had served had been selfish and left the world worse off than before.
5. A World War II soldier prayed that he would live through the war.	E. No one ever said thanks for the info and everyone took (her) for granted.
6. A genie in a bottle longed to grant a noble wish.	F. (She) was lonely and wanted to know if (she) had any brothers and sisters.

Ans: 1-C, 2-E, 3-B, 4-F, 5-A, 6-D

Allow your class to discuss these answers to ensure that all students see the direct link between character and goal and the corresponding motive.

Activity Review

Motives serve two key functions in a story. They explain why a character wants a certain goal, and they make that goal seem exceedingly important to the character. We'll look at that process in the next exercise.

Activity 25: More Motive _____

What Students Will Learn:

Students will learn to link motive to goal and will see the role of motive in increasing story suspense. Finally, they will see how motive changes reader expectation for how a story will end.

Time Estimate: 20 to 30 minutes

Directions:

Begin by discussing suspense and motive with your students using the following three paragraphs as a discussion guide. Then have students complete their worksheets before reviewing the answers.

Many motives might explain the existence of a particular goal, but few of those motives will make the goal seem important to the main character and to readers. The more important a goal is, the more readers will care about this character and this story. If a goal is made critically important to a character, readers will be anxious, needing to know whether or not the character will achieve this goal. They will wonder about the goal.

There is a writing term for filling readers with wonder and anxious expectancy. It is called suspense. Suspense drives readers through a story and makes them need to find out what happens in the end. Mystery writers use suspense to make readers wonder about who did it, or what will happen at the end. Spooky stories use suspense to make readers wonder (and imagine) what scary things are about to happen.

Sus•pense *n*. The state of anxious expectancy while waiting for an answer, decision, or outcome. Suspense makes readers read and enjoy your story. The easiest way to create suspense is by making the goal of the main character more important (motive) and by making it less likely that they will reach that goal (conflicts and problems and risk and danger).

In the short stories your students will write, suspense comes primarily from making readers wonder about the goal of the main character ("Will they ever get it?"). That suspense comes from making the main character's goal important. Your students will always make readers more interested in their stories by building suspense.

Let's look at the particular relationship between goal and motive and see how different motives either build or diminish the sense of suspense and interest in the story. Two combinations of character and goal are listed in the following example. Four possible motives for the goal are shown below each.

Tell your students to pick the one motive for each combination of character and goal that they think makes the goal most important and builds the most suspense. Their worksheet also asks them to justify their selection by explaining why that motive creates the most importance, interest, and suspense.

1. *A young colt galloped across the rolling pasture, his tail streaming behind him. But that colt dreamed not of prancing across grass but of streaking across the finish line in front of 100,000 screaming people to win the great derby race.*

Possible motives:

    A. The oats given to the horses in the neighboring farm tasted better.

    B. He hated the thought of any other horse winning anything.

    C. He needed to win the cash award so he could buy his mother and keep her from being sent to the slaughterhouse where she would be ground up for dog food.

    D. He liked to run.

    Ans: C

2. *Once a little engine needed to haul a long, loaded train over the mountain to a town on the other side. It thought it could. It thought it could. It hoped it could.*

    Possible motives:

    A. The little engine felt smugly superior to all the other engines and figured it could do anything.

    B. The little engine needed a tune-up.

    C. The little engine wanted to retire.

    D. The little engine wanted to be a hero by delivering the supplies and saving the town on the other side of the mountain.

    Ans: D

Let's look at the possible answers.

> For the first story, A and D might be true, but they don't explain why he wants to win the big derby race.
>
> B and C both do. Both make winning important to the colt. Yet these two different motives make readers *feel* differently about the colt, don't they? Answer **C** makes readers care about the goal; answer **B** doesn't. In picking motives for your character, think about how you want readers to feel about your characters.
>
> For the second story, neither answer B nor C explains why the little engine wants to make this haul. Actually, both could be made into problems that will make it harder for the engine.
>
> Choices A and D do. But, again, only one of these, D, will make readers root for the main character and care if character reaches its goal.
>
> Now, let's look at the link between goal, motive, and how a story ends. We have already seen that goal defines the possible ending points for a story. Now, let's see how different motives affect which ending fits best with the story.
>
> Students are asked to create their own version of each story's ending using two different motives. For Story #1, they are asked to first use motive B and then motive C. For Story #2, they are asked to first use motive A, and then motive D.

Remind students that they should not outline the entire story plot that leads to the ending point they choose. They should only describe what will happen at the very end of the story.

Let several students read their answers to the class. Enjoy the creativity and originality of students' ideas. Debate the appropriateness of each suggestion. Remember, the story's end must resolve the goal of the main character—either the character gets it or gives up on it. Generally, motive determines which of these two general endings readers prefer.

Activity Review

In every successful story, the main character's goal and motive are closely linked and determine the best ending spots for that story. Characters may have more than one motive for a given goal. In fact, the more motives a character has for needing to achieve a goal, the better. Those motives create suspense for readers—making them wonder all the more whether or not a character will reach this essential goal.

Just as games played with other students helped develop character traits to make a character interesting, students can use friends and family to help them develop the goal and motive for their stories. Writers need not grab the first ideas that come to mind. Students should explore as many ideas as they can. They never know when a great idea will leap into their mind.

ELEMENT #5: CONFLICTS AND PROBLEMS

What *conflicts* and *problems* block the character from the goal?

Discuss conflicts and problems with your class before beginning activity 26. Use the following paragraphs as a guide.

A character wants something (a goal). If the character already had it, there would be no story.

Nikko wanted a bag of marbles. He had one.

That's a statement of fact, not a story. It only becomes a story if Nikko hasn't reached his goal yet—hasn't gotten his marbles. That means that something must be preventing Nikko from getting marbles. If nothing stood in his way, he'd get them.

What blocks a character from reaching a goal? **Conflicts and problems**. That's their job. Conflicts and problems are often collectively called **obstacles** since they lie across (block) a character's path like obstacles on an obstacle course. Over the next few activities we will look at conflicts and problems—at their function, their nature, and at the difference between the two.

Obstacles may be internal (inside the character) or external. They may be big or small, deadly dangerous or trivial. Anything that keeps a character from reaching his or her goal is an obstacle.

What's the difference between conflicts and problems? Both block a character from a goal, but conflicts bring the character into conflict with a story character while problems do not.

A quick demonstration will help.

Vlad wanted to drive (character and goal). But he was only fourteen (a problem). He would have to wait two years to get his license to drive legally. (Another problem. Vlad is blocked from his goal. But it's not very exciting yet, is it? Problems don't easily create excitement in a story.) Besides, Officer Grumpus prowled the streets and had vowed to throw any kid in jail who tried to drive without a license. (Now the story's getting better. Why? We added conflict. Someone for Vlad to struggle against.)

Conflicts are the royal road to excitement in stories. Conflicts get characters into trouble, and trouble is always exciting. Excitement does not come from the action in a story—action alone is always boring. Excitement comes from the conflicts the main character must face. Conflicts can be against another character, against the main character, him- or herself (the best fighting is always against yourself), or even against a nonthinking element in the story (a storm, a river, etc.), as long as the main character treats that object or event as if it were a character and struggles against that object.

Obstacles are the root of story plots. Characters struggle to overcome obstacles to reach a goal. Know the obstacles, and you pretty well know what has to happen in the story. Once character, goal, and motive have been established in a story, it's time to create obstacles so that the character will have something to do (overcome those obstacles).

Activity 26: Goals, Motives, and Obstacles _____

What Students Will Learn:

Students will be introduced to the role of obstacles (problems and conflicts) in a story and will learn the link between obstacles, goals, and motives.

Time Estimate: 15 to 20 minutes

Directions:

Obstacles block a character from a goal. Without a goal, obstacles don't work. If obstacles don't block a character from reaching the goal, they make no sense in the story. Without obstacles, there is no story.

Have students read the story segment on their worksheet and answer the questions that follow.

Ob•sta•cle *n*. An obstruction that prevents forward movement. Story obstacles block the main character from reaching a goal.

> *Carlotta wanted an "A" on the history test* (character and goal). *But she hadn't studied* (a problem). *Even though she knew it was wrong and hated to do it, she was thinking of cheating.* (A conflict; Carlotta is now in conflict with herself—her desire for an "A" versus her values.) *But what scared Carlotta most was that Mrs. Slidewinkle, her teacher, was famous for catching cheaters, and she always sentenced them to stay after school for a month and polish all the hallway floors by hand in disgrace* (another conflict to add more excitement).

On the worksheet, there are spaces for students to create two important reasons (motives) why Carlotta might need to get this "A" and two spaces for them to invent two new conflicts or problems that Carlotta must face that will add excitement to the story. Students should not describe *what* happens, just identify the new problem or source of conflict. Finally, students are asked to explain how their new obstacles will add to the story's excitement.

Allow students to present their ideas. Start with their creations for Carlotta's motives. Note how strong motives instantly make everyone more interested in the story. Allow students to discuss the appropriateness of each offered motive. Motives must explain why a character wants a particular goal and should make that goal seem more important to readers.

Shift the discussion to student ideas for new obstacles. As they offer each obstacle to the class, students should explain how each will create excitement.

We can already guess that, during the story, Carlotta will have to struggle with her conscience and will eventually come face to face with Mrs. Slidewinkle. During a story, characters try to overcome the obstacles writers place in their path.

Certainly, writers use both problems and conflicts to torment their story characters. But students should plan their story's conflicts first and most carefully to ensure that the story will be exciting. Conflicts are the muscle that powers the plot of your story. Give your story plenty of muscle and the story will be a delight for readers.

Also notice that, if the goal of the main character becomes more important, the character will be willing to face greater, more exciting (dangerous) obstacles in the struggle to reach the goal. If Carlotta only sort of, maybe, I guess, kind of wants an A, it wouldn't seem believable for her to risk very much to get one. The more she *needs* the A, the more readers will believe that she will be willing to violate her own values and risk Mrs. Slidewinkle to get it.

Activity Review

Characters, goals, and obstacles work in concert to make a story powerful, effective, and fun. Obstacles block characters from established goals. Big obstacles that create risk and danger for a character make a story exciting. Without obstacles, there is nothing for a character to do during a story. The plot of a story, after all, is the actions characters take to overcome obstacles and reach a goal.

Activity 27: Recognizing Strong Obstacles _____

What Students Will Learn:

Students will learn to recognize, select, and create strong obstacles for their stories. They will also be introduced to the difference between problems and conflicts.

Time Estimate: 60 minutes

Directions:

This activity is divided into five parts. First review the general role of obstacles in a story using the following paragraph as a guide. Then, have students proceed to Part 1 of this activity. Pause after each part to briefly clear up any confusion they may have, to review the choices they made, and to keep them on the correct path for the next part.

Obstacles must block a character from reaching a stated goal. Anything and everything could be an obstacle—depending on the character and the goal. The job of obstacles is to create excitement in the story and provide opportunities for the main character to struggle. For an obstacle to effectively do its job, readers must be able to recognize that the obstacle blocks the character from the goal and that trying to get past this obstacle creates risk and danger for the main character.

Con•flict *n.* A clash of feelings or interests.

Prob•lem *n.* A matter that causes worry or perplexity.

Conflicts and problems form the obstacles that block characters and drive stories.

Part 1. Let's start by simply recognizing obstacles and then find ways to anticipate which will be truly effective (good) obstacles.

> *Once a young circus elephant named Dumbo, who had embarrassingly large ears (that his mother was sure came from his father's side of the family), wanted very much to fly.*

Which of the following fourteen items could logically become obstacles in this story? Circle the number of each item you pick.

1. His mother wanted to eat oat cakes and talk with friends.
2. He was hungry.
3. Other elephants laughed at his ears.
4. He was embarrassed at being the smallest elephant and having the biggest ears.
5. He was afraid of heights.
6. A mouse knew the secret of the flying feather.
7. The circus tent was very high.
8. The circus owner kept Dumbo locked in a cage.
9. Dumbo was afraid of mice.
10. The circus band played very loudly.
11. There was a big crowd in the circus tent bleachers.
12. Dumbo didn't know how to fly.

13. Dumbo's mother told him he was a naughty elephant for wanting to fly and forbade him from ever trying to fly.

14. The Senior Elephant Council passed a rule that no elephant could fly. Anyone caught trying to fly would have to leave the herd and become a pig.

Ans: 4, 5, 8, 12, 13, 14

Let's look at each item.

> Number 1 has nothing to do with Dumbo. It isn't an obstacle to Dumbo's flying. In fact, it might help Dumbo by distracting his mother while Dumbo practices.
>
> Number 2 could distract Dumbo and could make it harder for him to think about flying, but it doesn't directly block him from flying. It's not an effective obstacle, but it could be used in the story as a minor problem.
>
> Number 6 sounds like a help to Dumbo, not an obstacle.
>
> Numbers 3, 7, 10, and 11 aren't directly about Dumbo and don't directly keep him from flying. But they could relate to his flying and might make it harder for him to fly if we make up other information about Dumbo that would turn these into effective obstacles. We'll work to improve these obstacles in Part 2.
>
> Number 9 is a character trait and could be a problem. However, with the information we now have, it doesn't keep him from flying.

The other items, Numbers 4, 5, 8, 12, 13, and 14 all act to effectively block Dumbo from flying or from ever trying to fly. We could use any or all as effective obstacles in this story. Have students count how many of these six they circled and put on their list. As a class, discuss how these obstacles would make it harder for Dumbo to fly.

Part 2. Have students individually pick two of the four items mentioned previously (3, 7, 10, and 11) and describe what they'd have to make up about Dumbo or about this story to turn these into effective, exciting obstacles that would make it significantly harder for him to fly.

As examples, for Number 7, they could add that Dumbo is afraid of heights and that the elephant act begins with the smallest elephants entering at the top of the tent. The added information for Number 3 could be as simple as saying that Dumbo felt embarrassed when others laughed and always hid his ears, rolling them into tight curls against his head. Numbers 10 and 11 could be turned into obstacles if Dumbo is afraid of loud noises and crowds.

Certainly, those are only a few of the many ways the information in Numbers 3, 7, 10, and 11 could be turned into effective obstacles. There are no single correct answers for these questions. Anything that effectively and efficiently turns the chosen items into effective obstacles (something that would clearly block Dumbo from flying) will do. This part teaches students how to improve any ineffective obstacles they create as they plan, develop, and revise a story.

Allow several students to read their answers to compare their answers with those of other students. As a class, decide which answers create the most exciting obstacles and why.

Part 3. Have students individually complete Part 3 of this activity. Their instructions are "If you had to pick three of these six obstacles (Numbers 4, 5, 8, 12, 13, and 14) to use as the principle obstacles in this story, which three would you pick and why?"

Allow various students to nominate their choices and justify their picks. Let students debate the merits of different obstacles for a time before you ask, "Is it important that you all pick the same three?"

No, of course it isn't. Each writer will pick the obstacles that appeal most to them and will pick those that it will be easiest for them to turn into an exciting story. Different writers will work best with different obstacles. However, Number 12 is the only problem in this group of five obstacles and is the weakest. Few, if any, students should have picked this obstacle as one of their three favorites. Numbers 4 and 5 are internal conflicts. Numbers 8, 13, and 14 are external conflicts.

Part 4. The worksheet asks students to consider Number 9 on the list (Dumbo is afraid of mice). Students are asked to create one simple bit of new information that will turn Dumbo's fear into a solid conflict that will make it much harder for Dumbo to fly.

Allow various students to read their new information. Let students debate the merits of the various ideas. Have the class look for those that are the simplest and yet most effective in creating a powerful new obstacle for Dumbo. The actual story contains an excellent idea for that information. A mouse holds the secret to flying. Dumbo's fear would then keep him away from the one character who can help him.

Part 5. We have already said that Number 1 on the list is not an effective obstacle. The worksheet instructs students to turn that item into an effective obstacle that would keep Dumbo from flying. What other information about Dumbo and his mother would the writer have to create for this item to become an exciting, effective obstacle in this story?

Allow several students to read their answers to the class. Notice the wonderful variety in the strategies that could be used to make Number 1 work as an effective obstacle in this story. Were some of the ideas more effective than others? Why? Discuss each idea as a class and decide which ones are effective and why (or why not).

Activity Review

Problems and conflicts (collectively called obstacles) only do their job in a story if it is apparent how that obstacle prevents a character from reaching a known goal. Obstacles cannot do their job in a story unless the writer has created an interesting character and given that character a definite, important goal. When obstacles are allowed to do their job effectively, they create excitement in the story and provide opportunities for the character to struggle.

Activity 28: Conflicts and Problems _____

What Students Will Learn:

Students will learn to rank potential obstacles and will learn the difference between conflicts and problems in story planning.

Time Estimate: 30 to 50 minutes

Directions:

This activity uses the character Cecelia Sue, the spider first created in Activity 3. Review that story with students if they need to refresh their memory before continuing with this activity. After a brief introduction using the next paragraph, have students complete the entire activity before regathering as a class to discuss their results.

In the last exercise we didn't differentiate between conflicts and problems. We didn't focus on how effective an obstacle was. We just tried to identify the obstacles. But it is important for writers to evaluate each obstacle they create and pick those to use in a story that will create the most excitement.

It might help to review these three terms with your class before they begin this exercise.

Obstacle   Anything that blocks a character from reaching the goal. There are two types of obstacles—conflicts and problems.

Conflict   An obstacle that brings a character into direct conflict with another character or story element (a storm, a mountain, a bully, herself, etc.)

Problem   An obstacle that does not bring a character into conflict with any story character or element (a lack of money, being too young, etc.)

While creating the story of Cecelia Sue, the spider, students were given eight possible obstacles:

A. A hungry lizard wants to eat all the spiders in the spooky woods.

B. A friendly fly will carry a message to her parents.

C. She gets lost.

D. A mean tarantula won't let her enter the spooky woods.

E. She doesn't know where her parents are.

F. She doesn't have a map of the spooky woods.

G. She doesn't have enough money to rent a car.

H. Cecelia Sue is afraid of the dark.

Ans: There are three conflicts in the list: A, D, and H. There are four problems: C, E, F, and G.

1. The best obstacles create the most excitement in a story. They get the character in the greatest possible trouble. They create the most risk and danger for the character as that character attempts to get past that particular obstacle. The worksheet provides spaces for students to rank the eight

possible obstacles for Cecelia Sue from best to the worst. They are also asked to explain and justify their ranking.

Certainly, there is more than one plausible order for ranking these obstacles. Different writers will rank the obstacles differently depending on how each writer sees and plans to develop the story. However, students' rankings should reflect the following points:

Option B is not an obstacle at all. It should be at the bottom of every student's list.

Options A, D, and H are all excellent obstacles and will be the easiest to develop and the most exciting. They should be at the top.

Options C, E, F, and G are obstacles but are not as exciting as A, D, and H. These four belong in the middle of the list (below A, D, and H but above B).

Review how your students ranked these obstacles and the reasoning behind their ranking. Discuss any uncertainty or confusion.

Trou•ble *n*. Misfortune; a difficult situation. Conflicts and problems get characters into trouble. Trouble is always exciting and interesting to readers.

2. The worksheet instructs students to divide the listed obstacles into **conflicts** (obstacles that place Cecelia Sue in direct conflict with another character or with herself) and **problems** (obstacles that make it harder for Cecelia Sue, but don't put her in conflict with another character).

   Review the lists of conflicts and problems. Allow several students to read their lists aloud. Continue the discussion until all students clearly understand the difference between these two lists. Notice that the three conflicts (A, D, and H) are the ones we put at the top when we ranked the obstacles. Conflicts create more excitement in a story and are better obstacles than are problems. Writers typically use both but plan their story around conflicts.

3. Problems can often be turned into more powerful, exciting conflicts. Two of the four problems facing Cecelia Sue are listed here. The worksheet instructs students to write how they would turn each into a conflict. They may create new characters, and any new story information, that they need to.

   There is no single correct answer for these questions. Any answer that effectively and efficiently turns the listed problem into a strong conflict is acceptable.

   F. She doesn't have a map of the spooky woods.

   > *Ans: As one example, the owner of the map store could be a spider-eating army ant. If Cecelia Sue is going to get a map, she has a new dangerous conflict to face.*

   G. She doesn't have enough money to rent a car.

   > *Ans: As one example, Cecelia Sue could decide to rob a bank to get the money she needs. Now she is in conflict with the police.*

4. Finally, students are asked to create one new conflict and one new problem for Cecelia Sue to face that could be effectively used in this story. They are told to explain how that conflict and problem will block Cecelia Sue from saving her parents and are asked to explain why they picked those particular obstacles.

   Now review questions 3 and 4. Have students share their ideas for turning problems F and G into exciting conflicts. Let the class discuss which ideas are most effective and why.

   Finally, allow several students to read their new conflict and problem for Cecelia Sue. The class should make sure that each student created one conflict and one problem and that each clearly blocks her from her goal. Point out again how much more exciting and interesting conflicts are than problems.

Activity Review

Conflicts and problems (collectively called obstacles) do their job by blocking a character from a goal, but they are also supposed to create excitement in a story. While both conflicts and problems block a character, conflicts do a much better job of creating excitement. Plan your story around conflicts and fill in with problems as they are needed.

Activity 29: Obstacles and Plot _____

What Students Will Learn:

Students will learn the link between obstacles and plotting events and see that plot depends on obstacles and that obstacles must be created before plot.

Time Estimate: 15 to 20 minutes

Directions:

Before your students begin the worksheet for this activity, use the story of Sharky, the shark, (see Activity 23) and the different motives provided in this activity to again emphasize the need to create strong motive to allow writers to create exciting and dangerous obstacles.

Without a strong motive, characters will never be willing to face great risk and danger and the writer will struggle to make the story fascinating and interesting.

Here is a story segment:

> *Once a great white shark, named Sharky, wanted to get a puppy. Sharky was bored with just swimming and eating, and he didn't want to do any of his chores around the reef where he lived. Sharky thought that a puppy could entertain him. Maybe he'd even be able to teach the puppy to do tricks—or even to do Sharky's chores and work, so Sharky could just lie around all day.*
>
> *But Sharky couldn't get to the dog pound where all the puppies lived. Eight fierce giant squids guarded the channel through the reef. Deadly chemical pollution filled the bay. A thick cluster of shark fishermen cruised the reef and bay in radar-equipped boats. Lions and tigers guarded the path through the woods to the dog pound where all of the puppies were locked inside a triple-thick 100,000 volt electrified fence with double strands of barbed wire all around the top. Besides, a volcano was erupting and thick streams of molten lava flowed down to the shore that Sharky would have to cross. Even worse, it was night, and Sharky was afraid of the dark.*

These obstacles could make for an exciting story. But if Sharky's only motive is that he is bored, no one would believe that he'd be willing to face all this risk and danger to get a puppy. The shark needs a stronger motive that is more important to the shark if readers are going to believe the story. Let's change Shark's motive:

> *Sharky has pledged his life to maintaining world peace. But an angry feud between land and sea animals was about to boil into all-out war. Sharky has to stop the war from starting. He believes that his only hope is to show that land and sea animals can live in harmony, and he would do this by adopting and raising a puppy. So he wants—he needs—to get a puppy.*

Now the story segment makes sense. To have exciting obstacles, a story must provide enough motive to make the main character willing to face the risk and danger those obstacles create.

When the *Get It Write!* Eight Essential Elements were first introduced, the text said that conflicts and problems are the root of every plot and every action (event) in a story. Let's see what that statement means.

Have your students list all of the conflicts and problems blocking Sharky that they find in this story segment.

> *Ans: Four conflicts are listed: octopi, fishermen, lions and tigers, and Sharky, himself. (He must fight against his own fear of the dark.) Three problems are listed: pollution in the bay, the volcano, and the fence.*

Discuss these lists and make sure that students agree on the division between problem and conflict before you proceed.

The worksheet instructs students to list six events they think will happen in this story and how they think the story will end. Remind them to provide only a one-sentence summary of each event.

Allow students to read their individual lists of story events and to explain why they picked the events they picked. Watch for the same (or very similar) events to appear on many of the students' lists. Ask students why different students created the same events for this story.

E•vent *n*. An occurrence, especially one of significance or importance. A connected series of events makes up the plot of a story. *Incident* is another word for story events.

How many of the events your students created were based on the conflicts and problems they listed earlier? Probably all of them. In stories, characters act to overcome conflicts and problems to reach their goals. Events that don't help Sharky overcome obstacles, or that don't introduce new obstacles for him to struggle against, don't seem to make any sense in the story. Each of the events your students created should have either described Sharky's attempts to get past the obstacles already listed or should have presented new obstacles he would have to overcome.

Make sure your students wrote that the story will end either when Sharky gets his puppy and preserves peace in the world, or when he fails to get the puppy and war erupts. Stories always end when the main character finally resolves the goal.

Activity Review

Plotting events (the action of a story) must be based on the obstacles a writer has created for the character to overcome. Create powerful, exciting obstacles first. Then it will be easy to decide *what* is going to happen in the story. Your main character will act (do things) to try to overcome those obstacles and reach a stated goal.

If the obstacles are good, the plot will be easy to create. However, if the writer doesn't take the time to create effective obstacles, there won't be enough for the character to do in the story, and it will be a struggle to write from start to finish.

ELEMENT #6: RISK AND DANGER

How do the chosen obstacles create risk and danger for the main character?

   Before asking students to complete Activity 30, lead a general class discussion on the concept of risk and danger in stories. Use these paragraphs as a guide.

   Risk is a measure of the likelihood of failure. Danger measures the consequences of failure. The greater the risk, the greater the danger, the greater the excitement in a story. Conflicts and problems are supposed to make the story exciting. But how do they do that? They do it by creating **risk and danger** for the main character. If there is no risk and danger, there is no excitement.

   A boy walks home after school to find his mother angrily tapping her foot as she glares at him from the front porch.

   Every reader eagerly perks up thinking, "Oh, boy! He's in trouble now. This is going to be exciting." Why? That one sentence creates conflict *and* risk and danger for the boy. The same conflict could be created by having the person on the front porch be a 109-year-old man from the retirement home next door, or a 5-year-old neighbor girl—same conflict. But now the risk and danger are gone and so is the excitement.

   If the bears in the story of Goldilocks were koala bears or teddy bears, the story would lose most of its punch, power, and excitement. Why? Risk and danger for Goldilocks would be reduced, if not eliminated.

   We love to watch someone else face risk and danger. We are, in effect, risk junkies. We are drawn to watch risk and danger like a moth is drawn to a candle flame. Imagine placing a twenty-foot long 2 × 4 plank of wood on the floor. Almost anyone would be willing to walk the length of that plank. No one would pay to watch someone else walk it. Why? No real risk or danger.

   Now, imagine raising that same 2 × 4 a thousand feet in the air and suspend it high over jagged rocks and shark infested waters while hurricane-force winds buffet and snap the board making it vibrate like a violin string. *Now* would you be willing to walk the length of the plank? Probably not. But it is the same plank and the same action as before. All that has changed is the amount of risk and danger you, the main character, must face while doing it. If you found a volunteer willing to walk the plank, you could easily fill a stadium with people who'd pay to watch. Why? They'd want to watch someone else face risk and danger. Tell your students to remember that for their stories. Risk and danger make stories exciting.

   Excitement is really a feeling in the reader. It is created by the risk and danger writers build into the conflicts and problems they create for their characters. Suspense is also a feeling. Suspense is created by making readers wonder about the goal of the main character. Suspense and excitement propel readers through stories.

Activity 30: Conflicts and Problems for Fred _____

What Students Will Learn:

This activity will reinforce the characteristics of effective obstacles in students' minds and will demonstrate how to create risk and danger from existing obstacles.

Time Estimate: 60 minutes

Directions:

This activity is divided into five parts. Pause to discuss each and to allow students to voice their opinions and ideas before moving to the next part.

Part 1 Let's look at the role of risk and danger in stories. In Activity 28, we revisited the obstacles blocking Cecelia Sue. Now let's do the same for Fred du Frog (see Activity 4). As the story was presented at the end of Activity 4, what conflicts and problems were explicitly stated in the story? Have students list all they find in the lines provided on their worksheet.

Ans: There are two conflicts—frog-eating crocodiles and frog-eating bears There is one stated problem—no frog food on the frogs' side of the lake.

Risk *n.* The possibility of danger, injury, loss, and so on.

Dan·ger *n.* Peril, exposure to harm, injury, loss, and so on.

Risk measures the probability of failure (how likely it is that a character will fail to overcome an obstacle). Danger measures the consequences of failure (what happens to the character if he or she fails).

Part 2. Learning that the frogs have no food doesn't, itself, create excitement. It is a problem. However, the crocodiles and bears (conflicts) do instantly create interest and excitement.

Students are asked to write their answers to two questions: What makes those two conflicts exciting, and would it have been as exciting if it were goldfish instead of crocodiles in the lake and crickets instead of bears in the woods?

While the answer seems obvious, it's worth reinforcing with a brief class discussion. Students should have written that bears and crocodiles are more exciting because both the crocodiles and bears will kill (eat) the frogs. Crocodiles and bears create more **risk and danger** for the frogs than do goldfish and crickets. Risk and danger (created by the conflicts a character must face) are the source of excitement in a story. Facing risk and danger is how characters get in trouble. Stories are always exciting when characters we care about get into big trouble.

Part 3. Now let's work on increasing risk and danger. Have students look back at the conflicts and problems for Fred that they listed earlier. Every student should think of two things they could invent to increase the risk and danger to the frogs from these obstacles. (They'll know when they create a good one. It will make the story instantly seem more exciting.) Have them write their ideas on the lines on the worksheet.

Allow several students to share their ideas with the class. Discuss which ideas work the best and why.

Part 4. As the story has been presented so far, Fred and the three little frogs are safe in the mud because it's too soft and squishy to hold either a crocodile or a bear. Have students think of how to use that information to create a new obstacle for Fred and to increase the risk and danger to the frogs. Have them write their ideas on the worksheet and then let several students share their ideas with the class. Discuss which worked best and why. The answers will always come back to creating risk and danger.

Part 5. Here are two new character traits for Fred:

   A. Fred hates to be called chicken. When someone calls him a chicken, he begins to tremble and snort and will do anything—anything—to prove that he isn't.

   B. Fred is allergic to pine needles. His skin breaks out in a burning itch and he begins uncontrollable sneezing when he touches them.

Ask students to explain how they would use these new character traits to get Fred in trouble and to increase Fred's risk and danger and the story's excitement.

Finally, have students think of something that Fred is afraid of—something that hasn't been mentioned in this story so far, something that will be surprising to readers. Then, have them write how they'll turn that new character trait into another new obstacle that Fred will have to face and describe how it will create exciting risk and danger for the frogs.

Again, allow several students to share their ideas and discuss which work best and why. Notice that these new obstacles and dangers for Fred all come initially from additional character traits students created. The more students know about their story characters, the more information students can create about them, the easier it will be for students to create interesting obstacles and risk and danger. Spending time developing characters is never wasted.

Activity Review

Every conflict and problem in a story creates some risk and danger for the main character. It is the job of writers to find and emphasize that risk and danger to make a story exciting. The idea for an obstacle can come from character traits, the goals and motives of the character, or from problems and conflicts the writer creates. Find as much as you can. Then, pick what you want to work with most in this story.

Activity 31: Love to Hate—Finding Antagonists _____

What Students Will Learn:

Students will learn the purpose and function of an antagonist and learn the difference between an antagonist and other obstacles.

Time Estimate: 20 to 30 minutes of class time and one out-of-class assignment

Directions:

This activity is an introductory activity, designed to help students focus on the nature and characteristics of a good antagonist and is divided into three parts. Part 1 should be completed outside the classroom as homework. Pause between parts to discuss student ideas and opinions and to allow them to revel in their favorite antagonists before creating their own in the next activity.

Before assigning Part 1 as homework, lead a general class discussion about the fun of, the role of, and the importance of antagonists using the following paragraphs as a guide.

> **An·tag·o·nist** *n.* An open enemy or rival. Antagonists are the enemy readers love to hate.

One of the most popular and most effective conflicts a writer can create is a villain, the bad guy. In writing terms, a villain is called the antagonist. More correctly, an antagonist is the embodiment of the biggest and most dangerous of all the obstacles the main character must face. A story's climax is that moment when the main character confronts the antagonist for the final time.

Why should your students care? Because the antagonist is a character—a character they can make into both an interesting character and a major source of excitement in their story.

A hero can only become a hero if the hero has a worthy antagonist to struggle against. Heroes can rise no higher than their antagonists will let them rise. To make the main character into a hero, don't develop the hero, develop the antagonist into a bigger, badder, meaner, more powerful, fiercer antagonist. Then the main character automatically becomes a hero because he or she has to face this terrible brute of an antagonist.

The antagonist is the character readers love to hate. But it is important for writers to develop that character almost as fully as they develop the main character. It is possible for the main character to be his or her own worst enemy (antagonist) and for the climax scene to focus on that character's final confrontation with him- or herself.

Part 1. Let's learn to recognize and develop an effective antagonist. Have your students find two antagonists they enjoyed in stories they recently read. On the student worksheet, have students list these antagonists and describe what makes the character a successful antagonist. This is normally assigned as homework.

Remind students that not every story has a well-developed antagonist and that a successful antagonist does not need to physically threaten the main character. The antagonist will create risk and danger, but any kind will do.

Part 2. Allow students to share their top antagonists with the class. Discuss whose is the best antagonist of all. Have students take several minutes to write down what they think makes an antagonist a great antagonist.

Part 3. Discuss these answers as a class and create a master list of what you think it takes to make a great antagonist. Finally, the worksheet provides space for students to write what they think the difference is between an antagonist and an ordinary obstacle blocking the main character.

Conclude the activity by allowing students to compare their answer with those of other students. Build a class list of the best ideas. Generally, an antagonist is the biggest and most dangerous of the obstacles blocking a character and is also intentionally, purposefully dedicated to blocking or harming the main character. An antagonist not only is in the way but also wants to be in the way.

Activity Review

Obstacles block characters' paths and give them something to do in a story. Conflicts are those obstacles that place a character in conflict with some other story character or element. Conflicts create risk and danger, the source of story excitement. An antagonist is the embodiment of the biggest and most dangerous obstacle blocking the main character. Remind students to develop their antagonists as fully as they do their main characters, and they will be set to create powerful and delightful stories.

Activity 32: Creating Antagonists _____

What Students Will Learn:

Students will learn to recognize and create the character traits of an effective antagonist.

Time Estimate: 40 minutes

Directions:

This activity is divided into two parts. Begin with a general discussion about antagonists using the following paragraphs as a guide.

What does an antagonist look like? Anything. A friend could become an antagonist, so could a storm or a river, or a worm, or a mosquito, or a bear, or a bank president, or a football coach, or even the main character. Any character can become an antagonist if that character is the most important and dangerous obstacle blocking a main character from a goal.

Does every story have an antagonist? Yes . . . almost always. There are always obstacles. The physical embodiment of the biggest, most dangerous obstacle becomes the antagonist. There are stories where that biggest obstacle (societal prejudice, desert heat and dryness, a character's struggles to overcome physical limitation, etc.) cannot easily be represented by a single physical entity. But such stories are the exception, not the rule.

> **Ex·cite·ment** *n*. Being excited; to cause the emotions of a person to be intense. Excitement is created from the risk and danger the main character must face. The embodiment of the biggest of those risks and dangers is the story's antagonist.

Far more commonly, a story's antagonist exists but isn't developed. The main character simply struggles against a cluster of obstacles, but always one of them is the biggest and most dangerous. Always one of them is confronted last (during the climax scene). That one obstacle could be developed into an effective antagonist if the writer chooses.

Can a story have more than one antagonist? It is not recommended. Pick one that is the biggest and that the main character deals with during the story's climax scene. Let that one be the antagonist. If a student writer tries to develop more, it will likely confuse both readers and writer.

Part 1. Tell the class that they will each create an antagonist for Fred du Frog. Fred faces two major conflicts: a crocodile and bears. For this activity, let's turn the crocodile into a true antagonist for Fred du Frog. (As an example, the crocodile in *Peter Pan* acted as an antagonist for Captain Hook. It was specifically after Hook—hunting him, stalking him, blocking him from capturing Peter and ruling Neverland. That's an antagonist.)

The crocodile is already a dangerous obstacle for Fred. After reviewing results from the previous exercise, students should decide what they'll need to create and add to the story to turn the crocodile into a worthy antagonist. The worksheet provides space for them to list that information.

Compare different students' ideas through a general classroom discussion. Build a master list of the most popular bits of essential new information on the board.

Many writers have found that they need to create the following information to create a working antagonist out of an ordinary obstacle or conflict. Discuss this list with students and compare it to the one they created.

1. Every antagonist needs a name and physical form. You can't have an anonymous, amorphous antagonist.

2. The antagonist must have enough details written about him or her to make the character interesting and vivid.

3. The antagonist must have some specific, cruel habits and ways of dealing with others. The antagonist must act and be mean and cruel (at least from the viewpoint of the main character).

4. The antagonist must be a powerful character with enough abilities and resources to overcome the main character.

5. The antagonist must block the main character from a known goal.

6. The antagonist must be dedicated to blocking or destroying the main character.

7. The antagonist must have a goal of his or her own as well as compelling motives for that goal. (It's best if the goal helps explain why the antagonist is dedicated to blocking the main character.)

8. The antagonist must have struggles of his or her own.

9. The antagonist should have at least one important flaw. (Antagonists can't be perfect.)

10. Antagonists must work in the open. A secret antagonist can't deliver story excitement like one who is openly opposed to the main character.

Be sure to compare this list to the class list and create examples (or pull examples from stories the class has recently read) to show students the value of any bits of information that do not appear on their composite list.

Part 2. Have your students each create a new antagonist for Fred du Frog. They should try to make it one that will be unexpected and interesting as well as dangerous and exciting. They should describe the antagonist, provide any significant character traits, explain why this new antagonist wants to block Fred, what this antagonist is after, and how this antagonist will create risk, danger, and excitement in the story. You may want to give them this as a take-home assignment to give them more time to complete this character creation.

Allow several students to share their creation with the class. As a class, discuss how effective each new antagonist is and what will make the best antagonist for the story of Fred du Frog. Remember, it is not important that all students agree on the best antagonist. Different writers will have different viewpoints and opinions. It is important, however, that they justify their opinions in terms of the criteria for a strong antagonist and in terms of the role of an antagonist in this story.

Activity Review

Antagonists are a powerful writing tool for your students to use to improve their stories. Have students regularly search through stories they read for antagonists and write down what the authors do to make their antagonists work. Creating strong antagonists is an easy way to boost the power and excitement of stories.

If conflicts are the key to planning the plot of a story, then antagonists are a key to planning conflicts. After character, goal, and motive are developed, students should identify the antagonist of their story, then they should create any additional conflicts the main character must face. Then they create other problems and obstacles their character will have to face along the way.

ELEMENT #7: STRUGGLES

How does the main character struggle to get past conflicts to reach the goal?

Finally, it's time to think about plot about the events that will pepper your students' stories with thrilling action. Now, we will plan *what* is going to happen in their stories—the action. However, having already planned the first six *Get It Write!* elements, students are ready to create plotting events that will make sense, and have importance, to readers. To make the writing easy and successful, don't plan the action first, plan it last—after the first six elements have been created but before creating the details that make the story vivid and real.

Before turning to Activity 33, lead a class discussion based on the information in this section. Focus the discussion on the reasons to have something happen in a story, on the meaning of the term *struggles*.

First, let's review several definitions that were listed in Activity 3:

Action   Anything that a character does is an action. Lifting a glass, sighing, and raising a hand are actions, just as much as being chased over the edge of a 1,000-foot cliff by a fire-breathing, black-belt, motorcycle-riding dragon.

Event   Event and scene may be used interchangeably. An event is an occurrence that could contain a great number of separate actions. Two people meeting for a chess match is an event, as is a dragon chasing someone over a cliff and a person staying home to curl up on the couch with a good book.

Plot   A plot is the sequence of events that tells a story. Actions build into events that writers string together to create a plot.

Struggle   To struggle is to make a strenuous effort, a great effort, to progress with great difficulty. Struggle is when characters strain, strive, battle, toil, face torment, and are perplexed. Struggles are the actions a character takes to overcome obstacles and reach a goal.

Writers create big obstacles with maximum risk and danger so that their characters will have to exert a great and strenuous effort when they confront and contend with these obstacles. Readers need for characters to struggle. If the obstacles blocking a character are big and loaded with risk and danger, then it will not be easy for the character to overcome them. The character will have to struggle. Thus, struggle is the criterion for whether events belong in a story. Writers choose the events that allow them to show their characters struggling.

Why should a writer bother to have anything happen in their stories? Why take the time and effort to write action events and to create all the accompanying necessary detail? What do events and actions do for a story?

Here are four reasons to have something happen in a story. As a general rule, cut out every scene, character, setting, and event that doesn't accomplish at least one—and preferably more than one—of these four goals:

- Provide an opportunity for your characters to struggle at some risk and danger against conflicts and problems to try to reach a goal
- Create new obstacles, risk, and danger for the main character
- Reveal character (show readers more interesting information about the character)
- Resolve a goal, which eventually must happen.

The key to successful plots is struggle. Your characters are revealed through how they act and react during struggles. Struggles release the excitement created by conflicts and their risk and danger. It is through struggle that goals are resolved.

Notice that it is the struggle against a conflict or problem and not the solution of that obstacle that readers need. Struggle adds energy and interest to a story. Solutions suck energy out of the story. Don't rush to solve every problem. Instead, linger on the struggle as long as possible. An example will be helpful.

Fred du Frog needs to get past frog-eating crocodiles and bears to get the food to keep his fellow frogs from starving to death. Picking up from the end of the text presented at the end of Activity 3, here is the next sentence of the story:

> *Big Fred hopped into his froggie powerboat, sped across the lake, got the food, and raced it back to the other frogs who had a grand picnic and lived happily ever after. The End.*

Not very satisfying, is it? Yet this ending solves the conflicts and resolves the goal. Why won't readers like it? It's too easy on Fred. If Fred hops into his powerboat, you want the boat to spring a leak and sink halfway across the lake. You want the motor to explode and leave Fred wallowing in the water as the crocodile circles in for the kill. You want Fred to struggle mightily—maybe even to suffer before he ever reaches the frog food across the lake.

Two final notes need to be considered: First, point out to your students that struggle often implies (even requires) failure. Study the stories your students read. Most often main characters try a number of things that fail before they find a successful strategy for reaching their goal. Each struggle and failure adds more interest and suspense to the story. Any success pulls excitement out. Encourage your students to be mean to their main character. Make life hard for the character. Make the character struggle and fail. Readers will thank them for it.

Second, it is a bad idea to kill the main character before the end of the story. You have spent considerable time making the character interesting. Kill the character and you lose all that hard work. You have also spent considerable time and effort making readers interested in the character. Kill the main character and you lose the interest of readers. Finally, if the main character dies, you can't make him or her struggle any more. You know how this character talks, acts, and reacts better than any other character. If that character is gone, you will have to work harder through the rest of the story. Make the main character struggle. Make the character suffer if you want. But keep the character around through the climax of your story. Both you and your readers will be much happier and more satisfied.

Activity 33: The Plot Thickens _____

What Students Will Learn:

Students will learn to think of plots as strings of events created to provide a series of discrete opportunities for their characters to struggle within a story framework created by the goal, motive, and obstacles their character must face.

Time Estimate: 30 to 40 minutes

Directions:

This activity is divided into two parts. Complete and discuss Part 1 before turning to Part 2. Plots are built from scenes. Before beginning this activity, discuss the nature of plots and scenes with your class using the following paragraphs as a guide.

Plots are like a garden path constructed of flat stones. The stones lead you safely and logically through the overgrowth and tangle of the garden. You step on one stone, pause to look around and enjoy the garden, and then move on by, stepping to the next stone.

Story plots work the same way. Instead of stones, writers build scenes (events). Readers step into a scene, gaze around at that part of the story by reading the scene, and then move on to the next scene. A path built from individual scenes guides readers safely and logically through the garden of your story from opening, through climax, and to final resolution.

The job of the writer is to identify the necessary scenes and to lay them out in a logical order—just as you would if you were building a garden path of flat stones.

What, exactly, is a scene? A scene is a ministory, a specific event or encounter that comes to a specific close or resolution. Each scene has a main character who must have a goal (something the character wants to do or get in that scene). The goal must be blocked by one or more obstacles that cause the scene's main character to struggle. The scene must then come to a close by resolving the goal of that scene. Scenes are just like stories, but they tell about only one small bit of the whole story.

Strug·gle *n.* A great effort; a strenuous contending. Story struggles realize a story's risk and danger and release the story's excitement.

Part 1. It's time for your students to practice building plotting events and ordering them into a logical sequence. Let's go back to Fred du Frog. Assume that there is no powerboat. That's too easy. Without the boat, how will Big Fred try to get across the lake?

Have each student invent six schemes or ways Fred could try to reach the far side of the lake. They may not invent new conflicts and obstacles for Fred. They must use the ones that have already been created in this book and by the class. Students will write a one-line summary of each of their schemes in the spaces provided on the student worksheet. They won't describe *what* is going to happen, just identify the plan. Remind your students that this is still the creative part of story writing, the fun part. It's all right for them to be as inventive as they like.

A final reminder must be mentioned: each of the events of their stories should provide opportunities for Fred to struggle.

The worksheet directs students to pick their three favorite schemes and to summarize those three plans, the key character traits that will figure into each plan, and how each plan will ultimately fail and land Fred back on his lily pad without any food.

Have as many students as time permits share their plans. Allow the class to acknowledge the merits of each suggested plan and to debate its merits and possible improvements on the scheme. As a class, pick three favorite schemes and discuss why those are the most popular.

Still missing are transitions between these events—Fred's three tries. The easiest transition between events is to show how Fred and the little frogs react when Fred returns without any food. Each time the little frogs will ask, "Did you bring us any food?" Fred will have to answer, "Weeeeell, no I didn't. I think I have to think about it some more!" This transition between scenes (between blocks of action), which gives readers a chance to check in with the characters, is called a sequel. We will talk more about sequels later.

Think of the plot of Fred du Frog's story as being built out of five big stones or scenes. You have just identified three of those stones—the three ways Fred will try to cross the lake that won't work. The story segment presented at the end of Activity 3 will serve nicely for the first part, the introduction. We meet the characters, learn about Fred, and discover his goal, motive, conflicts, and danger.

Part 2. The final part of the story (the climax and resolution) has not yet been identified. Your students must invent Fred's final plan that leads to resolution of his goal—either he gets the food or he has to give up trying.

For this activity, let's assume that the frogs do get food. Divide the class into pairs or trios of students. Each group will create four things:

1. How the frogs finally get their food (it doesn't necessarily have to be through Fred's efforts)

2. Fred's final try to get across the lake—what he does on his final attempt to get across the lake to the frog food (Remember, this is the climax of the story. This plan should bring out the greatest risk and danger for Fred and should bring him face to face with his antagonist, if there is one.)

3. How Fred and the rest of the frogs feel after this attempt

4. Why you think this ending will be satisfying to readers

Have each group write that information in the space provided on the student worksheet.

Allow several groups to share their ideas. It is important for students to see what their peers have done with the same situation and instructions they had. It typically expands the range of possibilities they will consider during future writing assignments.

Point out to your students the importance of checking in with the characters at the end of the story to see how they feel about what has happened. This is called a final sequel and will be discussed in Activity 37.

Your students have now defined a complete story. They created and developed a character and the first seven elements of the story, and laid out a five-part story line. All that is left to do is to create the details that will make each event, character, and place seem real and compelling to readers.

Activity Review

The words *action, events,* and *plot* all refer to the same element of a story. The best word for student writers to use to describe this element of every story is struggles. Through a series of events and actions, characters struggle to overcome obstacles and reach a goal. This sequence of events is what writers call a plot.

A plot is constructed from a series of scenes—separate events—strung together in a logical sequence that presents the characters, traits, goals, motives, struggles, and resolution of a story. The time to plan the plot and action of a story is after you have developed the characters and the other story elements. Remember, if an action or event doesn't show your main character struggling, create new or improved obstacles, reveal character, or resolve a goal, it probably doesn't belong in the story.

Activity 34: Plotting Strategies _____

What Students Will Learn:

Students will learn two comprehensive plotting systems that they can use whenever necessary.

Time Estimate: 75 minutes

Directions:

This activity presents two general plotting systems. The first includes four specific strategies for breaking a story into discrete events that can be individually created. The second system leads students through a seven-step progression to help them define and prioritize the events they will use in a story.

It is valuable—though not essential—for the class to see how each of these strategies works. To do this, divide the class into five groups. Assign one group to use each of the four strategies of the first system and one group to use the second system. (Each system is listed in this section and on the student worksheets.) Each group, using the assigned strategy, will create a plot sequence for the same story—the story of Cecelia Sue.

Provide a brief introductory discussion based on the following paragraphs. Then, talk the class quickly through the concept of each strategy before students begin their group work. The group using System #2 will need the most time since they have the most to do. All groups will need twenty minutes or more to complete this activity. Monitor each group's progress and adjust time accordingly. Have each group complete the assigned strategy before you review and discuss each strategy with the whole class. Space is provided on the worksheets for each of the student groups to use.

Plot *n.* A sequence or plan of events.

Se•quence *n.* A succession of things, connected in a logical way.

The individual events of a story must be logically connected in a meaningful sequence to form a successful plot.

Sometimes writers have already developed the main character, goal, motive, and obstacles and still struggle to decide *what* ought to happen in their stories. If your students find that they aren't sure of what to have their characters *do* in the story, or if they're confused as to how to organize their story events, two systems described in this section can help.

Before trying any plotting system, however, the best way past this dilemma is for student writers to spend more time getting to know their characters. Work on the goals, motives, fears, hopes, and flaws of their characters. Define exactly what conflicts and problems stand in their way and how they create risk and danger. Usually working on these story elements helps to suggest story events that will effectively show these elements to readers.

If your students are still stuck for plotting ideas, the following two plotting systems will help them create meaningful events for your story.

Plotting System #1: Four Plotting Guides. You know who (character) and what (goal) the story is about. You have decided how the goal will finally be resolved (the ending). The stumbling block happens when a character tries to reach the goal. If you jump straight to resolving problems and goal, the story is boring. If you create meaningless events just to fill up the story, the story seems pointless. Here are four strategies to help you create a logical and meaningful pathway from opening to resolution.

You can combine several of these strategies together to complete a strong plot line. For example, a writer could space two failures and two things that go wrong over a two-day period before reaching the final plan, which is broken into four steps.

Strategy A: Time. Identify a certain amount of time that will pass between the start of your story and the final resolution. Then, decide what your main character will do during each block of that time to try to reach the goal.

Let's say that two days will pass between the time Cecelia Sue decides to cross the spooky woods to find (and save) her parents and the time she reaches their small house. Split each of those days into three blocks: morning, afternoon, and night. Students decide, and briefly outline, what she does (and what happens to her) in each of those blocks of time.

Each of these time blocks can be turned into a separate event in the story. In each, students will give Cecelia Sue a specific goal and obstacle to overcome (get by the tarantula, get a map for the woods, etc.).

Strategy B: Failure. Most often, characters fail before they succeed. We made Fred du Frog fail at each of his first three attempts to cross the lake. Making your main character fail before succeeding is a great plotting strategy.

Let's agree that Cecelia Sue's first two attempts to get across the spooky woods to find her parents will end in failure—that is, she will create and attempt a plan but will end up either no closer to getting across the woods than she was when she started or in a worse predicament than when she started. Each of her plans will fail to get her closer to her goal.

Tell students in this group to invent and briefly outline two plans she can try that will each fail. Describe why and how each plan will fail.

Just as in the story of Fred du Frog, these failures will form the story line that leads Cecelia Sue to a final plan that succeeds and gets her across the spooky woods to find her parents and save them from the hungry, spider-eating lizard.

Strategy C: Things Go Wrong. In Strategy B, Cecelia Sue tried things that didn't work. Here, things beyond her control happen to make it harder for her to reach her goal. Technically, you will now create new obstacles for her to overcome. Each time something goes wrong, it creates a new obstacle in the story. Cecelia Sue must confront and overcome this new problem or conflict before she can go on with her journey.

What could go wrong? Maybe rain falls and turns the babbling brook into a raging torrent of a river that Cecelia Sue can't cross. Maybe a forest fire rages through the woods and blocks her path. Maybe her map turns out to be for the wrong woods or written in a language she can't read. Maybe a snippity beaver won't let her cross his dam. Literally anything could happen as long as it creates new obstacles that Cecelia Sue has to face.

Have students in this group invent and briefly outline three things that could go wrong for Cecelia Sue. They should describe how each will create a new and dangerous obstacle for Cecelia Sue to face. Be sure that each is something beyond her control.

Each of these can be turned into a story event. Stringing the events together as Cecelia Sue bounces from problem to problem creates a plot line.

Strategy D: Break Up the Event. Even the simplest plan by your main character involves more than one single action or step. Usually one thing needs to be accomplished to make it possible to do the next. Look at the following example:

Maria needed to go to the store to get butter to make her cookies.

This seems like one simple action, but think. First, she needs to find enough money to buy butter. Then, she needs to walk to the store, get the butter (unless the first store is out of butter), and carry it back home. That's four steps just to accomplish one simple task. Each could be turned into a separate event—if not into an entire story—with it's own conflicts, problems, and struggles.

Try using this technique for Cecelia Sue. Assume that she decides that the only way she'll get across the spooky woods is to charter a helicopter to fly her across.

The students will break this plan into separate steps. (The worksheet provides spaces for six steps. However, students should use as many steps as they need.)

These students will additionally create two things that can go wrong and two failures that will occur during these various individual steps.

Again, when complete, students have outlined the individual events of a plot line.

Plotting System #2: Seven Plotting Steps. This system involves the use of the seven sequential steps in this section. Use the story of Cecelia Sue to practice the seven steps. The steps of this system are listed here using the same wording that appears on the student activity sheet.

Step 1. List six to eight events, encounters, or scenes that could form the important moments in your story.

Step 2. On the lines below, write why each of these events is needed to tell this story.

Step 3. Think about these events and decide which should happen first, second, and so forth, and list them in the order you think will make the story easiest to write and most effective for readers.

Step 4. Write a one-paragraph summary of this story. Try to make clear the elements as well as the flow of events of your story.

Step 5. Look at the events you listed in Step 1 and ordered in Step 3. Is each really needed to tell the story you summarized in the paragraph of Step 4? Are there any events you could drop and still effectively tell the story? (If you don't absolutely need it, cut it.) Are there any events you did not include in Step 1 that you would need to include to tell the complete story as summarized in Step 4?

Step 6. Write a one-sentence summary of the story. This sentence should tell what the story is about. (In this summary, did students summarize the plot or list the main character and goal? Remember, every story is about the goal of the main character.)

Step 7. Review the list of events as amended in Step 5. Will each be useful and helpful in telling the story defined in Step 6? Are there any events that could be eliminated and still adequately tell the story defined in Step 6?

This seven-step process should leave students with an ordered list of events they can individually write and string together with good transitions to tell the story of Cecelia Sue.

Allow groups to share their results and to briefly present their strategy's strengths and weaknesses they encountered while working. Let the class discuss each group's results and the steps to create successful plotting structures.

Activity Review

Plots are pathways through a story. There can be many different plot lines to lead readers through the same story, just as there can be many different paths to lead viewers through a garden. Each scene in a story must have a purpose and must act like a ministory with its own goal, struggles, and resolution.

Plots may be carefully planned and laid out before writing the story, or they may be built as the writer progresses through the story. The advantage of preplanning is that it usually eliminates much of the rewriting and revision that would otherwise become necessary.

Activity 35: Problem Solved . . . or Not! _____

What Students Will Learn:

Students will learn what informational elements are essential to a satisfying story resolution and will gain experience in recognizing and creating those elements.

Time Estimate: 15 to 20 minutes for Part 1; 30 to 40 minutes for Part 2

Directions:

This activity is divided into two parts. Part 1 should be completed out of class. Part 2 is an in-class activity.

Introduce the activity by leading a brief class discussion about what makes a story ending a good ending. What has to happen at the end? What do your students—as readers—want to know at the end? When does the end of a story begin? Allow students to voice their opinions and to discuss this important element of a story before you continue.

Creating a satisfying ending to a story is often a big challenge. Story goals dictate the general end of every story—either the main character gets his or her goal or gives up on that goal. But that information alone seems unsatisfying. Readers need a feeling of resolution, of completeness. How does that happen? What, besides the goal, must be resolved to give readers a feeling of satisfaction and completeness?

Cli·max *n.* The last in a series of events or situations to which what has gone before seems in retrospect to have been building up. In the climax scene of a story, the main character confronts the antagonist for the final time.

Story resolution (the end of the story) is everything in the story following the climax scene. The climax scene, of course, is the scene in which the main character confronts, for the final time, the last and greatest obstacle standing between the character and the goal. A climax scene is usually an exciting, dramatic, intense scene. It is the high point of tension in the story. Everything is on the line with the outcome of that scene. After the climax comes the resolution of the story.

Part 1. Start by examining satisfying stories students have recently read. Assign students to select two stories, carefully examine the ending of each story, and complete Part 1 of their worksheet. This step may be assigned as homework.

Part 2. Lead a class discussion about the information that appears in a resolution. What did your students find there? Did they all find the same types of information in each story? Were there types of information that always appeared? Allow your students to debate the questions to come to their own collective conclusions. Try to create a class master list of the information readers need to find in the resolution of a story.

Writers have found that readers need four key bits of information after a climax. All four of these bits relate to the main character and to the goal:

1. Can the character now reach the goal?
2. Does the character still want it?
3. Does the character actually get it?
4. How does the character *feel* about it (how has the character changed)?

In summary, these questions resolve the goal (does the character get it?) and provide a final sequel for the main character. We will introduce sequels in Activity 37.

Have students review the lists of information they created for their two stories. Does the information they found fit within those four questions? Do the elements on their composite list fit the questions?

Let's practice creating effective resolutions by finishing the story of Fred du Frog. In previous activities, we created a goal (get the frog food from across the lake—Activity 4), an antagonist (Activity 32), and a final try for Fred (Activity 33). The final try will become the climax of this story. We also decided that Fred and the other three frogs don't starve to death but do get food—though not necessarily through Fred's efforts and actions.

Let each student decide how they want to end the story and answer the four questions. Then have each student complete the rest of the activity worksheet.

Allow several students to share their resolution scenes. Have the class discuss whether the information answers each of the four questions. Debate which student's ideas are most satisfying and why.

As an option, post each student's written resolution scene on the board, so students can see what others did with the same information and assignment.

Activity Review

The resolution of a story provides a satisfying sense of completeness and closure. To get closure, readers need to see the goal resolved and need to see how the main characters feel about the outcome.

The resolution (ending) of a story includes everything beyond the story's climax scene. Writers are often tempted to ramble on during the resolution, including much more information than readers want or need. This rambling will always dilute the power and satisfaction of the ending for readers. It is best to answer the four questions listed in this activity and end the story. Save additional events involving these same characters for the next story.

Activity 36: Cause and Effect Game _____

What Students Will Learn:

Readers expect the laws of cause and effect to apply to the world of stories. In this activity, students will learn the meaning and value of cause and effect planning.

Time Estimate: 10 minutes

Directions:

This activity is a class verbal story-building game. There is no student worksheet for it. Following the directions below, you will lead your class to see and understand the value of cause and effect planning in building their story plots.

Nothing is more basic in stories than the idea of cause and effect. One thing leads to another. Actions today cause events tomorrow. What you sow today, so shall you reap tomorrow. It is a powerful and reliable story structure.

This is a verbal group activity that begins with one student (Student #1) inventing and describing a fictional event. The student tells about something that happened but does not explain why it happened. The student simply makes up and tells *what* happened.

Cause *n.* That which brings about a result.

Ef·fect *n.* The result produced by a cause.

Writers use cause and effect to create logical order and meaning to the sequence of events they use to create a story plot.

> *Example:*
> *Student #1: "A cat wandered, howling, down an alley."*

A second student (Student #2) then invents *why* that event happened. That is, Student #2 defines what actions in the past caused this action to happen in the story's present.

> *Example:*
> *Student #2: "The cat was howling because it was lost and hadn't eaten in six days. On a family vacation, it had jumped out of the arms of the girl who owned it. The family couldn't find the cat and had to leave for home without it."*

If the class isn't satisfied with, or isn't sure of, this causal relationship, have Student #2 explain and justify it. If necessary, the class can amend Student #2's event so that the class understands and accepts the cause and effect relationship between the events provided by Students #1 and #2. This is an important part of this activity. It is always surprising to see how much more interest is created in Student #1's event after Student #2 has provided its causal background.

A third student (Student #3) then makes up why the situation and events described by Student #2 came to be. That is, Student #3 invents a cause for the actions described by Student #2, which were made up to be a cause for the action described by Student #1.

> *Example:*
> *Student #3: "The family loved the cat, Scooter. But they knew Scooter would never survive on her own while they left for a three-week driving vacation. Scooter was scared of everything and needed lots of love and attention. They decided to take Scooter with them on the car trip."*

Every cause leads to an action or event that becomes the root cause for the next action. Every action has a root cause lying somewhere in the past. Again, the class must come to agreement that Student #3's description forms a plausible cause for Student #2's action—not for Student #1's action or for some other plausible action but for the specific event created by Student #2.

Now go forward. Another student (Student #4) creates the next event in the story that follows after, and because of, the original event described by Student #1.

> *Example:*
> Student #4: *"A man threw a shoe at Scooter and yelled at her to be quiet. Scooter collapsed, trembling with hunger and fear behind a slimy dumpster, where she met a cockroach."*

Again the class debates and approves Student #4's event, which must follow logically based on the events created by Students #3, #2, and, especially, #1.

Finally, Student #5 creates yet another event, which flows after and because of the event described by Student #4.

> *Example:*
> Student #5: *"Scooter found that the cockroach was part of a large, friendly family. Scooter moved in with the cockroaches (even though her room was much too small) and lived happily ever after."*

A string of five cause-and-effect events has been laid out. Do these events define a story? No, not yet. Some character traits and some struggles have been created, but no goal, no motives, and no clear picture of obstacles are present. More important, the character, Scooter, has not been adequately developed to create a successful story. From this string of events, however, students could track back to the character and story information that define a story.

Can the class members see how this whole flow of cause and effect leads from step to step? Is Event #5 more interesting because you know its causal background of Events #1 through #4?

Activity Review

Every reader expects story events to flow logically from one scene to the next. Readers often can't anticipate the exact nature of this flow but should be able to see it as logical, if not inevitable, in hindsight. As writers lay out the scenes of a story, they can use this concept to first plan, and later review and edit, the sequencing of scenes they created.

If the story seems to drift without purpose, one way to repair it is to check scenes that lead up to any dull, aimless spots and make sure causal actions are laid out in these scenes, which must be lived out during the present scene. The causal action is like hearing one shoe hit the floor—readers can't put the story down until they've heard the other shoe fall. That is, once they've seen the cause, they need to keep reading until they see the effect.

Activity 37: Scene and Sequel Game _____

What Students Will Learn:

Students will learn the meaning of, power of, and use of a sequel as a form of transition between blocks of story action.

Time Estimate: 15 minutes

Directions:

This is a verbal story-building game to play with the whole class. There is no student worksheet for this activity. Following the directions and guidance in this section, you will lead your students to see and appreciate the value of sequels following their scenes (or blocks of action).

Many people think *sequel* means "the second movie in a series." In writing it has a slightly different meaning. A sequel is a result or an aftereffect. It is the effect (on a character) of something (an action).

A scene is a block of action, an event, a confrontation. A sequel is a chance to check in with the main characters following that event to see how the action event has changed their thinking and feeling. Nothing physically happens during a sequel except that the main character reflects on the previous event and ponders (or decides) what it means. If a scene is *what* happens, a sequel is the *so what*. Sequels tell readers what the preceding event means to the character. Scenes are typically long and detailed. Sequels are usually short, often only a sentence or two.

Sequels serve the following valuable functions. They:

Scene *n.* A division or separate part of a story.

Se·quel *n.* A result or aftereffect.

A scene is an event, a block of action. The resultant and following sequel shows the effect of that action on the thinking and feeling of the main character.

- Reconnect readers to the characters after the action of a scene has concluded.

- Reveal more about a character's thinking and feelings.

- Provide effective transitions between scenes.

- Let readers see inside the main character to understand and anticipate what will happen next.

Sequels are powerful writing tools for your students to practice building into their stories—especially because so many beginning writers forget to reveal their characters' thinking and feelings following each event. Readers see *what* happens but never see the *so what*—what it means to the story's characters.

In this game, one student will invent a sequel after each story event created by the rest of the class. The class will then see how much easier it is to decide both what should happen next in the story and why it should happen once they know the sequel.

Let's examine the power of sequels by playing a game as a whole class. Assign one student to be Mr./Ms. Sequel. This student will stand near the door and watch what the rest of the class creates.

Have a student volunteer make up a character, a first impression for that character, and a goal. The student should also include an obstacle that blocks the character and—optionally—a motive for the goal.

> *Example:*
> *Once there was a young brown bear named Squirt who wanted some honey. But he was very small. So the other bears shoved him aside when they found a honeycomb and wouldn't let him have any. Even worse, Squirt was afraid of heights and couldn't climb trees, so he couldn't get his own honey from a beehive. But Squirt* really *wanted some honey.*

This paragraph contains a first impression, a goal, and two obstacles. A second volunteer creates an event or interaction involving the main character and the specified goal and obstacles.

> *Example:*
> *One day Squirt saw a fat bee buzzing through the meadow and decided to follow it back to its hive. Maybe he'd find a way to get the bee's honey.*
> *But the bee angrily turned on Squirt. "Don't you follow me! I know you just want to steal our honey. But you can't have any. And if you try to get some, a thousand bees will sting and bite you and make you so miserable you'll wish you never heard of honey!" And the bee flew off.*

Now have Mr./Ms. Sequel step out of the room. Once the door is closed, allow several class volunteers to guess at what they think might happen next in the story—that is, guess at what the next action or event in the story might be.

> *Example guesses:*
> *Guess #1: The bear swats at and kills the bee.*
> *Guess #2: The bear says he's not afraid of a bee and follows the bee home and pushes over the tree to get at the hive and the honey.*
> *Guess #3: The bear is terrified and runs away to chase butterflies.*

The class must ensure that each guess describes only an event—an action—that might follow logically after the action first described.

Now bring Mr./Ms. Sequel back into the room and ask him or her to tell the class how Squirt *felt* and what he *thought* after that first scene. (That is, ask Mr./Ms. Sequel to provide a sequel for that first scene.) Mr./Ms. Sequel did not hear the guesses made by other students for the next action event in the story, so this sequel may not have any relevance to those guesses.

> *Example:*
> *Squirt realized how mean and unfair it was for bears to steal honey from hard-working bees. He wanted honey but realized he couldn't steal it anymore. If he were going to get some honey, he'd have to find a way to get it fairly.*

That's a sequel. Nothing physically has happened in this sequel. Nothing should, except for the character's reflections on the previous scene, internalizing it, deciding what the action and interaction of the scene means.

If Mr./Ms. Sequel includes any major actions taken by the main character, or any interactions with other characters, the class should stop the sequel and correct this incursion of scene into sequel. Review with the class the difference between scene and sequel and the purpose of each.

Now the class can see how close or how far off their guesses were about what is actually going to happen next in this story. After they hear the sequel, students should have a much better idea of what must happen next in the story. Creating the next scene, or event, is now easy.

That's the point of this game. Scenes follow from sequels, just as sequels follow from scenes.

The reason Mr./Ms. Sequel is sent out of the room is so the nature of the sequel they invent won't be influenced by other students' guesses about the action of the next scene.

Sequels lead us from scene to scene by showing how the main character interprets the last scene and plans for the next.

Have a volunteer now create the real next scene based on Scene #1 and its sequel.

> *Example:*
> *Squirt went to the grocery store and asked for a job to earn the money to buy his honey.*
> *He volunteered to be a stock boy, a cashier, even a sweeper.*
> *But the store owner said he didn't trust bears, and besides health codes said bears weren't allowed in grocery stores because of all the moldy bear hair.*
> *The owner said, "Go away!" and slammed the door in Squirt's face.*

Note that a scene should include a goal, a conflict or problem that is addressed, a character interaction, and a conclusion to that action or interaction.

Again have Mr./Ms. Sequel leave the room while several other students guess at what event might happen next. Mr./Ms. Sequel then returns and reveals the next sequel—how the character feels about this last interaction and what it means to and for the character.

Continue in this way through four or five scenes to the end of the story and a final sequel.

It is the class's job is to ensure that each student providing a scene presents a complete and valid scene but only one scene, that all offered scenes are consistent with the story's basic information and past scenes and sequels, and that Mr./Ms. Sequel provides a plausible sequel for every scene.

As an optional follow-up activity, assign students to find sequels in books they have read and to report these back to the class for extra credit.

Activity Review

The information in sequels is essential to readers' understanding of both character and story. Readers want to view all scenes through the eyes of the main character, but they can only do that when they understand the character's interpretation of, and reaction to, the events of the story. That's a sequel.

Sequels are the intersection of the events of the previous scenes and the personality of the main character. Sequels reveal how characters reflect on and understand events and action. Sequels lead the reader to understand and sympathize with a character. If action is the *what* of a story, then sequels are the *so what*.

Activity 38: Story Mapping

What Students Will Learn:

Students will be introduced to the concept of, and general design of, story maps.

Time Estimate: varies depending on which mapping system is used

Directions:

This is a brief classroom discussion activity that can easily dovetail with other writing guides you may be using and their story mapping systems and forms. There is no student worksheet for this activity. Many effective mapping systems have been published. The best one to use is the one that works best for the individual student writers.

Many students like to work with story maps. But what is a story map? The street maps and land maps we use every day form a picture of part of the earth and show you the parts, contours, and features of the ground. Story maps provide the same information for a story. Story maps lay out a picture of the story and of its major features: characters, elements, sequence of events, how the characters felt during those events, settings where events take place, and any major details the writer needs to remember while writing.

Map *n.* A visual representation that shows the main parts and features of the area being mapped. Story maps should reveal the Eight Essential Elements of the story and lay out the general sequence of events the writer will use to tell the story.

Some writers draw pictures (even stick-figure pictures) of the characters, settings, and scenes to use as a story map. Some write an outline of the story. Some use file cards, writing one file card for each character and one for each scene. This makes it easy to reshuffle the scenes to explore different plotting paths. Previous activities in this book laid out simple story maps for Fred du Frog and for Cecelia Sue the spider.

The following elements should appear on any effective story map:

1. At least a good first impression for each major character and additional significant detail for the main character(s)

2. A statement of goal, motive, and the ending (resolution of goal) that the writer chooses

3. A listing of major conflicts and obstacles

4. A sequence of major events, with a description for each event that includes the goal for that scene, the conflict the character must confront, and the outcome (resolution of the scene's goal). (It is beneficial to add a sequel as a transition—how the character feels at the end of the scene about the scene's events and how those events have changed the character's feeling and thinking.)

5. The climax event, with a brief description of that event during which the main character confronts the last (and greatest) obstacle that stands between the character and the goal

Have your students try writing or drawing a story map for Fred du Frog and Cecelia Sue. Encourage them to experiment with different formats and styles, searching for one that is comfortable for each student to use.

Allow several students to share their maps and discuss what they liked and didn't like about the format and structure of the map they created. Students should feel free to copy ideas from other students for future story maps they make.

Activity Review

Story maps are organizational tools to use if and when they help you organize your thoughts about a story. If used effectively, they will speed the process of story planning and will greatly reduce story revision after the first draft has been completed. Story maps come in a wide variety of forms and styles. Some are done as outlines, some as word maps, and some as a series of cartoon picture sketches of the story. The form to develop and use is the one that works best for you and your story.

ELEMENT #8: DETAILS

What details will make the story real and vibrant to readers?

Details are the eighth and final of the Get It Write! Eight Essential Elements. Student writers use Elements #1 through #7 to create a compelling, satisfying story. Then, they must write the story—in words, on paper. To do that, writers must convert their mental images of characters, places, actions, and objects into details. It is the details writers write that make a story seem vivid and real in the minds of readers. When you write, write details.

In the next fourteen activities, we explore what details are, what a writer has to describe in a story, and—especially—how students can successfully describe.

During these activities, you and your students will encounter some new lists. Your students have already become familiar with one list—the Eight Essential Elements. To understand details, we have to create several more lists.

Why bog students down with more lists? Because these lists consistently help students write more effective details and help them improve the caliber of their writing.

Students typically struggle to include sufficient description in their stories. Much of what they do include is vague, general, and ineffective. Students and teachers both consistently identify this as one of their biggest writing problems.

A story will not be interesting, intriguing, or satisfying to readers unless they can successfully visualize the characters, places, and events of the story in their minds as they read. Those images always come from details, which means that student writers will not achieve their writing goals unless they include strong, specific details throughout their stories.

Breaking the vast subject of details into smaller chunks helps students better understand and manage their story details. Those chunks are called **aspects** of a story. There are four of these aspects.

Giving students lists of the specific kinds of information they can use to create each aspect helps them create consistently better and more effective details and helps them create these details more easily.

We will develop three new lists while exploring details and will revisit a long list developed in Activity 12 that listed fifteen categories of information students can use to describe their characters.

The new lists are as follows:

- The four aspects of a story writers must describe (characters, settings, actions and events, and objects that appear in the story)
- The Five Criteria students can use to distinguish effective details from ordinary description
- The Five Categories of Information students can use to create details about an object or setting.

This exploration of details uses fourteen activities and is thus a long section. In it, we examine how student writers can effectively create the details to describe each of the four aspects of a story. The following list helps to summarize how these fourteen activities are organized.

Activity 39: Deciding What to Describe

What Students Will Learn:

Students will learn to identify *what* they must describe in a story and will begin to focus on what it means to describe something in a narrative.

Time Estimate: 5 to 10 minutes

Directions:

This is a quick introductory activity designed to help students organize the giant topic of description and details. You may either have students complete their worksheet individually or conduct the exercise as a class discussion. Student worksheets do not include the narrative discussion presented here.

Once the elements of a story and its plot line (struggles) have been laid out, it's time to create the rich details (the eighth of *Get It Write!* Eight Essential Elements) that will make the story vivid and real to readers. Everyone has heard of details. But what are details? What do they do in a story? Why do we need them?

We'll begin with a simple question: What does a writer have to describe in a story? There are four general aspects of every story a writer must describe. See if your students can name them. Before you go on, have students write their ideas on the lines provided on the worksheet.

De·tail *n.* A small part of a composition considered in isolation. Writers use details to describe the characters, places, actions, and objects of a story.

Through class discussion, determine if students wrote characters, settings, actions, and objects (things), which are the four aspects. A writer must describe every character, place (setting), action (movement or event), and object or thing that enters a story if readers are going to be able to create vivid, detailed images of those story events in their minds.

Must a writer describe every object, setting, character, and action? The answer is to describe everything you want readers to see. Don't describe parts of the settings and stories you don't want readers to actively visualize while they read. Include only as much description as readers need to vividly picture and understand the story. If you put in few details, readers won't be able to "see" the story in their minds and will become bored. If you bog down the story with excess description, the story loses its energy, emotion, and pace; readers, again, will edge toward boredom.

Still, virtually every word written in a story is a detail describing one of the four aspects of the story. That's why details are so important. Writers create their story first, and write second. Writers create stories, but they write details.

Here are some activities to help your students better understand what effective details look like and how to consistently create them for each of these four aspects of stories. We begin with the simplest of the four, objects, or things, and then proceed through settings, actions, and characters.

Activity 40: Details versus Description _____

What Students Will Learn:

Students will learn the Five Categories of Information they can use to describe an object and will learn the difference between description and details.

Time Estimate: 10 minutes

Directions:

There is no student worksheet for this verbal activity. This is important activity, with which we begin our exploration of details, one that teachers must lead verbally with their whole class. We begin by exploring how to describe objects, or things—the simplest of the four aspects.

You should begin with this introduction: "Everyone has heard the word *details* as well as the word *description.* Is there a difference in the meaning of these two words, or is this a case where English has two words that mean the same thing?"

Allow the class to first vote on whether these two words have different meanings and then define the difference (for those who thought that there was one). End this discussion by saying, "*He wore a faded red-checked shirt with a jagged, lightning-bolt-shaped tear in the back.* Was that description or detail?"

If students answer "details," you answer, "But didn't it sound like I was *describing* the shirt?" If they answer "description," you answer, "But didn't those sound like *details* I was using to describe the shirt?" The idea is to make them question their own concepts about these two words and to create increased curiosity about both the difference in meaning and about the real meaning of details.

Ob·ject *n.* An identifiable body or thing. Objects (things) differ from characters in that objects cannot and do not think and act on their own behalf.

Then say that you want to show what writers mean when they use these two words by having the students describe a simple object, a thing (one of the four aspects of a story identified in Activity 39).

Pick up a chalk- or marker-board eraser. Hold it and turn it so that your students can see all sides. Say, "Here is a thing. I want you to describe this thing, and, in the way you describe it, I want to see if we can identify all five of the ways you can describe an object. Then I'll show you the difference between description and details."

On the board write "description of an Object" and under it the numerals 1 through 5 in a column.

Continue to hold the eraser so that students can see it and ask them to describe it. As volunteers correctly identify one of the five categories by using it to describe the eraser, write the name of that category on the board next to its appropriate number. The words I write are in boldface in the following list.

The Five Categories of Information are as follows:

1. **Name:** Every object has a name. Students can say, "It's an eraser." That accurately and specifically describes the object.

2. **Sensory information:** This category includes any information that could be directly obtained through the five senses—what the object looks like, sounds like, feels like, smells like, or tastes like. Students will always begin this activity by using visual sensory information to describe the eraser—"It's black. It's rectangular. It's small."

   Sight is only one of our five senses, so I usually don't give students credit for identifying this category (i.e., I don't write the words "sensory information" on the board) until they have mentioned three individual senses. Before that, I will write an "L" in the margin next to the numeral

2 when someone gives me information they got by looking at the object (visual sensory information), an "F" if they offer tactile information (what it *feels* like), and so on.

3. **Function:** What the object does, what you do with it, is its function. This includes both the object's intended purpose and as well as any inventive, unintended uses—"You erase the board with it. You can throw it across the room and bonk someone on the head with it."

4. **History:** We often describe places, people, and things by describing where they came from, where they have been, and what has happened to them. Rarely do students identify this category when trying to describe an eraser. I usually ask a volunteer to make up answers to the following questions: "Where was this eraser made? When? How did it get to (whatever town you are in)? How did it get to this school? How long has it been in this classroom?" Then ask the class what the volunteer created for the eraser. This usually triggers the correct answer—history.

5. **Comparison** (what it reminds you of): I usually have to give the class this category, even though they use it all the time—themselves. We regularly describe one thing by comparing it to other things with which the listener (or reader) is already familiar. We regularly describe objects or people by saying what they remind us of. These comparisons can be physical ("looks like a black pillow or a black river barge") or functional ("reminds me of school"). This is where metaphor and simile fit into a writer's descriptive tool bag.

Having led them to identify all five categories, I say, "In a story, I am going to write that John picked up the thing and used it. But I know that would be bad writing. I'm supposed to describe this thing in my story. Right? So I will name it (state here the complete company and brand name); say what it looks like, sounds like, feels like, tastes like, and smells like on all six sides, inside and outside, day and night; I'll list thirty-eight things I can do with this eraser; I'll include the entire history of this eraser (summarize here the history invented by your volunteer); and I'll list twenty-seven things this eraser reminds me of (include a few here—a soft, black pillow; a blackened coal car on a train; etc.)."

Take a deep breath and ask, "Should I do that? Should I include eight pages of description for this one eraser?"

The answer, of course, is "No! It would be boring."

If you don't include enough description, the story is boring because readers don't have sufficient details with which to visualize your characters, settings, events, and objects in their minds. But if you include too much description, the story again becomes boring because the excess description bogs down the pace of the story and sucks out its energy.

Too much description, and its boring; too little, and its boring.

So what is a writer to do? Here is what writers do. In their minds, they sift through the hundreds of bits of possible description in each of the five categories for each of the objects they include in the story, searching for one or two individual bits of description they think are the most effective, the most powerful, the most descriptive. Then, they include only those one or two best bits of description in their story.

What do we call these one or two best bits of all the possible description? We call them **details**.

This is the difference between details and description: Details *are* description, but they are the best bits of description the writer can find to describe the thing being described.

Activities 41 through 47 explore how writers describe an object—a thing—in their stories. Activities 41 and 42 look at what turns a bit of description into an effective detail. Activities 43 through 46 explore one of the five categories—Sensory Information. Activity 47 explores a second of these categories—Comparisons. The other three categories (name, function, and history) are equally important but are not addressed in separate activities.

Activity Review

Details are the one or two best, most effective bits of description a writer can find for the objects being described. There is only time and space in a story for writers to include a few descriptive details, so it is important for writers to search out the best bits of description to use each time they describe a character, setting, event, or object. It is important to get the most descriptive "bang" for every descriptive word stuffed into a story.

Activity 41: Characteristics of Good Details _____

What Students Will Learn:

Students will learn the characteristics of effective details, will develop the five Criteria of effective detail, and will practice creating details for an object.

Time Estimate: 15 minutes

Directions:

Introduce this activity with the questions in the following paragraph. Then review the rules and directions in this section, which also are included on the students' worksheets. They can follow along while you describe what they have to do. Time the students while they write their description.

Activity 40 identified the Five Categories of Information writers can use to describe an object. That game also showed that details are the best individual bits of all possible description. But which ones are the best? How does a writer know which ones to use as details? What writers need is a list of criteria to guide them in crafting and selecting the best description to use as their story details.

This is a group activity for the whole class. Without getting up from their desks, students will secretly select one object in the room. They may not let anyone else know what object they have chosen. It may *not* be a human or an animal. It must be an object.

Have students think about all the ways they could describe their object. Think about each of the Five Categories of Information identified during the previous activity: name, sensory information, function (what it does), history, and a comparison to some other object (what it reminds you of).

The student worksheet provides space for students to write as much description about this object as they can in three minutes while following these five rules:

1. They may not name their object. They should try to use each of the other four categories of descriptive information, but they may not say what the object is.

2. Spelling doesn't matter for this activity, as long as they can read what they wrote.

3. They do not need to write in complete sentences. They should just get down as much description as they can.

4. They may not get up from their desks to hold, feel, or otherwise inspect their object. They should describe it while sitting at their desks.

5. They may infer (guess at) any information they don't know for this object. If, for example, they wanted to say where the object was made (its history) or how long it has been in this room (history), or what it feels like (sensory), they will have to write down their best guess since they can't get up to find out for sure.

U·nique *adj.* Being the only one of its kind.

Un·u·su·al *adj.* Rare, different from others.

If a trait of a character, object, or setting is unusual or unique, it will always be interesting.

Continue the activity following these directions. They are not included on the students' worksheets.

Have one student (the reader) stand and read his or her description—slowly—one bit of description at a time, pausing between each individual bit to allow the other students to consider this new descriptive information.

The rest of the class has three jobs:

1. They need to figure out exactly which object in the room is being described. It is not enough to identify the general group of an object ("one of the ceiling tiles"). The class must identify the individual, specific tile (object) being described.
2. They need to determine if the reader uses all four available categories of descriptive information.
3. They need to pick their favorite single bit of description being read.

After the entire description has been read and the object has been identified, the student who first correctly identifies the object should say exactly which bit of description led him or her to the correct answer. (Good details uniquely and accurately identify an object.)

The reader will reread each bit of the description. As each individual bit is read, the class should call out which category of descriptive information it is. This helps all students gain a feel for the different categories. Decide if the reader used all four available categories.

After this second reading, the class members get to pick their favorite single bit of description: the bit that created the best and most interesting image in their minds, the bit they thought was the most fun. Good details are vivid and interesting.

Have a second, and even a third, student read his or her description, repeating all of the steps. If a student fools the class so that no one can correctly identify the single object being described, does that student win or lose? The student loses. The goal of all description is to uniquely and accurately identify the object being described. The easier a writer makes the identification process for readers, the better.

Good details make it easy for the reader to specifically picture the object being described. Thus, the details must be specific. Additionally, the best details are interesting. They create vivid, interesting images in a reader's mind. Thus, good details *must* be:

- **Accurate:** Incorrect or misleading information always confuses the reader.
- **Specific:** General or vague description—for example, "It was big"—does not correctly or uniquely identify the item. Specific description does—"It was the biggest snake I had ever seen, stretching out longer than two school buses."

To be interesting, good details *should* be:

- **Unique:** Description that shows how one object differs from all others helps to specifically identify it. Another word for *unique* is *different*. Good details show how the object being described is different from all others.
- **Unusual:** Details that identify unusual or unexpected characteristics of an object create the most interest. Writing that a pencil is yellow is accurate and specific but neither unique nor unusual. Saying it is glow-in-the-dark neon orange that is as bright as a forty-watt lightbulb is unique and interesting but not unusual. We commonly describe the color of pencils. Writing that the pencil speaks French is more interesting because it is both unique and unusual.

• **Vivid** Effective details paint vivid images in the minds of readers. Notice that description that compares the object being described (says what it reminds the writer of) usually creates the most interesting and vivid images.

As you write these criteria on the board, cite examples (positive or negative) from the student descriptions that have just been read.

Review the class's votes for the favorite bit of description and for which bit of detail gave away the objects being described. See if these details meet the criteria for good details.

Have one more student read his or her description. After the class has identified the object being described, have the student reread the description, one bit at a time. The class must change or add to this information to turn each of these bits of description into vivid and interesting details.

They do not have to stay truthful and accurate while they do this. If they need to fictionalize their description to make it vivid and interesting, they may. Guide them to use each of the other four criteria of effective details as guides to turning each bit of ordinary description into intriguing, vivid, interesting details.

Finally, compare this list of criteria for effective details to the list created in Activity 11 for effective character description. They are the same. As we will see later, students were creating details while trying to describe a character and make the character interesting.

Activity Review

Effective details are those specific bits of descriptive information that accurately and uniquely identify an object being described and that create specific and vivid images in the minds of readers. The rest of the information is just description. As you write, search for strong details to describe the four aspects of your story.

Most of the words in a story are details, there to describe the characters, settings, actions, or objects of the story. First, the writer must create an interesting story and then create the interesting details that communicate the images of the story to readers. Writers don't have space in a story to include a barrage of mediocre description. Rather, they must squeeze as much descriptive power as they can out of every word. To find those few, best bits of descriptive detail, writers must search through each of the Five Categories (name, sensory information, function, history, and comparisons).

Activity 42: Describe a Leaf

What Students Will Learn:

Students will practice describing an object and will clearly see the difference between description and effective details.

Time Estimate: 30 minutes for homework; one day during which students read and evaluate the descriptions; 30 minutes for final class review

Directions:

Let's look further into how writers describe objects and at the tools writers use to create effective details.

As a homework assignment, students must pluck a single leaf from a tree or bush and write at least a half-page description about that leaf on their worksheet page. They should not write their name on the paper, should not name the variety of leaf (or the bush or tree it came from), and should not show their leaf or description to anyone in the class. Each student should try to use all four of the other categories of possible descriptive information.

The next day, students turn in their leaves and descriptions in closed, brown paper bags. You must develop an alphanumeric coding system for the leaves and descriptions. Give each leaf a letter label on a piece of masking tape fastened to its stem. Write a number on each description and create a master code linking each leaf letter with its description number. All leaves and descriptions are then spread out on a table for the rest of the day. During available time, students must read the descriptions, study the leaves, and write down which leaf they think goes with each description.

Ac·cu·rate *adj.* Precise; exact; correct and truthful. Description and details must be accurate, or readers will stop believing what the writer says.

Then, read each description, allowing students to call out which leaf it describes. Writers win if most students correctly identify their leaf. Good description uniquely describes an object.

The class must decide which exact bits of information in each half-page description uniquely identified its leaf. These bits should be highlighted. They are effective details that uniquely identify and describe an object. The class should also decide which bits of description were the most interesting and which painted the most vivid and interesting images in their heads. These bits should also be highlighted. Effective details paint strong, interesting, vivid images in readers' heads.

The leaves may now be discarded, but leave the descriptions out for students to review. Each contains a half-page description with highlighted bits that could serve as effective details in a story to describe a leaf and thus demonstrate the difference between general description and effective details.

Activity 43: Sound Details

What Students Will Learn:

Students will explore the use of sound (sense of hearing) as one sensory detail they can use to enrich their descriptions.

Time Estimate: one day during which students complete their worksheet; 20 to 30 minutes to review and discuss

Directions:

Sensory information is one of the Five Categories we identified that students can use to describe objects. This category, however, deserves closer study. The next four activities focus on using specific senses in creating effective sensory details.

Each of these activities requires out-of-class time for students. Student worksheets include basic directions. More detailed directions and discussion are included here.

We begin with the sense of hearing. Tell students to pick a specific location (preferably at or near home) where they can comfortably and safely sit with eyes closed for one minute. They should carry a watch or clock that can time one minute. They should also bring the worksheet for this activity and a pencil.

The worksheet instructs students to sit at their chosen spot for one minute with eyes closed and concentrate on hearing and remembering individual sounds. After the minute is over, they are to write down and describe every sound they can remember.

Students are then told to pick two of these sounds, the two they think best describe the place where they sat, and to write effective descriptions of the two sounds. Remind students to search for descriptive words that allow readers to vividly picture the spot and the sounds in their imagination.

Have several students read the descriptions of their chosen sounds to see if the class can guess where they were sitting and what they were hearing. Then the class should review and critique students' description, stating whether descriptions were accurate, specific, unique, unusual, and vivid. Which bits of description were most interesting? Why? As a class, can you improve on these descriptions and make them stronger and more interesting?

As a class, discuss how and when sounds are effective and powerful details to incorporate into descriptions of objects, characters, events, and settings.

Finally, the class should agree on one specific place that each student can easily visit (bedroom, kitchen, sidewalk, closet, yard, etc.). On the worksheet, students should describe the two most interesting and descriptive sounds they hear in that place.

Sense *n.* Any of the bodily faculties (sight, sound, smell, touch, and taste) by which the organism becomes aware of its surroundings.

Sen·so·ry *adj.* Of or relating to the sensations carried by the sense organs.

Compare the descriptions created by different students. Discuss how effective each proposed detail is. Allow the class to reword and improve the offerings of individual students. How did each student describe his or her sounds? Did students describe the tone, pitch, and volume, of the sound? Did they compare the sound to another sound? Did they say what the sound reminded them of? Did they say how the sound made them feel? Which of these descriptive tools was most effective? Which got the best reaction from the class?

Activity Review

Hearing is one of a human's five senses. Sensory information is one of the Five Categories of Information writers can use to describe objects in their stories. When writers describe using one of the senses, readers are encouraged to envision the object using their senses and thus enrich their imagery of the story. Effective use of hearing requires that the sound description be specific, unique, and vivid.

Activity 44: "Seeing" Your Details _____

What Students Will Learn:

Students will explore using their sense of vision (what things look like) to enrich their descriptions.

Time Estimate: one elapsed day for students to complete their worksheet; 20 to 30 minutes to review and discuss

Directions:

This activity focuses on students' sense of sight, or vision. Vision, what objects look like, is the most commonly used sense in story writing. Tell your students to pick two places and two objects to describe. For each, they are to pick two visual details that they think are most important and that uniquely define the place or thing they are describing. They will write these visual details on their worksheet. They may not name the places or objects in their description.

Remind students that details are specific and unique. They should find specific, interesting things to describe that will be easy for readers to visualize.

Have several students read their descriptions to see if the class can correctly identify the place or object being described. Then the class should review and critique each visual detail to see if the descriptions were accurate, specific, unique, unusual, and vivid. Which bits of description were most interesting? Why? As a class, can you improve on these descriptions and make them stronger and more interesting?

As a class, discuss how and when visual sensory details are effective and powerful and when to incorporate these details into descriptions of objects, characters, events, and settings.

Viv•id *adj.* Providing a very strong stimulus to the eye or to the imagination. Details are most interesting (and, thus, most effective) when they create vivid images in a reader's mind.

Finally, the class should agree on one specific place that is easy for students to visit (bedroom, kitchen, backyard, closet, desk, grocery store, bed, etc.). In the space provided on the worksheet, students should write two visual images that they think are most interesting and descriptive of that place.

Compare the descriptions created by different students. Discuss how effective each proposed detail is. Allow the class to reword and improve the offerings of individual students. How did students describe their visual impressions? Did they describe the shape, size, color, or placement of the object? Did they compare the object they were describing to another object? Did they say what the vision reminded them of? Did they say how seeing the object made them feel? Which of these descriptive tools was most effective? Which got the best reaction from the class?

Activity Review

The sense of vision, what things look like, is the most commonly used of all senses and accounts for a majority of the description students use in their stories. But vision is just one of the five senses that, collectively, make up one of the Five Categories of Information writers can use to describe objects in their stories.

Visual details are important, but they must be developed with care to ensure that they create accurate, vivid, and specific imagery in the minds of readers and meet the criteria of good details. When writers describe using one of the senses, readers are encouraged to envision the object using that sense and thus enrich their imagery of the story.

Activity 45: Good "Feeling" Details _____

What Students Will Learn:

Students will explore using their sense of touch (what things feel like) to enrich their descriptions.

Time Estimate: one elapsed day for students to complete their worksheet; 20 to 30 minutes to review and discuss

Directions:

We gain tremendous amounts of information through our sense of touch. Yet student writers rarely include this sense in their descriptions. This activity lets them focus on what can be contributed to their story details by this underused sense.

The worksheet instructs students to pick three common objects and describe only how they feel. Students may not name them, use any other sense, or use the object's history or function in their description. They are to describe only what they learn through their sense of touch and are to write their descriptions on the worksheet.

Instructions tell students to place an asterisk (*) next to the two individual bits of their description that they think best and most interestingly describe the objects or create the most vivid and interesting images in the minds of readers.

Have several students read their descriptions to see if the class can correctly identify the objects being described. Then the class should review and critique each student's description to see if the descriptions were accurate, specific, unique, unusual, and vivid. Which bits of description were most interesting? Why? As a class, can you improve on these descriptions and make them stronger and more interesting?

Have the class discuss how and when the sense of touch is an effective and powerful detail to incorporate into descriptions of objects, characters, events, and settings.

Finally, the class should agree on one specific object or place that each student can easily study (pencil, pillow, shirt, TV, bedroom, living room, locker, desk, etc.). In the space provided on the worksheet, students should write two sense of touch details they think are most interesting and descriptive.

Touch *n.* The sensation conveyed by contact with the skin.

Feel *n.* The effect on the sense of touch. The effect conveyed by the sense of touch. Direct contact between you and another person or object is emotionally powerful and can be used to create strong, effective details.

Compare the descriptions created by different students. Discuss how effective each proposed detail is. Allow the class to reword and improve the offerings of individual students. How did each student describe what the objects felt like? Did they describe the texture, smoothness, temperature, and weight? Did they say what the feel of the object reminded them of? Did they say how it made them feel? Which of these descriptive tools was most effective? Which got the best reaction from the class?

Activity Review

Touch, one of humans' five senses, is a powerful and intimate sense. Sensory information is one of the Five Categories of Information writers can use to describe objects in their stories. Describing using the sense of touch brings readers intimately and powerfully into the midst of a scene. When writers describe using one of the senses, readers are encouraged to use that sense to envision and thus enrich their imagery of the story.

Activity 46: The "Taste and Smell" of Success _____

What Students Will Learn:

Students will explore using their sense of smell (what things smell like) and taste (what things taste like) to enrich their descriptions.

Time Estimate: one elapsed day for students to complete their worksheets; 20 to 30 minutes to review and discuss

Directions:

Odors evoke strong memories and strong emotional reactions. Rotting garbage or curdled milk smells revolting. Thanksgiving dinner smells enticing. Air smells fresh and invigorating after a summer rain.

The sense of taste is not regularly used for story details. Still, it is a strong sense. That is, we have strong reactions the taste of things. Tastes we like, we like a lot; tastes we dislike, we hate. Those strong reactions make this sense a powerful tool for students to use in their stories.

Tell students it's time to practice using their senses of smell and taste to create descriptions that evoke strong images for readers.

The student worksheet instructs students to sit quietly in their home kitchen for thirty seconds, both in the morning and in the evening, and concentrate on everything they smell. During each time period, they are to identify three separate odors that dominate the room. These odors should be recorded on the worksheet.

Spe·cif·ic *adj.* Clearly distinguished. The more specific a descriptive detail is, the more vivid it becomes and the more likely it is to make the object being described appear to be unusual and unique.

After naming each odor, students should pick one from the morning and one from the evening and describe these two odors by creating two effective descriptive details for each. They may not name the source of the odor. Rather, they are to describe the odor, itself. Remind students to search for details that will conjure images of the odor in the minds of other students and that will help them identify the item being tasted or smelled.

Finally, they are told to pick one item associated with each of the two smells they have described and taste that item. The chosen item must be edible and should be the source of the smell or closely linked with the source of the smell. As best they can, students should describe the taste of the item. The worksheet contains space for them to list both the item tasted and to describe the taste. Again, this description may not include the name of the item being tasted.

Have several students read their descriptions to see if the class can correctly identify the source of the odor and the item being tasted from the provided descriptions. Then the class should review and critique each student's description to see if the description is accurate, specific, unique, unusual, and vivid. Which bits of description were most interesting? Why? As a class, can you improve on these descriptions and make them stronger and more interesting?

As a class, agree on one object that each student has (a food item, a place in the house, a pencil, a sweater, etc.). In the space provided on the worksheet, students should write two details about how the object smells and one about how it tastes. These details should be the details students think are most interesting and descriptive.

Compare the descriptions created by different students. Discuss how effective each proposed detail is. Allow the class to reword and improve the offerings of individual students. How did students describe the odors and tastes of the items? What kinds of information did they provide?

Activity Review

Odors and tastes are emotionally powerful and personal. In a story, they draw out the emotions of a reader and pull them deeply into the moments and images of the story. When writers describe using one of the senses, readers are encouraged to use that sense to envision and thus enrich their imagery of the story.

Activity 47: Exploring Comparisons: What Things Remind You Of

What Students Will Learn:

Students will learn to recognize and use effective comparisons in their writing.

Time Estimate: 20 to 30 minutes

Directions:

Begin this activity with a class discussion on the meaning of and look of comparisons in general and of similes and metaphors in particular. There is no need to introduce similes and metaphors as new and advanced concepts. Your students have used them for years in their daily conversation. They just didn't have a formal name for these comparative forms of detail.

Comparisons (what things remind you of) is one of the Five Categories of Information writers can use to describe objects, or things, that appear in a story.

This activity is divided into three parts. Set the activity aside for an hour or more after Part 1 before revisiting these details and finishing Parts 2 and 3. There is a brief guide to the follow-up discussion between Parts 2 and 3.

Let's explore one additional category of descriptive information before moving on to look at other aspects of a story every writer must describe. The previous four activities explored the five senses (sensory information). Now, let's turn to comparisons, to what things remind you of, the only other of the category of information we will explore with a separate activity.

Often comparisons are the most vivid, interesting, and effective category of information to use when creating story details. While humans naturally use this type of descriptive information every day, it often feels awkward and forced to include such comparisons in stories. Student writers need only practice writing these comparisons to master the knack of creating powerful and appropriate comparative details in their writing.

Two writing terms describe the ways we compare things: simile and metaphor. When writers directly compare two things with the words *like* or *as,* they are using simile.

> *She was as fast as a snake. His mind spun as fast as a computer. Her arms were like tentacles of rotting seaweed.*

Com·par·i·son *n.* An attempt to discover what is like and unlike. Writers compare one thing to another to show readers what a new object is like or not like.

Sim·i·le *n.* A figure of speech in which one thing is likened to another. Similes use the words *like* or *as* in their wording.

Met·a·phor *n.* A figure of speech in which a quality of some other object or being is attributed to something to which it is not literally applicable.

Similes and metaphors are consistently the most powerful and effective ways to compare two things.

These are similes. We use similes all the time in our everyday conversation.

In a metaphor, the writer directly attributes the attributes of one thing to another.

> *His arm was a rock. Grandma's lap was a soft pillow where I curled up.*

These are metaphors. We know that his arm isn't really a rock or that grandma's lap isn't really a pillow. The writer is using the form of a metaphor to make a comparison.

Comparisons—both similes and metaphors—describe a new object by ascribing the attributes, abilities, or characteristics of a known thing to this new object. Readers will understand the new object if they are familiar with the known thing. Similes and metaphors are valuable writing tools because they are so appealing to readers' visual sense. They create strong, interesting images in readers' minds—characteristics of good details.

Describing a new object by saying what it reminds you of is a broader category of description. Direct comparisons are one way to say what an object reminds you of. However, you are not limited to physical comparisons. One object might evoke a feeling that reminds you of the feeling created by some other (known) object or event.

> *The breeze reminded me of a summer day at the beach with kites gliding and the smells of countless barbecues mingling in the air.*

An object could also evoke a memory. You would describe the object by saying what it reminds you of.

> *I smelled the musty storeroom and was reminded of my grandmother's attic when I was six and such smells were new, exciting, and smelled like adventures waiting to be discovered.*

When you tell readers what something reminds you of, you create rich images in readers' minds that will enhance their enjoyment of your story.

Part 1. Let's practice using comparisons in our writing. The student worksheet lists the following three objects. For each, students are to create two comparisons of this object and another common object and then identify two things the object reminds them of. You may substitute other common items if any of these are unavailable in your classroom.

> **Object #1:** *a round, electric, school clock on the wall*
> **Object #2:** *a common classroom blackboard or whiteboard eraser*
> **Object #3:** *a thirty-six-inch wooden ruler*

Have students set these comparisons aside for at least an hour so that they can look at them with a fresher eye when they start the task of editing and molding them into effective details.

Part 2. Each student should pick their favorite of each pair of descriptions in Step 1 and refine, improve, and rewrite each of these six descriptions. Have them search for ways to make their wording more specific and interesting.

Have several students read what they have written. Monitor how the class reacts to these descriptions and determine whether students can correctly identify the item being described. Then the class should review and critique each student's wording to see if it formed an effective detail. Which details were most interesting? Why? As a class, can you improve on these details and make them stronger and more interesting?

Have the class discuss how and when comparisons are effective and powerful and when to incorporate them into descriptions of objects, characters, events, and settings.

Part 3. Finally, the class should agree on one place that each student has ready access to. In the space on the worksheet, students should write two bits of comparative detail about that place. Remind them to search for a new way to compare this place to other places or common memories or to find new and fresh things the place reminds them of.

Again, have several students read what they have written. Monitor how the class reacts to these descriptions and assess how these descriptions compare to the ones created by other students. Which details were most interesting? Why? As a class, can you improve on these details and make them stronger and more interesting?

Activity Review

Comparisons are a powerful and effective category of descriptive information. As you read stories, watch for how and when writers use these types of description. Remember the images the comparisons create in your mind and how you react to them. You will likely find that you enjoyed the vivid imagery created by comparisons and that it increased your enjoyment of the story.

There are two ways to use comparisons in your descriptions: by directly comparing one thing with another known object or by saying what an object reminds you of. These forms for making direct comparisons are similes and metaphors. Have students search for similes and metaphors when they read and practice writing them whenever they try to describe a character, setting, or object.

Activity 48: Describe a Setting

What Students Will Learn:

Students will explore how to describe the second aspect of every story—settings—and will learn the categories of information appropriate for them to use to describe settings and places.

Time Estimate: 20 to 35 minutes

Directions:

Begin this activity with a class discussion about settings—the second of the four aspects of a story every writer must describe. What is a setting? How can you describe a setting? What categories of information could you use? Are there any of the five categories we used to describe an object that you could not use when describing a setting? Are there any new categories you could use to describe a setting that did not apply when describing an object? Discuss these questions as a class before you read on.

Did the class decide that the categories for a setting were different than those for an object? Probably not. They are exactly the same. A setting is simply a collection of things all in one place. Writers can name the place, provide sensory information about it, describe its function (what happens there), describe its history, or compare this place to another place. A meadow has grass, weeds, flowers, air, trees, and insects. Those are all things. A room has chairs, a floor, walls, rugs, desks, and so on. Those are all things.

Set•ting *n*. The place where an event occurs. Every event in every story takes place in a setting. It is difficult for readers to visualize the actions of a scene if they can't visualize the scene's setting.

Here's the problem. Remember how much description students were able to create for one object in your classroom during Activity 41? Think of how many individual objects are in the classroom. In describing the classroom as a setting, students could describe any or all of them. The problem is that a setting has much more possible description for a writer to pick through when selecting the best details to include in a story.

Settings are not difficult to describe once your students have had some practice. For this activity, divide the class into pairs of students. Each pair will describe the same two places (settings): the classroom and the school. It is not essential to complete this activity in pairs, but it's fun and a good change of pace from previous activities.

Here are the rules to give to your students. They are reproduced on the student worksheet.

1. Each pair will write and revise (to make them into stronger details) three descriptive details for each of the two settings.

2. They may use any of the possible categories of description for these details but should try to use as many of the categories as they can.

3. The pairs must search for details that are unique, unusual, and interesting and that suggest the setting's typical activities and mood or feeling. Also remind students to be specific.

Having written three details for each setting, each pair should select their strongest detail from each list and rework their choices to make them more specific, more vivid, and more unique.

Allow each pair to share their two final details with the class. Which categories of information did each pair use? Were all five categories used? How many combined more than one category of information into their final details?

Which details for each setting were most interesting? Why? Did they follow the criteria for good details?

Activity Review

Settings are simply collections of many objects in one place. Writers use the same Five Categories of Information to describe settings that they use to describe objects.

However, settings are often harder to effectively describe because they contain so much that could be described. Remember to describe those parts and aspects of a setting that are important to the story and that you want readers to focus on as they visualize the scene. Then describe those few elements of the setting with strong, vivid, interesting details. Trust readers to fill in the rest of the scene in their minds.

To pick the best elements of a setting to describe, writers must hold a vivid, detailed, multisensory image of that setting in their own mind. Verbal games (such as the Scene Game described in the next activity) are most effective for helping student writers create the necessary vivid and detailed picture of each setting.

Have students think of how well they can visualize their own bedroom—the look, smell, history, and use of each thing; how light and temperature vary over the day and year; the feel and emotional significance of each object; and so on. They should be able to visualize each setting in just as much detail when they write a story. Verbal games with other students can help.

Activity 49: The Scene Game _____

What Students Will Learn:

Students will learn to use additional powerful tools to assist in developing scenic details.

Time Estimate: 20 minutes

Directions:

This is a verbal classroom game. There is no student worksheet for this activity. The Scene Game is designed to help student writers create a fuller, richer image of the various settings in their stories. It is best used after the elements of a story have been created and before actual writing has begun. This description was taken from *Write Right*.

The more detailed a writer's image of a setting, the easier it will be for the writer to create a vivid, detailed picture of the setting in the reader's mind. Student writers rarely take time to thoroughly visualize each scene (setting) of a story in rich detail. It's valuable to get outside help when creating expansive, detailed mental images. For this activity, students should have already developed their story's characters, story elements, ending, and general plot sequencing. Now it is time to work on the detailed description of the setting.

Divide the class into groups of four or five students. Six students per group is unwieldy and slow; three doesn't allow for enough group input.

One student at a time in each group is "it." That student gets thirty seconds to describe to the group an important scene and setting in his or her story. This description should mention who is present and generally what happens but should concentrate on a description of the setting—the physical place—itself.

The group then gets two minutes to ask any question about the setting. The group acts like suspicious police officers grilling a suspect. No question is too detailed or trivial. The goal is to either catch the student contradicting information he or she provided or to ask questions that momentarily stump the writer. These questions cause the student who is "it" to think of aspects of the scene never thought of before. And that's good.

The student who is "it" must answer every question, even if it means the student has to make up an answer on the spot. The student may not answer "I don't know" or "It doesn't matter." The student, of course, isn't committed to that answer and may change it later while writing. But having to answer will expand the student's image of each story scene.

The groups should be encouraged to explore all five senses and all five of the categories of descriptive information during this questioning and to search for possible inconsistencies or gaps in the writer's story.

After two minutes of being peppered by the group's questions, the student who is "it" shifts off the hot seat, and a second student moves on.

Activity Review

Writers never think of all the aspects of a scene, even though they visualize it in as much detail as they can. It is valuable to have others help widen the writer's horizon and make the writer think about aspects of a scene and a story he or she hadn't considered. Every writer needs this help. The tougher the group's questions, the more help they are to the writer.

During this exercise, all group members benefit from each question—even if they aren't on the hot seat. They still consider the answers to each question as if it had been asked about their own story.

Activity 50: Describe an Action _____

What Students Will Learn:

Students will learn how to effectively describe actions, the third of the four aspects of a story writers must describe.

Time Estimate: 15 minutes

Directions:

This is a verbal in-class game that explores how writers describe actions. There is no worksheet for this activity.

In past activities, we explored two of the four story aspects writers need to describe in detail: objects and settings. Next, we turn to actions. How does a writer describe an action or event in powerful detail?

You should write the sentence "She _____ (into) the room" on the board and then fill in the blank with the word *entered*. The word *into* is in parentheses because it may be used or omitted depending on what is written in the blank. If you are a male teacher, write "he" instead of "she."

Ac•tion *n*. The process of doing; the thing done. Every movement and bit of progress in a story constitutes an action. A series of actions constitutes an incident or event.

Ask the students if they can see in their mind's eye exactly how she entered the room. Ask them to describe, in detail, their image of this person entering the room. Their images will all be vague, general, and mostly inaccurate. Why? The verb *enter* is vague and general.

Tell students that you want to show them how she really entered the room. Step out of the room and then reenter. You may enter any way you choose—saunter in, burst in, crawl in, dash in, creep in, trip in, back in, skip in, storm in, and so on.

Having reentered the room, ask, "What's a better word than *entered* to describe how I came in?" They may not substitute a whole phrase for the blank space. They can't use similes and metaphors. They may only insert a single better verb.

Make a list on the board of the plausible words that are offered. Have the students vote for the one they think most accurately and specifically describes how you entered the room. They will pick the one that creates the most vivid and interesting image in their minds. Remind them that these are the best details to use to describe your action of entering the room.

Again, tell the class that you want to show them how she really entered the room. Erase the old list and step back into the hall and reenter. You may enter any way you choose—as long as it is different from the way you entered the first time.

Repeat this process several times. You may let one or more of the students enter the room. Your goal is to encourage debate among the students as to which is the most accurate, imaginative, and interesting verb to use to describe each entry.

Finally, summarize the game by asking the class which kind of words writers use to create the details that describe actions. The answer, of course, is verbs. Verbs describe actions. The same criteria we developed for picking details while describing objects and settings still apply. The verbs writers use must be accurate, specific, unique, unusual, and vivid to act as effective details describing the actions of a story.

Activity Review

Verbs define the action, motion, and much of the emotional tone of a story. Careful choice of verbs during story writing and editing creates a much stronger sense of the energy, emotion, and drama of the story's events.

What are better verbs to choose? Verbs that provide more accurate, specific, unique, and vivid information about the action and event being described. The excessive use of adverbs is one sign of weak verb choices. Strong, descriptive, action verbs don't need the assistance of many adverbs. Using strong verbs allows the writer to cut needless words out of the story.

Activity 51: Describe a Character _____

What Students Will Learn:

Students will complete their exploration of details by examining the fourth aspect of a story to describe—characters—and will compare the categories and criteria for details with earlier activities in which they developed tools to create interesting characters.

Time Estimate: 20 to 30 minutes

Directions:

The fourth of the four story aspects each writer must describe is characters. However, we have already spent much time and effort (Activities 8 through 19) describing characters and making characters interesting. What did you create in each of those activities as you tried to make a character more interesting?

Details! Details about the character. Writers make characters interesting by selecting and crafting effective details from the fifteen categories of character information first developed during Activity 12.

Effective details must be:
• Accurate
• Specific

Effective details should be:
• Unique
• Unusual
• Vivid

Take a minute to review Activities 8 through 19 with your class to notice the following:

1. In each activity, you strove to make a character interesting by creating information that was accurate, specific, unique, unusual, and vivid. Those are the same five criteria we are using for creating effective details. When you created character traits to make a character interesting, you were crafting details.

2. The first five categories of character information listed in Activity 12 exactly match the five categories identified in Activity 40 for describing an object. After all, characters—like objects—are physical things. The other categories of possible character information refer to the inner workings of the mind, conscience, heart, and soul of the character. Those inner workings separate characters from objects.

It takes effective details from a variety of the fifteen possible categories of character information to make a character interesting. With that in mind, the one thing we have not done for Cecelia Sue is to develop enough character details to make her truly interesting. Here are the character traits for Cecelia Sue we agreed on in Activity 3.

• She has only seven legs.
• She wears dark glasses as a disguise.
• Her favorite food is fried snails.
• She has painted yellow racing stripes on her sides to make her look faster.

- She is afraid of flies.
- Her name is Cecelia Sue.
- She loves the moon because it was the first thing she saw when she emerged from her mother's sac.

That's not a bad start. But it isn't enough to make her truly interesting to readers or to make it easy for your students to write her story. The more your students create about their characters, the easier it will be for them to write the story. In this activity, their job will be to invent twelve bits of character information (details) for Cecelia Sue, using at least eight of the possible fifteen categories of character information (see Activity 12). Tell them to make her truly interesting by the details they create. Remember, each one of those details should be specific and accurate (consistent with already created information), should make her seem unique and unusual, and should paint vivid images in readers' minds.

You may have students work individually or in pairs for this activity. In the spaces on the worksheet, students should write the details they create and the categories of character information they are using for each detail.

Have several students read their lists. The class is tasked to ensure that each is an effective character detail and that the reader correctly identified which of the fifteen categories he or she used in creating that detail.

As a class, agree on which details make her most interesting. Would knowing this final class list of interesting characteristics for Cecelia Sue make it easier for your students to create conflicts and struggles for her? It should. Would knowing this new character information have made Activities 3, 28, 34, and 38 (those that involve Cecelia Sue) easier and more productive? It should. Time spent developing a character is never wasted. It always makes it easier to develop the story.

Activity Review

Every writer's most important job is the creation of interesting characters. Effective details about the characters make them interesting. Those details may be drawn from any—or all—of the fifteen categories of possible character information. Each bit of detail should adhere to the five criteria for effective details.

Activity 52: Where Images Come From _____

What Students Will Learn:

Students will learn to recognize the contribution of the three major word groups (nouns, verbs, and modifiers) in forming the details of a story.

Time Estimate: 10 to 30 minutes

Directions:

This activity is a verbal class exercise. There is no student worksheet.

Images in a reader's mind come from all forms of details—not just modifiers. Students rarely stop to consider which words produce the images of their story or what contribution different types of words make to a reader's understanding of the story events, characters, and places. However, it is individual words that form a writer's details.

Im•age *n.* A mental picture or concept. Details create vivid images in readers' minds and make the events and characters of a story seem real.

For this activity, you will read three versions of a paragraph to the class, one without any modifiers, one without any verbs, and one without any nouns. This exercise is most effective if each version is read to a different group—groups that can then compare their images of the scene. However, it is more often used as a class activity followed by a discussion of the images evoked by each reading.

Almost any exposition paragraph will do. The following paragraph works well since it relies on an even mix of nouns, verbs, and modifiers to create the overall scene.

The paragraph without **nouns** or **pronouns**:

> *A scraggly old shuffled down the twisty. Looked for a comfortable to sit. Found on the of a fallen, and sat, gazing at the pastoral around. In the heard a deep, resonant. Slowly stood, rubbed aching, and continued to.*

The common reaction to this version is that it is comical and makes no sense. Nouns create the basic images in a reader's mind.

The paragraph without **verbs**:

> *A scraggly old man down the twisty, blacktop road. He for a comfortable place. He one on the stump of a fallen tree, and, at the pastoral scene around him. In the distance he a deep, resonant church bell. He slowly, his aching back, and his walk to town.*

The common reaction to this version is that it is a disconnected string of separate images. Verbs create motion and action, and they connect and complete a reader's images.

The paragraph without **modifiers**:

> *A man shuffled down the road. He looked for a place to sit. He found one on the stump of a tree, and sat, gazing at the scene around him. In the distance he heard a bell. He stood, rubbed his back, and continued his walk to town.*

The common reaction to this version is that it is clear but flat and colorless. Modifiers paint the rich pallet of story colors in a reader's mind.

The whole paragraph:

> *A scraggly old man shuffled down the twisty, blacktop road. He looked for a comfortable place to sit. He found one on the stump of a fallen tree and sat, gazing at the pastoral scene around him. In the distance he heard a deep, resonant church bell. He slowly stood, rubbed his aching back, and continued his walk to town.*

In all discussions, focus the class on what contribution each type of word (noun, verb, modifier) makes to our understanding of even this simple scene. As they reread and edit their own work, students' understanding of the role of each type of word can lead them to identifying easily corrected weaknesses in their writing.

Activity Review

Basic images come from nouns. Without nouns, a paragraph is meaningless. It makes no sense. Readers don't know what to picture.

Action and movement come from verbs. Without verbs, readers don't know how to interpret scenes. They are left with disconnected images and are hungry for information about what happens.

Supporting details come from modifiers. Without modifiers, a paragraph is colorless and boring. However, all three provide details about the characters, settings, actions, and objects in a story. Details come from every kind of word.

Chapter 3

Building Stories

It's time to look again at how the *Get It Write!* Eight Essential Elements fit together to form successful stories. In Chapter 2, we studied each element individually. Now we'll look at how they link together in combination. Along the way, your students will have a chance to review the purpose and look of each element. But we will now focus on how each appears in, and contributes to, the functioning of a smooth story segment.

A segment is a part of a story. Complete stories are too long to be practical for our purposes here. So we'll look at a few story segments to examine combinations of individual elements.

Assessing these story segments is harder than the previous activities that focused on one element at a time. These activities require some thought and careful observation by your students. However, having completed Chapters 1 and 2 of *Get It Write!*, your students should be able to be both specific and articulate in their assessments of these story segments. Every activity that helps them get in the habit of recognizing and understanding the Eight Essential Elements will make it easier for them to both create and to comprehend any literature they write or read.

Through these activities they learn to recognize each of the story elements in the context of a story and to know when each is successfully performing its job. Use these activities as springboards for review of one or more of the elements if your students struggle with some aspect of these exercises.

Here, again, are the *Get It Write!* Eight Essential Elements for every narrative. This information is repeated on the CD-ROM at the beginning of Part 3.

1. **Characters**	Stories are all about characters.
2. **Character traits**	Character traits make a character interesting.
3. **Goal**	A goal is what the character is after in the story.
4. **Motive**	The motive is *why* that goal is important to the character.
5. **Conflicts and problems**	Conflicts and problems are the obstacles that block a character from reaching a goal.
6. **Risk and danger**	Excitement comes from the risk and danger created by the conflicts that the main character must face.
7. **Struggles**	A character must struggle in his or her attempts to get past obstacles and reach a goal.
8. **Details**	The details make a story seem real and vivid to readers.

Activity 53: Ingredients of the Story Stew _____

What Students Will Learn:

Students will have a chance to recognize the need for, and then create, elements missing in a provided story segment.

Time Estimate: 20 to 30 minutes

Directions:

Have your students read the story segment below and then answer the following questions.

> Fifth graders Jimmy and Jason were twins. Each night their father marched into their room and made up a little bedtime story. Unfortunately, Jimmy and Jason's father was the worst storyteller in the entire state.
>
> Tonight's story was as awful as ever: "Okey-dokey, boys, hee-hee. Once there was a boy . . . and . . . ummm, well . . . he walked down the street and . . . well, he . . . ummm, he found a ball. Ummmm, I guess he played with it all day long . . . and then, well . . . it must have flown away into the sky. The end. Goodnight!" And he clicked off the light and left.
>
> But the next morning Jimmy did find a ball. And he played with it all day long until late in the afternoon when, after Jimmy slammed the ball down onto the sidewalk to see how high it would bounce, a seagull flew by, snatched the ball out of midair with its beak, and flew off toward the hills.
>
> It happened just like their father's dumb bedtime story!
>
> "Hey, Jason . . . I think maybe Dad's stories are beginning to come . . . true?"

Scene *n*. A division or separate part of a story.

In·ci·dent *n*. An event seen as part of a whole situation.

E·vent *n*. An occurrence, especially one of significance or importance.

Events and incidents are strung together in some logical order to create a scene. Scenes are the basic building blocks of a story plot.

Students should answer the following six questions based on this story segment.

1. What kind of information is presented in the second and third paragraphs of this story segment? Are any of the Eight Essential Elements included in those two paragraphs? *Ans: Those two paragraphs tell about something that happened—plot, actions, incidents. None of those actions could become part of the story's struggle until readers know the main character, his goal, and the conflicts that block him. Then, maybe, these actions could become part of the struggle.*

   The second paragraph presents details about Dad's voice. Voice is a character trait that makes him interesting because it is unique, unusual, and specific.

2. Which elements are included in this story segment? Which are missing? *Ans: Characters are identified, and some information is included to make Dad interesting. A tiny bit of detail—but not nearly enough—is included. All other elements are missing.*

3. To make this story work, name two elements we should create immediately. *Ans: We need a goal and we need to make Jimmy and Jason interesting with new character traits.*

4. Based on the events listed in this story segment, create two plausible goals for Jimmy and Jason.

   Ans: Any answers will suffice if they fit with existing story material.

5. Pick your favorite goal and explain what will make that goal important to Jimmy, Jason, and readers. *Ans: Acceptable answers depend on the writer's use of relevant story information to justify his or her answer.*

6. After incorporating the goal you chose in Question 5 into the story, which of the following would be the most useful to include next in the story and why?

   A. Jimmy and Jason argue over whether or not their father's stories are coming true.

   B. Jimmy finds another ball the next day.

   C. Jimmy and Jason decide not to have any more bedtime stories.

   D. Dad talks about how he makes up his stories.

   Ans: A. See the following paragraphs for an explanation.

Review the answers to Questions 1 through 3. These questions call for students to locate factual information in the story or to extrapolate from presented information.

Questions 4 and 5 tell students to create new information based on what they have read. Let several students present their answers and have the class discuss their appropriateness and effectiveness. Insist that students use *Get It Write!* Eight Essential Elements and concepts established in Parts 1 and 2 and information in this story segment to justify and defend their arguments.

Use the following paragraphs to guide the discussion of Question 6.

Choice B is another event. It would make sense only as part of the boys' struggles to reach a goal. We have no reason to watch another event until the first six elements have been established. In Question 5, you created a goal and explained why it is important. The story presents characters. What we need is not another event but conflicts for Jimmy and Jason to struggle against.

Choice C might serve as a final conclusion for the story—after Jimmy and Jason face struggles and dangers. But there is nothing presented yet to indicate that they wouldn't want to hear another story to find out if they are coming true.

Choice D asks readers to care about Dad and his stories. Dad's stories are awful. He probably makes them up as he goes. Based on what we've read so far, no one cares how he makes them up. We only care that they are terrible, and we care to find out whether or not they are going to come true. We have also established that Jimmy and Jason will be the main characters, not Dad. Thus, D is a poor choice to include in the story at this time.

That leaves choice A. A is a form of conflict. Conflict, of course, must block a character from reaching a goal. Since you invented your own goal in Question 5, we can't be sure that this particular conflict is the best one to insert into the story at this time. However, some conflict is needed here to give purpose to any future actions. Struggles have to be attempts to overcome obstacles. A is the best answer.

Activity 54: Find the Flaw

What Students Will Learn:

Students will have a chance to identify what's wrong with a given story segment and propose ways to correct and improve it.

Time Estimate: 20 to 35 minutes

Directions:

Some of the Eight Essential Elements are missing from the following story segment. At least one element—as stated—is inappropriate and doesn't fit with the rest of the segment. Students should read the story segment, decide what's missing and what doesn't fit, and answer the questions that follow the story segment.

> *Jack nervously shifted from foot to foot. "There is that flame there and . . . what? It must be six inches high . . ."*
> *"Jack, be nimble. Jack, be quick. I know you can do it."*
> *"Do I have to? How will this help me get what I want?"*
> *"Don't think, Jack. Just run and jump over the candlestick."*
> *"Okay. Here I go . . ." Jack rocked back and forth. "I'll go on three. One . . . Two . . . What if I trip? What if my foot forgets to jump and hits the flame? What if I burn up in a ball of fire?"*
> *"Jack! It's just a candlestick. I've blown out the flame. See? It's not even lit. Just jump over the darned thing!"*
> *"Okay. Here I go . . ." Jack rocked back and forth. "I'll go on three. One . . . two . . . But it might light itself just when I get there."*
> *"Neagh!!! It won't! Just run and jump!"*
> *"Okay. Here I go . . ." Jack rocked back and forth. "I'll go on three. One . . . two . . . But what if I make it? What then? I mean, what do I have left to do after I've jumped over the candlestick?"*
> *"Please, Jack! I'm on my knees begging. Pleeeeeease, jump over the candlestick!"*
> *A monstrous bear crashed through the window roaring and slashing with its claws.*
> *Jack nodded, "See? I knew that would happen."*

Hu•mor *n.* Something that arouses laughter and amusement. Humor is a powerful tool for making stories interesting, appealing, and enjoyable for readers. In general, if you can add humor, do it!

1. What's wrong with this segment? What's missing? *Ans: There is no goal or motive for Jack, no identification of the character he's talking to, and no motive for that character who seems to want Jack to jump over the candlestick. The bear doesn't fit with anything that comes before and Jack's last line makes no sense based on what we know.*

2. Which elements are expressly included in this segment? *Ans: Character, character traits, probably conflict (between Jack and the other person), details, and—presumably—struggles*

3. Which elements aren't included? *Ans: Goal and motive, certainly. Without those two, it is difficult to assess conflict and risk and danger that may or may not be present depending on the goal.*

4. What makes Jack interesting? *Ans: His voice, his worry and fearfulness, his pattern of hesitation, and his repeated line about going on three*

5. Is there anything in the story segment that doesn't seem to fit, that seems inappropriate based on the information you are given? If so, what and why? *Ans: The bear and Jack's reaction to the bear*

6. What is the bear an attempt to create in this story? *Ans: Presumably conflict and risk and danger, but without a goal, it's difficult to tell for sure*

7. Change the bear into something else that serves the same purpose but fits better with the story segment. *Ans: Any idea will do that creates conflict, risk and danger, and fits with the given characters and story information.*

8. From the information given, can you guess Jack's goal in this story? *Ans: No*

9. If you had to invent a goal for Jack, what would you choose and why? *Ans: Any answer will suffice as long as it clearly creates a goal for Jack and fits with the given story information.*

10. What creates humor in this story segment? *Ans: Exaggeration and repetition are used in this segment to create humor. Jack seems overly worried about a harmless candle (exaggeration). The other person seems overly determined to make Jack do something insignificant (exaggeration). Three times Jack repeats the line beginning "Okay. Here I go . . ." (repetition). It is possible that some might think that the bear's arrival is humorous. If so, it is because this represents an unexpected surprise, something that can also create humor.*

Review and discuss your students' answers. The first six questions are factual, asking students to assess and extract information from the provided story segment.

Questions 7 and 8 ask them to create new story information to fill gaping holes in what was originally provided. There is no one correct answer to these two questions. Allow students to offer individual ideas for a new conflict and for Jack's motive. Which offerings work best? Why? Insist that your students use the *Get It Write!* concepts from Chapters 1 and 2 and information in this story segment to justify their ideas and arguments.

Activity 55: What's the Difference? _____

What Students Will Learn:

Students are given a chance to compare two versions of a story, assess the difference, and evaluate each version.

Time Estimate: 15 to 20 minutes for each set

Directions:

This activity has two sets of story segments. In each set, the second version contains additional story material not presented in the first version. Discuss student answers for the first set before proceeding to the second set.

Ten·sion *n*. A state of emotional distress. Feeling tension forces readers to continue reading a story. Tension is created by excitement and suspense.

First Set. Two versions of a story segment are presented here. The student worksheet provides space to compare the two versions and to describe the difference between them. Which story elements appear in both segments? Are there elements that appear in only one segment? How do those added elements affect the way you view and understand the story segment?

Version #1

> *Alyssa played outside in the far corner of her backyard by four tall apple trees. She picked up each fallen apple and lined them up in a long, neat row on the grass—biggest one on the left end all the way down to the littlest, shriveled, worm-eaten apple on the right end. She was having a wonderful time!*
>
> *High above her, hanging onto the trunk of the biggest apple tree, standing on one of the branches, stood the ooshiest, gooshiest mud puddle that you have ever seen. That mud puddle sloshed his way across the branch and then jumped all over Alyssa!*

Version #2

> *Alyssa played outside in the far corner of her backyard by four tall apple trees. Her mother called out the kitchen window, "Stay neat and clean until your grandmother gets here."*
> *Alyssa answered, "I will, mom!"*
> *She picked up each fallen apple and lined them up in a long, neat row on the grass— biggest one on the left end all the way down to the littlest, shriveled, worm-eaten apple on the right end. She was having a wonderful time!*
> *High above her, hanging onto the trunk of the biggest apple tree, standing on one of the branches, stood the ooshiest, gooshiest mud puddle that you have ever seen. That mud puddle sloshed his way across the branch and then jumped all over Alyssa!*

1. List the story elements that appear in both segments and those that appear in only one of the segments. How do those added element(s) affect your understanding of the story?

   Elements in *both* segments: *Ans: Main character, character traits, probable conflict (with mud puddle—but we can't be sure since there is no stated goal and a conflict must block a character from reaching a goal)*

   Elements in *only one* segment: *Ans: Goal (stay neat and clean), motive (grandmother is coming), and an additional conflict (with mother when Alyssa fails to "stay neat and clean")*

How do the extra elements affect your understanding of the story? *Ans: The goal (stay neat and clean) tells readers what the story is about and sets up both the conflict and the story's risk and danger. Once readers know Alyssa's goal, they understand the importance of, and the danger of, the mud puddle. The additional conflict (with her mother) increases story excitement by adding additional risk and danger to the main character—she is now in trouble both inside and outside.*

2. Which version do you prefer and why? *Ans: Students should prefer the second version since its additional information creates greater reader understanding of, and involvement in, the character and her story.*

3. What do you think should happen next in Version #2 of the story and why? *Ans: Goal, motive, and conflict (with the mud puddle) have been established for Alyssa. Two possibilities exist for the next story event. First, Alyssa could do something to deal with the mud puddle (and then, presumably, deal with her muddy clothes before she goes back in to see her mother and grandmother). Second, Alyssa will have to face her mother after being covered in mud. That will establish the second conflict between Alyssa and her mother (Alyssa has lied to her mother and didn't do what her mother asked). That will give Alyssa two conflicts to deal with—one inside the house (mother) and one outside (the mud puddle).*

4. How do you think this story will end? Why? *Ans: Alyssa has already failed to meet her goal (stay neat and clean). Usually, this means that she must conquer the source of her failure (defeat the mud puddle) and regain her mother's good graces (overcome that conflict) to regain her goal (become neat and clean again and in her mother's good favor). This is the most likely (commonly expected) outcome but not the only possible outcome for this story.*

Discuss the answers to these four questions with your class. There should be agreement on the answers to Questions 1 and 2. Question 3 is open to students' creative imaginings. However, insist that they be able to justify their answer based on the story information in Version #2, on the Eight Essential Elements, and on normal cause-and-effect plotting.

Question 4 allows some room for student invention. However, their ideas must bring the story to some form of goal resolution and to a final sequel. (Does Alyssa achieve her goal and how do Alyssa and her mother feel about it?)

Second Set. Once you have thoroughly reviewed these answers, have your students read the two story segments of the second set. Again, students will be asked to decide how they are different and to answer the following questions.

Version #1

> *Grettel slowly shook her head. "Poor father is becoming so forgetful. I do worry about him. He will feel terrible when he realizes he forgot us in the forest."*
>
> *Hansel smiled confidently as they walked the twisting forest trail. "Don't worry Grettel. Just follow the trail of bread crumbs. They'll lead us home."*
>
> *"I'm not worried," said Grettel. "I know you cleverly left a trail of bread crumbs for us to follow. It will be wonderful to be home again with dear mother and father!"*
>
> *"Just a little farther," said Hansel, beginning to whistle as he walked. "Great day for a walk, isn't it?"*

Version #2

> *Two parents huddled around the kitchen table at dawn. "We must get rid of our two children. It's the only answer. They're eating us out of house and home." The father sighed and nodded. "I'll leave them deep in the forest when I cut wood today. They'll never find their way out." Both parents clinked their coffee mugs together.*

Late that afternoon, Grettel slowly shook her head. "Poor father is becoming so forget-ful. I do worry about him. He will feel terrible when he realizes he forgot us in the forest."

Hansel smiled confidently as they walked the twisting forest trail. "Don't worry Grettel. Just follow the trail of bread crumbs. They'll lead us home."

"I'm not worried," said Grettel. "I know you cleverly left a trail of bread crumbs for us to follow. It will be wonderful to be home again with dear mother and father!"

"Just a little farther," said Hansel, beginning to whistle as he walked. "Great day for a walk, isn't it?"

From behind a tree, an evil witch peered through her binoculars and cackled. "Those fool children haven't noticed that I moved their bread-crumb trail. Soon they'll reach my candy house, and I'll dine on juicy children tonight!"

At the same time the Big Bad Wolf sniffed his way down the same forest trail. "I smell children just ahead. Even better than pig for dinner, and I won't have to blow down any houses, either!"

Now, answer these questions about these two story segments.

1. List the story elements that appear in both segments and those that appear in only one of the seg-ments. How do those added element(s) affect your understanding of the story?

   Elements in *both* segments: *Ans: Character, character traits, goal (get home), motive ("It will be wonderful to be home again with dear mother and father"), and struggles (actions taken to reach a goal)*

   Elements in *only one* segment: *Ans: Conflicts (parents, witch, wolf) and risks and dangers*

   How do the extra elements affect your understanding of the story? *Ans: Conflicts give meaning to the struggles of the main characters and provide obstacles for them to struggle against. Risk and danger create excitement in the story.*

2. Which version do you prefer and why? *Ans: Students should pick the second version. Conflicts and risks and dangers create excitement that is lacking in the first version.*

3. What do you think should happen next in Version #2 of the story and why? *Ans: Before Hansel and Grettel can get back home and confront their parents (climax and final resolution), they now have two other conflicts to deal with—the Big Bad Wolf and the witch. The next story event should involve the two children with one (or both) of these conflicts. Any specific event your students invent that falls within this general area will suffice.*

4. How do you think each of the two versions of this story should end? Why? *Ans: There are several op-tions your students could create. However, each of their versions must resolve Hansel and Grettle's goal (get home) and must address their motive (be with their dear parents) and the conflict with their parents (even though the children don't yet realize there is one).*

Discuss the answers to these four questions with your class. There should be agreement on the an-swers to Questions 1 and 2. Question 3 is open for students' creative imaginings. However, insist that they be able to justify their answer based on the story information in Version #2, on the Eight Essential Elements, and on normal cause-and-effect plotting.

Question 4 allows some room for student invention. However, their ideas must bring the story to some form of goal resolution and to a final sequel. (Do Hansel and Grettel get home—their goal—and how do they and their parents feel about it? The resolution will resolve the final conflict, resolve the mo-tive of the children, and provide a final sequel.)

Activity 56: Getting Started

What Students Will Learn:

This activity gives students a chance to compare three different opening scenes for a story and to learn successful models and strategies for writing an opening scene.

Time Estimate: 25 minutes for Part 1; 30 minutes for Part 2

Directions:

This activity focuses on the opening scene of a story. How should a student start a story? What's the best thing to put in an opening scene? What does the opening scene need to accomplish? What can an effective opening do for a story? These are the questions we'll address in this activity.

The activity is divided into two parts. Part 1 requires some out-of-class reading and research time for students. Part 2 can be completed in class.

Part 1. Begin this activity with a class discussion based on the following paragraphs. Does any kind of an opening make sense for a story? Are some openings stronger and more successful than others? What kinds of openings should your students create when they develop their stories?

Hook *n.* The element in writing that first attracts favorable attention.

Tone *n.* A way of writing (word choice, sentence structure, etc.) that denotes a person's emotions, sentiments, mood, and so on.

Opening paragraphs should hook the reader and set the tone (mood) for the story.

First, what is an opening scene supposed to do? Discuss this with your class. Make a list of their answers. Most writers would agree that a story opening:

A. Must hook readers and make them want to read further.

B. Should set the mood and tone for the story.

C. Should set up the ending scene and paragraphs of the story.

Let's quickly look at each requirement.

A. Every writer wants to—needs to—hook readers into their stories. If readers don't like the opening, if it doesn't hook them into the story and make them want to read the rest, they will never get to the second scene. But what kind of openings do that most easily and effectively? This is the big question.

B. Mood and tone are advanced writing concepts—valuable to study and master but only after you have mastered the basic writing skills and concepts presented in *Get It Write!* Your students shouldn't concern themselves with mood and tone at this point in their writing careers.

C. Story endings involve goal resolution and character feelings and reactions. If the opening scene presents a goal and shows a character's initial feelings and reactions to the opening situation, it will seem to set up the ending of the story and create a satisfying sense of completion at story's end for readers. This feeling can also be created by using the same—or parallel—wording or by talking about the same things in the opening and ending scenes.

Have students review two stories they have recently read and enjoyed and two movies they have recently seen and enjoyed and describe what kind of information they found in each of these four opening scenes. Tell students to describe which of the *Get It Write!* Eight Essential Elements they found in each opening.

The student worksheet has space for students to summarize their evaluation of each opening.

Allow several students to describe the kinds of information (elements) they found in each opening scene. Help them search for common and successful patterns and opening options.

After hearing from a number of students, have each describe three kinds of openings the student thinks will be effective for his or her own story. Space is provided on the student worksheet for these ideas.

Discuss these lists as a class. Search for ideas that appear on many (if not most) of your students' lists.

In general, four types of scenes make for the best story openings:

- **Type 1: Present core story elements.** The most reliable opening is to tell readers what this story will be about (character and goal). Begin by introducing the main character and a character first impression, a goal, a motive (optional), and a conflict. This is the best opening to use unless you have a strong reason to shift to something else. It reliably propels readers straight into the heart of the story.

- **Type 2: Establish interesting character traits.** If the main character either is particularly unusual and interesting, acts in a quirky and unusual way, or does something unique and unusual, then the writer might start the story by showing this character doing what he or she does to make the main character interesting. Once an interesting character has been established, the next scene should reveal what this story is about by presenting a goal.

- **Type 3: Establish risk and danger.** This opening is particularly effective for stories with a strong, fascinating antagonist. Use the first scene to show the antagonist acting in a cruel, dastardly, and powerful way. This establishes risk and danger for the main character (once we meet that character in the second scene of the story and have established conflict between main character and antagonist).

- **Type 4: Establish goal and motive.** If the eventual goal of the main character is significant and important to most readers, an opening scene that establishes the goal and the importance of that goal (motive) within the story will be a strong and effective opening.

Compare this list with the ones your students created.

Part 2. Having looked at story openings in general, let's use that information to look at alternative openings for one specific story. Three alternative versions of the opening for the same story are printed in this section and on the student worksheet.

Students will read and compare these three openings as directed by the questions that follow. Tell your students to assume that the information in each of the three versions is correct and that each is a plausible opening for this same story.

Version #1

Humpty Dumpty climbed up onto a wall. Then he sat on the wall. Then Humpty Dumpty had a great fall. All the king's horses and all the king's men tried but couldn't put Humpty together again.

Version #2

Humpty Dumpty paced slowly below the wall surrounding the castle garden. "Am I really the biggest coward in the kingdom? Have I ever done something that's worth being told in stories for generations to come? No!"

He sighed and shook his head as he paced. "But I'm afraid of dragons, and battles, and horses, and knives, and cats, and stairs, and spiders, and loud noises, and heights, and . . . and . . ." Again he sighed. "Maybe I could grow braver in tiny steps. I'll start by climbing up onto this wall."

He tilted his egg-shaped body so he could see the top. "It's so high . . ." He clenched his fists. "No, I must do this. Don't let your fears rule your life!"

Eyes squeezed shut he climbed hand over hand, foot over foot to the top. Then he opened his eyes. "Oh, dear! It's such a long way down. What have I done? I'm such a fool! I'm not brave. I'm . . . I'm slipping. Ahhhhhhhh . . ."

Version #3

The evil castle bookkeeper, Count Softly, paced beside his counting table. "I swear, I'll get rid of the king and rule the world. But how? If only I could get close enough to the king to steal his magic sandals of power. But how? He's always wearing the sandals, and he's guarded by his soldiers. I need a diversion. But what?"

He paused to gaze idly out the window and saw dear Humpty Dumpty pacing beneath the garden wall. "Ahh, if the king's uncle, Humpty Dumpty, had an 'accident' and was splattered across the walkway, then all the king's horses and all the king's men will rush to put him together again. Even the king will come out. But he'll have to put on outside shoes. That will give me a chance to slip into the throne room and snatch the king's magic sandals of power."

With an evil chuckle Count Softly slipped out of the castle and toward the garden. Sure, Humpty Dumpty was Count Softly's godfather and dearest friend. Sure, he was a good egg and the nicest, kindest, being in the kingdom. Count Softly's face twitched with a deep pang of guilt and remorse. Could he do this awful thing to sweet Uncle Humpty? No! He couldn't let his feelings get in the way of his ambition. Uncle Humpty had to go if Count Softly was to rule the world!

Now students are to answer the following five questions:

1. Which essential elements do you find in each version?

   Version #1. *Ans: Two elements only: a character (mentioned by name only with no other character traits provided) and plotting events (struggles)*

   Version #2. *Ans: All are included—character first impression, character traits, a goal, a motive, an internal conflict, some struggles, and some details about the character, setting, and actions*

   Version #3. *Ans: Seven of the eight are included: character first impression, character traits, a goal (actually a goal— rule the world—and two subgoals, or interim steps—first create a diversion and then steal the magic slippers—which happens when the plotting strategy breaks a task into multiple steps, each with its own goal and obstacles), conflicts and problems (both external and internal), struggles, and details. No motive is given for Count Softly's desire to rule the world. Motive is the only missing element.*

2. Without knowing what the whole story is about, which version do you prefer as the story's opening? Why? *Ans: Students should pick either Version #2 or #3. Both provide the same elements. Version #3 contains more risk and danger and so normally receives the most votes. Version #1 should never be picked since it lacks goal and conflict provided by both of the other two.*

3. Let's combine Versions #2 and #3. Assume that Count Softly causes Humpty Dumpty to fall (though Humpty doesn't realize it and thinks he fell due to his own clumsiness). As a reader, what would you need to know next in this story? *Ans: The identity of the main character. Who is this story going to be about and what is the character's goal in this story? Is it Count Softly? Humpty? The king? What is that character after? Everything else (motive, ending, struggles, etc.) depends on letting readers know who and what this story is going to be about.*

4. Which of following could logically be the main character and goal for this story? Circle the choices you think could logically be used.

   A. The king, who wants to give the best-ever birthday present to his uncle, Humpty Dumpty

   B. A kitchen maid, who wants to marry Count Softly to escape the drudgery of the kitchens

   C. Humpty Dumpty, who wants to fly to the stars

   D. The king, who wants his daughter to marry a wealthy prince

   E. A knight, who wants to fight a dragon and become famous

   F. Bookkeeper Count Softly, who wants to rule the world

   Ans: All are logically possible main characters.

5. Four types of effective openings were presented and discussed earlier in this activity. What type of opening is each of the three versions? We will now assume that Humpty Dumpty will be the story's main character. What type of an opening is presented in each version? Which create effective hooks for readers? Which don't? Why?

   Version #1: *Ans: Version #1 includes plotting events only. It is an ineffective opening. By failing to include any of the first six story elements, readers are not drawn in to the story and don't care about any of the characters.*

   Version #2: *Ans: This opening (Type 1) presents a character, character first impression, goal, internal conflict, and even includes both internal and physical struggles. It draws readers in because it gives them the core story elements.*

   Version #3. *Ans: This version presents a compelling antagonist (Type 3). We meet the antagonist, learn of his goal, and see him act cruelly with malice. This clearly establishes conflict and risk and danger for the main character and draws readers in to the story.*

Review and discuss your class's answers. Question 1 is a factual review of the Eight Essential Elements.

Question 2 requires students to assess the three versions and make and support an opinion. Either Version #2 or #3 makes a plausible choice since both provide the same elements. Version #3 has more risk and danger and a more complex plot line, so it should receive more votes.

By combining Versions #2 and #3, Question 3 presents two equally well-developed characters. Readers can find both interesting but will need to know who the main character is to settle into the story and have it make sense. Readers can manage a chapter or two for a novel-length story without knowing who the main character is but only a scene or two for a short story. If this is a short story, it's time to identify the central character.

Any of the options in Question 4 is possible. The most difficult to write would be option F. Count Softly's goal, motive, intent, and actions are cruel. Readers like to identify with the main character but not with an evil character. It would be easier to write if Count Softly filled the roll of an antagonist. It's possible to make Count Softly the main character, but it will be more work for the writer. Notice that the goals and motives of each character determine whether or not readers will identify with, and root for, the character.

Question 5 reviews the four types (or models) of effective openings. Opening scenes must hook readers. The four general types of openings presented here are most effective at accomplishing this important feat and are described in the previous paragraphs. The best time to settle on an opening scene is after the first six of *Get It Write!* Eight Essential Elements have been created and after the general flow of the plot has been decided.

Activity 57: Building from Characters _____

What Students Will Learn:

Students will have an opportunity to experience building a story beginning with only character information.

Time Estimate: 20 minutes

Directions:

This activity focuses on the power of interesting character traits as an easy and effective way to begin a story. Have students read this story segment and then answer the questions that follow.

Twelve-year-old Patricia loved jelly beans. In her upstairs room Patricia had jelly bean book covers on all her books. She had twelve stuffed jelly bean–shaped pillows piled onto her bed. Fifteen inflated plastic jelly beans hung from the ceiling of her room. She had quilted jelly bean–shaped felt patches all over her comforter.

Patricia's little brother, William, liked jelly beans. So when Patricia had some jelly beans . . . she never shared any with William. Liking jelly beans wasn't nearly good enough to earn some of Patricia's jelly beans.

Patricia's best friend, Muriel, liked jelly beans very much. So when Patricia had some jelly beans . . . she never shared any with Muriel. Liking them very much was no better than just liking jelly beans.

Ob·ses·sion *n.* Something or someone that occupies the mind to an inordinate degree.

Pas·sion *n.* An intense or violent emotion.

If a character feels too much passion for something, it becomes an obsession. Such extreme emotional attachments are always interesting to readers.

1. List at least six things you know about the character Patricia. *Ans: She's twelve years old; she loves jelly beans; her room is upstairs; she has a brother, William; she has a best friend, Muriel; we know about her room decorations; she's stingy, greedy, and doesn't share.*

2. What information do you learn that makes Patricia an interesting character? *Ans: We learn about her passion. Seeing characters' strong emotional attachments (loves, hates, fears) always makes them interesting.*

3. What elements are included in this story segment? Ans: Characters and character traits

   Let's add one more paragraph to this story segment.

   Now you might think that Patricia ate jelly beans all the time and, so, grew hideously fat, and all her teeth rotted and fell out. But that's not true. Patricia's mother hardly ever allowed Patricia to get a new bag of jelly beans.

4. Which new story elements are in this paragraph? *Ans: Conflict. Her mother won't let her have what she wants.*

5. Is a story goal specifically stated in the text of this segment? *Ans: No*

6. Can you now guess Patricia's goal in this story? What goal would you pick? *Ans: Based on what is given in the story so far, the best guess for a goal is to get jelly beans.*

7. Why did you pick that goal? *Ans: Goal and conflicts are closely linked. If you know the main conflict, you can usually guess the main character's goal. Once you know the goal, you can decide what would and would not be a suitable obstacle (conflict).*

8. Which of the following would be reasonable goals for Patricia based on the story so far? Circle your choices.

   A. Go on a diet

   B. Learn to be nicer to her brother, William

   C. Find a better best friend

   D. Get more jelly beans

   E. Redecorate her room

   F. Study nutrition

   G. Brush her teeth more often

   Ans: Only D fits with what we know so far.

9. Invent a new goal for Patricia that will fit with existing story information and that you think will make for a great story. Explain why you picked that one. *Ans: Since conflict has already been established in the story, the most natural goal for Patricia is one that will be blocked by the existing conflict. Based on given story information, the goal must also be important to Patricia. Thus, get jelly beans is the most logical answer. However, a wide number of goals are possible—as long as the student proposing the goal can justify and support it using known story information.*

10. Invent four interesting, new characteristics about Patricia that don't contradict what you already know about her. See Activity 12 if you need to review the list of possible categories of information to create. Remember to be specific. Character traits should be in the form of good details. *Ans: Any character-related information is acceptable as long as it is presented as effective details—specific, unique, unusual, and vivid.*

11. In the following space list four conflicts or problems you might include in this story if you were going to write it. *Ans: Conflicts must block a character from a goal. Students may invent any obstacles as long as those obstacles clearly block Patricia from reaching her stated goal.*

12. How would you like to end this story? Why? *Ans: The story must end when Patricia resolves her goal. That ending should include a final sequel.*

Review and discuss student answers. Questions 1 through 8 are based on stated story information. However, Questions 2, 6, and 7 allow for student opinion. If students do not pick the obvious answers, have them explain and justify their answer based on the character and story information provided so far.

Questions 9 through 12 allow for greater individual creativity. Have students share and explain why their goals and conflicts will be valuable and workable additions to this story.

As a final option, have students write their versions of the story. In this assignment, students will naturally want to rush straight to the exciting plot elements they have imagined based on the conflicts and ending they created. You must caution them, however, that proceeding to plot before they have fully developed their character, goal, and motive (and so far we haven't in this story) is both the surest path to a boring story and the bad habit they have been working to break.

Activity 58: Recognizing the Elements _____

What Students Will Learn:

Students will reinforce their ability to locate and identify each of the Eight Essential Elements within the context of a complex story segment.

Time Estimate: 30 to 40 minutes

Directions:

Have students read this story segment and follow the directions that follow. No lead-in discussion should be necessary. Follow-up questions instruct your students to find and mark each of the Eight Essential Elements in this segment. Some of the Eight Essential Elements may not be included in this segment, and, if so, students should disregard those parts of the directions. The paragraphs in this segment are numbered for use in the first set of questions.

1. *Little's the name. Chicken—Chicken Little. I'm short. I'm yellow. And I'm all chicken!*

2. *I just want to be a good chicken and protect my barnyard. Everyone respects a chicken who protects the barnyard, who's the first to squawk at any sign of trouble.*

3. *Of course, it would be soooo embarrassing to give a false alarm. I don't think I'd dare show my face in the barnyard again if I gave a false alarm.*

4. *Three days ago, I strolled down the road on my usual patrol route around the barnyard when my nose caught a whiff of fox drifting on the breeze. I slowed down, being doubly alert. You see, Fox has the nasty habit of eating us barnyard animals. No one is safe when Fox is on the prowl.*

5. *When, bonk! Something smacked me on the head. Something big and hard. I looked down but nothing unusual was there. I looked up, and nothing was there, either. Then I put two and six together and realized a chunk of the sky had fallen on my head. That's why I couldn't see it. If one piece of the sky could break loose and fall, so could another. And the next piece might be the size of a house and flatten everyone in the barnyard! We could all be killed!*

6. *I admit to a moment of panic. I ran in circles squawking, "The sky is falling! The sky is falling!"*

7. *Fox bounded out of the bushes, his eyes bugged out. "The sky is falling?!" he wailed, running in circles with his paws over his head. "Help me! Help me! The sky is falling!" Henny Penny came running from the henhouse. "The sky is falling!" I yelled. She turned as white as a hen can turn and clucked in terror.*

8. *Why, in no time the entire barnyard was out mooing, bleating, crying, and woe-is-me-ing, all running in circles and glancing fearfully toward the high blue yonder. Fox was so frightened, he never noticed that his favorite foods—us chickens—were sprinting terrified laps around the barnyard right beside him.*

Part 1. Identify which story elements are included in each paragraph of this story segment.

Paragraph	Included Essential Elements
1.	*Ans: Main character, first impression for the main character, details (about the character)*
2.	*Ans: Goal and motive*
3.	*Ans: Risk and danger (embarrassment) and one character trait*
4.	*Ans: Struggle (patrol the barnyard), conflict (fox), and risk and danger (be eaten)*
5.	*Ans: A problem (falling sky), risk and danger (get flattened), character traits (put two and six together), and struggles (look down, look up, and think—something the character does to try to resolve a problem)*
6.	*Ans: Character trait (a reaction)*
7.	*Ans: Character trait (character creations)*
8.	*Ans: Same as Paragraph 7 (Note that Paragraph 6, 7, and 8 describe actions, things that characters do. These actions, however, do not qualify as struggles because struggles are a character's attempt to overcome and resolve a problem. These actions are merely characters' reactions to a problem.)*

Jeop·ard·y *n.* The state of being exposed to danger. That which creates the danger. Jeopardy is another word for the risk and danger a character must face.

Part 2. Students are asked to follow the directions in these ten questions.

1. Circle the first mention of the main character in red. *Ans: The first two sentences of Paragraph 1. "Little's the name. Chicken—Chicken Little."* Underline the first impression for this character in red. *Ans: The rest of the first paragraph: "I'm short. I'm yellow. And I'm all chicken!"*

2. Use a yellow highlighter to highlight the goal of this character. *Ans: First sentence of the second paragraph: "I just want to be a good chicken and protect my barnyard."*

3. In yellow, underline the main character's motive, why this goal is important. *Ans: Second sentence, second paragraph: "Everyone respects a chicken who protects . . ."*

4. Use a different color highlighter to highlight all character traits of the main character that are presented in the segment. *Ans: All of first paragraph—a name is a character trait; last line, third paragraph: we learn a fear—giving a false alarm; fifth paragraph, sixth sentence: Chicken Little jumps to wild conclusions—a personality trait; sixth paragraph: Chicken Little is easily excitable.*

5. Use a blue pen to underline all specifically mentioned conflicts or problems for the main character. *Ans: Third paragraph: an internal conflict between wanting to be the first to give an alarm and his fear of giving a false alarm; fourth paragraph: fox; fifth paragraph: falling sky.*

6. In pencil, circle the stated risk and danger associated with each obstacle identified in your answer to Question 5. *Ans: Third paragraph: "be soooo embarrassing," defines the danger of giving a false alarm, fourth paragraph: last two sentences define the danger of the fox: "Fox has a nasty habit of eating us barnyard animals. No one is safe when fox is on the prowl"; fifth paragraph: last two sentences define the danger of a falling sky.*

7. In black ink, underline the struggles of the main character, things this character does to try to reach the goal. *Ans: Fourth paragraph, first half of first sentence, "Three days ago, I strolled down the road on my usual patrol route around the barnyard . . ."*

8. In green, underline all sensory details. (For a reminder about sensory details, see Activities 43 through 46.) *Ans: Fourth paragraph, third and fourth sentences; fourth paragraph, "nose caught a whiff . . .";* *Fifth paragraph, third sentence, "something big and hard"; seventh paragraph, first sentence, "eyes bugged out," and second sentence, "paws over his head"; seventh paragraph, last sentence, "turned as white as a hen can turn"; last paragraph, first sentence, "mooing, bleating, crying, and woe-is-me-ing."*

9. Which of the Eight Essential Elements are here? *Ans: All of them—main character, character traits, goal, motive, problems, risk and danger, struggles, and some details. The story needs to finish the struggles and resolve the goal.*

   What is still missing? *Ans: The rest of the struggles (plot), the climax, and the goal resolution*

10. Are there any phrases or sentences that you did not mark? If so, why are they in the story? What do they do? *Ans: Fourth paragraph, phrase "Three days ago" is a transition; Fifth paragraph, last half is a sequel (main character ponders recent actions and decides what they mean to him); Seventh and eighth paragraphs show actions and reactions of other characters.*

Review and discuss your students' answers before proceeding to Part 3. Parts 1 and 2 ask factual questions. Still, allow students time to offer variations and alternatives. Have the class decide if these meet the mandates of each specific question. After you are satisfied that all students understand the answers to these questions, turn to the four possible additions of Part 3.

Part 3. This part includes four possible add-ons to this story segment. Decide if you think it would be good to add each to this story segment and then answer the questions that follow each addition.

> *1. Mr. Horse looked down and said, "Wait! It was just an acorn that hit you on the head, not the sky."*
> *"The sky isn't falling?" I cheeped.*
> *Everyone grumbled, "A false alarm!" But they also breathed a deep sigh of relief— until they realized Fox stood in their midst.*

Do you want to include this addition? (Yes/No) Why? What would it add that this story segment needs? Where would you place this addition? *Ans: Yes, this would be good to add because it resolves a central plotting question: did the sky really fall and hit Chicken Little on the head. It should be placed at the end of the provided story segment.*

> *2. A snarling, red-eyed bull stomped in from the pasture and bellowed, "Quiet!" He turned toward Chicken Little and snorted. His voice rumbled like a speeding avalanche. "This is all your fault. I'm sick and tired of your false alarms. This time you're gonna pay."*

Do you want to include this addition? (Yes/No) Why? What would it add that this story segment needs? Where would you place this addition? *Ans: This could be added because it adds a new conflict, excellent danger for the main character, and, thus, extra story excitement. However, we already have several good problems and conflicts in the story and don't need more. Too many conflicts could dilute the power and focus of the story. If added, it should be placed at the end of the original story segment but before Mr. Horse solves the falling-sky question and establishes beyond question that Chicken Little gave a false alarm.*

3. Henny Penny has been getting far too much attention in the barnyard lately—what with everyone making a fuss over her and saying that she's so smart. Well, I've got my share of smarts, too. She may be a hen, but I'm all chicken. If I save the barnyard from some great disaster, then the others will realize that I'm the one who deserves the attention.

Do you want to include this addition? (Yes/No) Why? What would it add that this story segment needs? Where would you place this addition? *Ans: Yes, this would be good to add since it provides both more motive for the main character and creates an additional conflict (Chicken Little is jealous of Henny Penny) that will be closely tangled with existing story events. If this paragraph is added, it should be placed after the second paragraph—after the goal has been mentioned.*

4. Late at night, while the other animals sleep, I stay up practicing my card playing. Come fair time, I'm gonna win the tournament and be crowned best Go Fish player in the county!

Do you want to include this addition? (Yes/No) Why? What would it add that this story segment needs? Where would you place this addition? *Ans: No, this should not be added to the story. This paragraph provides a new goal not at all related to the existing goal for the main character. We don't need and can't use a second goal for Chicken Little unless we plan to write a novel-length story.*

While several of the add-ons will be valuable, none of them completes the story. One conflict (Fox likes to eat chickens and is standing in their midst) still remains unresolved, and Chicken Little's goal (be the barnyard hero) remains unresolved. We still need climax and resolution scenes.

Activity 59: What's Here? _____

What Students Will Learn:

Students will have a chance to analyze a story segment and identify—and then create—the missing elements.

Time Estimate: 20 to 25 minutes

Directions:

Have students read the following story segment and answer the questions that follow. Students should complete the entire worksheet before you begin a review of the answers.

> *Jack and Jill climbed up the hill carrying an empty bucket. Jill stopped halfway, gazing up the steep slope. "Sure is a long way up this hill."*
>
> *"We have to fetch a pail of water," answered Jack.*
>
> *Jill huffed. "Why would some fool put the well on top of a hill instead of down at the bottom where it'd be easy to get to?" She dropped the bucket and crossed her arms. "Besides, why doesn't Mother turn on the faucet at home if she wants water?"*
>
> *Jack scooped up the bucket. "Mother said we have to."*
>
> *Jill shook her head. "I refuse. First, it's too steep. Second, I think she's just trying to get us out of the house. So, third, you should go tell her this is a dumb idea."*
>
> *"I won't say that to Mamma," answered Jack.*
>
> *"Well, I'm not moving until we get some answers."*
>
> *"Then I'll go up and get the water alone," sneered Jack as he started up the hill. "And then I'll be Mother's favorite."*
>
> *Jill yanked on his sleeve. "Oh no you don't!" Jack fell down and broke his crown. Jill slipped and came tumbling after.*

Work *vt.* To reach a satisfying state, position, or conclusion through effort. Every writer wants their stories to work. It takes some effort—both in planning and creating the Eight Essential Elements and in writing and refining the written details of the story.

Students are instructed to answer the following questions:

1. Which elements are specifically stated in this segment? *Ans: Characters, character traits, a goal (fetch water), conflict, and character struggles (both what they do to get the water and what they do trying to win their conflict with each other)*

2. Which elements are missing? *Ans: Motive (both why they need to get the water and why they want to quarrel and fight with each other), risk and danger (what will happen if they don't get the water), character traits (we learn very little about either child), and details about the setting and actions*

3. Do Jack and Jill share a common goal, or do they have different goals in this segment? *Ans: Officially, they are both going to fetch water, but individually they seem to have very different goals.*

   What do you think Jack is after? *Ans: Either to be his mother's favorite or to get Jill in trouble.*

   What do you think Jill is after? *Ans: To get out of work*

   Explain why your choices fit with the story information provided in this segment and compare your choices with those of other students. *Ans: Any answer that successfully uses story information and* Get It Write! *concepts to support the answer is acceptable.*

4. What do you learn of Jack and Jill's personalities in this segment? *Ans: Jack seems to have a strong sense of duty and wants to please his mother. They both seem to enjoy verbally sparring with each other. Jill seems to be lazy and to love inventing excuses for her laziness.*

    How did you learn this information? *Ans: Through action and dialogue.*

5. In Question 3 you chose personal goals for Jack and Jill. Now, create new conflict for these two children by describing the relationships between Jack, Jill, and their mother. You may introduce additional characters if you need them to create adequate conflict in this story. *Ans: There is no one correct answer to this question. Any conflict that blocks or interferes with the children's goals will suffice.*

    Explain why your choices fit with the story information provided in this segment.

6. Create your own version for two of the missing elements: motive and risk and danger. Explain why your choices fit with the story information provided in this segment. *Ans: There are no single correct answers to these questions. Students may be as creative as they wish, as long as their motives explain why the children want and need to achieve their individual goals.*

    Describe the risk and danger for these two children created by the conflicts you created in Question 5. *Ans: The correct answer will vary depending on the conflicts picked earlier.*

Review the entire activity with your class. Pay particular attention to Question 2 since those answers set up students' work in Questions 5 and 6. Let students debate their answers using story material to justify their versions until you are satisfied that everyone understands these two characters and this story segment.

Questions 5 and 6 are less factual (taken from provided story information) and are more creative (extending beyond existing story information). Allow several students to share their motives and risk and danger. The class should ensure that the stated motives really do explain Jack and Jill's goals and that the risk and danger each student creates does emanate from established obstacles.

As an optional add-on, have your class finish and write the story. Their individual versions will, of course, vary depending on the goals and motives they use.

Activity 60: Order Up!

What Students Will Learn:

Students will have a chance to unscramble the presented order of a story and observe how they naturally order the story elements.

Time Estimate: 30 to 40 minutes

Directions:

The following story segment is presented in short paragraphs. Each paragraph has a letter designation (**A** through **H**). However, the paragraphs are not presented in the most logical order. Tell your students to read the segment and then reorder the paragraphs so that the story makes sense. They will also be asked to locate each of the Eight Essential Elements within these paragraphs.

The Eight Essential Elements

Character

Character traits

Goal

Motive

Conflicts and problems

Risk and danger

Struggles

Details

A. *George gulped his last swig of latte, slid his books into his backpack, hooked his cell phone into his belt, set his face grim and hard, and sped off on his ten-speed.*

B. *"I will, mom," said George. "Be brave! I'm on the way home!"*

C. *Mother threw her arms around George's neck. "You made it! There's a teensy spider on the counter. Could you take it outside for me, dear."*

D. *George leapt from his bike onto the television broadcast building fire escape ladder moments before the bike was flattened by a government tank. George scampered twenty-eight stories to the roof where he looped a rope over one antenna guide wire that angled down to the defense department building across the deadly lava flow that snaked through the city. Sliding down the wire, George crashed into a roof support and tumbled to the ground. Now he had only a half-mile sprint home.*

E. *George, a tall boy of sixteen and president of the school physics club, sat at a university cafe table sipping a latte when his cell phone rang.*

F. *But civil war had erupted in Matsubutsu and rebel forces had seized half the city. George would have to fight his way through the combat zone and across the volcanic lava flows that had wiped out the French quarter.*

G. *His mother's voice sounded frantic. "George, come home right now! I need you desperately."*

H. *Bullets whined about him as he raced through the rebel lines. Both bike tires were shot flat, but he sped on, riding on the rims. Sirens whined as police and rebel soldiers chased him down an alley.*

1. Identify the elements included in each paragraph.

Paragraph Order	Paragraph Designation	Included Essential Elements
1st	A	_____
2nd	B	_____

3rd	C	_____
4th	D	_____
5th	E	_____
6th	F	_____
7th	G	_____
8th	H	_____

Ans: A—struggle and details of George's actions; B—goal; C—resolution of goal; D—struggle and scenic and event details; E—main character, first impression, character traits (character details); F—conflicts and problems, risk and danger, and scenic details; G—motive; H—struggle, risk and danger, and details of the setting and action (struggles) (Note: George is mentioned in paragraph A. Some students will want to claim that that is where we first meet George. However, it is obvious that that is not where readers are supposed to first meet him and that this mention of George only comes first because the order of paragraphs is scrambled. Paragraph E is obviously where we are supposed to first meet George.)

2. Reorder the paragraphs so that the story makes sense and flows in a logical sequence.

Paragraph	I'd reorder the story to make this Paragraph #
A	_____
B	_____
C	_____
D	_____
E	_____
F	_____
G	_____
H	_____

Ans: A-5; B-3; C-8; D-7; E-1; F-4; G-2; H-6 (Note: Some students may want to place paragraph A before paragraph F, thus switching their order. Since paragraph F contains background information only, this switch is plausible. However, the listed order reads better.)

3. In which paragraph (1st, 2nd, 3rd, etc.) is each of these elements located in the original and in your revised order?

Essential Element	Original Order	Revised Order
Character (first impression)	_____	_____
Goal	_____	_____
Motive	_____	_____
Conflicts and problems	_____	_____
Risk and danger	_____	_____
Struggle	_____	_____
Goal resolution	_____	_____

Ans: Main character—5, 1; goal—2, 3; motive—7, 2; resolution—3, 8; conflicts—6, 4; risk and danger—6 and 8, 4 and 6; struggles—1 and 4 and 8, 5 and 6 and 7 (first number is for original version; second is for revised version)

Have students compare the order of the elements as originally presented with their revised order. Notice several things:

- In the original order, we aren't given a motive to explain George's goal until paragraph **G.** When finally reading **G,** everyone thinks, "Ahhh, now I get it." In the revised order, motive is moved to second place—ahead even of goal so that the goal makes sense when readers see it.

- The original order doesn't make much sense until you reach paragraph **E.** It is there that readers realize they have met the main character. That's why **E** is placed first in the revised order.

- In the original order, struggles come early (Paragraphs 1 and 4). In the revised version, struggles are pushed back so that character, goal, motive, and conflict are explained first.

- In the original order, resolution comes early (Paragraph 3). In the revised order, resolution comes last, as it should.

- In the revised order, we meet the main character (**E**), understand his motive and goal (**G** and **B**), establish conflict (**F**), and then watch a character do something (an action) that increases risk and danger (**A, H,** and **D**).

- In the revised order, we present the elements to readers in order, Elements 1 through 7. Details (Element 8) are sprinkled throughout as needed.

Readers understand information best when its comes to them in this sequential order.

Activity 61: On the Fly _____

What Students Will Learn:

This activity affords students a chance to build improvisational stories and to assess those stories as they are being built.

Time Estimate: 10 to 20 minutes

Directions:

This is a fun improvisational story game. There is no student worksheet for this activity. It is designed to provide students with an opportunity to review the look of, purpose of, and position of the Eight Essential Elements.

One student volunteer (the teller) makes up a thirty-second oral story for the class while the teacher times his or her telling. There should be no preparatory discussion before this improvisation.

The teacher then asks the class to identify each of the story elements that were—and were not—included in this thirty-second story. The class must come to agreement both on which elements were present and on the specific information that constituted each element.

The teacher should then appoint other volunteers to create each of the first seven elements that the class agreed were missing from the improvised story. Their creations must fit with, and be consistent with, the original story. The class may then debate these elements, continuing to refine and improve them until the class as a whole is satisfied that this will be a great story.

The teacher should now summarize the final version of this story and lead a comparison of it to the original improvised thirty-second story. In particular, review the gradual and steady development of the final story and the process by which the class shifted from the original to the final version. Focus on identifying the elements with which the class struggled and on the elements that seem to do the most to define the final form and direction of the story.

Create first; write second.

- When you *create,* create the Eight Essential Elements.
- When you *write,* write the details.

As an option, tape-record the original version as it is being improvised. Replay the tape during this comparison to remind the class of what was and wasn't in the original version.

Pick a new volunteer teller and repeat the exercise.

As you recap this game, help your class notice the natural human tendency to start each of these made-up stories with action (events, plot); which is the counterproductive tendency your students have to break if they are going to make their writing flow easily and successfully. It is hard to make up an interesting character while you improvise a timed story. However, if they were to start each of these stories with a character first impression in the first sentence and a goal in the second, it would be much easier for the class to proceed through motive, conflict, and risk and danger to action.

Activity 62: The Write Time _____

What Students Will Learn:

Students will have an opportunity to work through the process of creating all Eight Essential Elements for a story.

Time Estimate: 20 minutes plus time to write the entire story

Directions:

In this activity students will be led through the progression of steps to create a complete story. This activity gives students a chance to put to practical use all of the concepts and strategies they have learned in *Get It Write!* To speed up the creative process, the student creations will be based on a well-known folktale.

We all know the story of Goldilocks and the three bears. In the opening paragraph, Goldi commits a felony—breaking and entering into the bears' house. Then she gobbles their breakfast, smashes much of the living room furniture, wanders upstairs for a nap, and is caught by the bears.

That is the outline of the story's basic plot line. But that certainly isn't the whole story. Your students will be asked to create their own version of this story—adhering to the known plotting events of the story.

The following questions guide students through the process. Minimal directions are included on the student worksheet. There are no single correct answers for the questions in this activity. Students may create anything they want, as long as they create the appropriate information for each element, as long as their ideas fit with the known plotting events of the story, and as long as their creations fit together and create an effective, logical story. Use the following descriptive paragraphs to talk students through this entire process before they begin.

Effective Details Must Be:

Accurate

Specific

Effective Details Should Be:

Unique

Unusual

Vivid

1. Tell us about this girl, Goldilocks. Who is she? How does she think? What is she like? Tell about her life, friends, and activities and what she's doing in the woods all alone. Take your time and invent as much about this girl as you can using as many of the fifteen possible categories of character information as you can (see Activity 12). The more you invent now, the easier it will be later to write the story. Nothing you invent may contradict the basic facts of the story: she is a girl, she has blond hair, and her name is Goldilocks.

   You may want to give students a fixed amount of time (ten to twenty minutes) to develop their version of this character before playing one or more of the character games introduced in Part 1 (see especially Activities 14 and 15). Then allow students another block of time to amend their written descriptions.

2. Why does she break into the bears' house? What is she after? Pick one of the following six goals and motives for Goldilocks to use in your version of the story.

   A. She wants to be elected county supervisor and is hoping to talk the bears (and all their relatives) into voting for her.

   B. She breaks into the bears' house to pass her initiation test into a secret club.

   C. She wants to make friends with all the forest dwellers, so she'll feel safe when she walks in the woods.

D. She just *has* to see how Mrs. Bear decorated the place. Goldilocks is compulsively, uncontrollably curious and can't stop herself from breaking in—even though she knows she should wait for an invitation.

E. She is soooo bored and looking for some excitement—any excitement—to fill up her day.

F. She wants to steal Mrs. Bear's recipe for honey-baked ham, so she can win first place at the county fair cook-off and become a famous chef.

3. All but one of the goals also includes at least one motive for that goal (a reason Goldilocks wants to reach that goal). Still, more motive will make the story better and easier to write. Create two additional motives for Goldilocks that provide additional reasons why she needs to achieve the goal you picked.

   Students should search through the character profile they have written, through Goldilocks's history, through her relationships and fears, through her passions to find strong motives for this character.

4. What problems and conflicts will block Goldi along the way and what risk and danger will she face? (Let's keep this a simple story by limiting the story to no more than three obstacles.)

5. Which of these do you want to make the biggest and most dangerous obstacle and how will Goldi confront this obstacle during the climax scene?

   This question requires students to create an antagonist if they are going to have one. If they choose to turn one of the conflicts Goldi faces into an antagonist, then they must develop that antagonist as we did in Activity 32.

6. How will your story end?

   Remind students that the ending they choose must resolve Goldilocks's goal and should provide a final sequel for that character. (Does she get her goal and how does she feel about it?) There is still plenty of room for them to incorporate any twist or surprise outcome their creative imaginings can produce.

7. Use any of the plotting strategies you like best and outline the major events of the story. Your story must be consistent with the information presented in the opening paragraph of this activity.

   This is a good spot for students to talk through their story with peers and to benefit from the feedback and ideas of their contemporaries. The more they talk their way through it, the more clearly they will see it when they begin to write.

8. Describe two settings (places) where important parts of this story will happen.

   Students often rush through creating their settings to get to the action. However, they will be well served by a pause here to consider the places of their story. It will make it much easier for them to write the action sequences that happen in these places. The Scene Game (Activity 49) is an excellent way for students to better develop their multisensory images of these places before they begin to write.

9. How and where will you start this story? By presenting character first impression, goal, motive, and conflict? By showing the main character in action to make her interesting? By creating an antagonist and showing him or her engaged in evil action?

   An option is to have students either turn in for your review, or present in class, their ideas and creations to this point. It is appropriate to include a quality control review (idea editing) before they launch into recording and writing their version of the story.

10. Now it's time to create the story.

    The longer students use verbal techniques to create their stories, the stronger their story details will become. Before writing, several steps are valuable:

- Have students sketch a quick picture of each scene. Stick-figure pictures are fine. These pictures should show the place, the characters, and the key action of each scene.

- Have students tape-record three versions of the story before they write. They will say the story, listen to it, and then make any editing notes to improve the story before the next recording. They should review their worksheet pages of notes before each recording but should look only at their sketched pictures while they say the story.

By the third taping, they will have a solid version of their story fixed in their minds and on tape. They then can write without fear of forgetting part of their story—it's on tape.

When they write, they can now focus on the details they need to create—details about the characters, settings, actions, and objects in the story. The story, itself, has already been created.

Space is not provided on the worksheets for them to actually write the story. They will need to provide their own paper for this part of the process.

11. As your teacher directs, set this story aside for several weeks before you revisit, evaluate, revise, and edit it. No one writes a perfect first draft. Every story can benefit from editing.

First drafts are starting points, not ending points. Your students should not be discouraged if this first draft of the story isn't all they had hoped for. It most likely is a good story that just needs a little editing. It is best to set a story aside for several weeks. Student writers will then be able to look at what they wrote with a fresh eye and more accurately evaluate, revise, and edit their work.

Chapter 4

Writing Assessment Preparation

The first three chapters of *Get It Write!* focused on stories. We worked with stories, uncovered story structure, mastered the Eight Essential Elements, and wrote story segments. Will this help your students write the kinds of narrative pieces that are assigned on standardized assessments? Will the Eight Essential Elements and the writing strategies we developed for stories help students excel when writing personal narratives or expository essays to persuade or to inform?

The answer, of course, is yes! The *Get It Write!* approach is specifically designed to directly support and greatly enhance *all* kinds of student narrative writing.

You and your students should treat all narrative writing assignments the same. When you write a story, you are *informing* readers about the characters, setting, and events of the story. You include specific information that will *persuade* readers to believe in and visualize your story. When you write to persuade, you persuade by providing information to convince the reader and you develop the same scenic and sensory details you would use in a story to make the writing vivid and believable. When you write to inform, you persuade the reader to accept your information using the techniques of good story writing to make the pertinent information seem vivid and compelling.

This chapter of *Get It Write!* is both a practical application and a practical demonstration of the power of the *Get It Write!* concepts and the Eight Essential Elements. Interestingly, students tend to make the same mistakes while writing expository essays and personal narratives that they do when writing stories—they barge straight into writing before they create the key elements of their essay, and they start by planning the essay's plot. These deadly expository pitfalls can be corrected the same way they were for story writing—by adhering to the *Get It Write!* concepts and approach students have just mastered.

Create First; Write Second

• **When you *create,*** create the Eight Essential Elements.

• **When you *write,*** write the details.

Teachers, school districts, and state standardized assessments unwittingly exacerbate the problem by handing students plot questions as writing themes: "What did you do last summer?" "Tell about a time you were surprised," or "Write about your favorite thing to do after school." Those are all plot questions and encourage students to bypass character and character development to the detriment of their writing. It makes successful expository writing a greater challenge and requires that your students be ever vigilant to guard against these pitfalls and to be well schooled in the habit of using the *Get It Write!* Eight Essential Elements.

In this chapter of *Get It Write!*, we fix the common errors in expository writing in the same way we fixed them for story writing. We advance students' expository writing skills with the same Eight Essential Elements and tools we used to advance their story writing.

This chapter of *Get It Write!* is broken into three sections, one for each of the three most commonly assigned varieties of expository writing: persuasive writing (Section A), personal narratives (Section B), and informational writing (Section C). Of course, they are really the same structures, but just to make it clear, we'll study each individually.

Let's begin with a quick review of the *Get It Write!* Eight Essential Elements.

1. Characters	All stories are about characters. Story events happen to characters.
2. Character traits	Character traits are any information that makes a character seem clear, real, vivid, and interesting to readers.
3. Goal	A goal is what the main character wants to do *or* get in this story. It's what the character is after in the story.
4. Motive	A motive explains why the goal is important to the character.
5. Conflicts and problems	Conflicts and problems are the obstacles that block a character from reaching a goal.
6. Risk and danger	Risk and danger represent the likelihood that something will go wrong and the consequences (what happens) to the main character when something goes wrong (the trouble the character gets into). Risk and danger create excitement.
7. Struggles	Struggles are what a character does (the action, the plot) to overcome obstacles and reach a goal.
8. Details	Details about the characters, settings, actions, and objects make a story seem real and vivid to readers.

SECTION A : EXPOSITORY WRITING TO PERSUADE

Expository means descriptive or explanatory. *Persuade* means to convince, to cause someone to believe something by reasoning. Combine the two and you have usually short explanatory essays written to cause readers to change their beliefs or opinions and to adopt those of the writer.

What's the difference between a persuasive essay and a story? Really, very little. The key is in the word *reasoning* in the definition of persuade. Through stories, writers cause readers to change opinions and beliefs all the time. We do it by making the reader view the world through the eyes (perspective) of a story character. We use perspective shifts to affect readers' beliefs. In persuasive essays, writers rely more on reasoning to get the job done. In a persuasive essay, it is not the actions (struggles) of the main character that hold readers' attention; it is the reasoning—the persuasive arguments—offered by the writer that do it.

There is one other difference. In a persuasive essay, the main character (the writer) talks directly to the reader. That's not true in a story. Story characters talk to other characters.

Do those differences create any changes in the structure, approach, or creative process of the writer? Let's see and then let's practice building effective persuasive essays.

Activity 63: Where's the Difference? _____

What Students Will Learn:

Students will see the applicability of the *Get It Write!* Eight Essential Elements to expository writing to persuade and will learn the specific identity of each element for this new format.

Time Estimate: 15 minutes

Directions:

This is an introductory activity. Before we pry inside expository essays to learn and understand them as we have done for stories, students should pause to decide if they will need these same elements for this new kind of writing.

Have students fill out Chart #1, the *Get It Write!* Eight Essential Elements in a Persuasive Essay, on their activity worksheet without preliminary discussion. They need to only circle yes or no in the righthand column for each element.

Ex·pos·i·to·ry *adj.* Descriptive and explanatory.

Per·suade *vt.* To cause someone to believe something by reasoning.

Chart #1
The *Get It Write!* Eight Essential Elements in a Persuasive Essay

Element	What It Tells Readers in a Story	Do You Need It in an Expository Essay?
Character	The main character	Yes/No
Character traits	Traits make the character interesting	Yes/No
Goal	What the main character wants to do or get	Yes/No
Motive	Why the character needs that goal	Yes/No
Conflicts and problems	The obstacles that block characters from their goals	Yes/No
Risk and danger	Probability of characters' failing and the consequences of failure	Yes/No
Struggles	What the character does to overcome obstacles and reach the goal	Yes/No
Details	Details of characters, settings, actions, and objects to make the story vivid and real	Yes/No

In the righthand column, all answers are "yes." Successful expository essays depend on the same Eight Essential Elements we have learned for stories. Further, these elements serve the same function and the same purpose as they did in a story. If that is true, then student writers should be able to clearly identify and create each element in the specific format for a persuasive element. Does each element look the same in a persuasive essay as it does in a story?

To find out, have students complete Chart #2 for this activity. Instructions ask them to identify, as specifically as possible, what each of the Get It Write! Eight Essential Elements is in the new format of a persuasive essay. Students should not need more than three or four minutes to complete Chart #2.

Chart #2
Role of the Eight Essential Elements in a Persuasive Essay

Element	What Is It in an Expository Essay to Persuade?
Main character	*Ans: Me, the author****
Character traits	*Ans: Traits that show main character's relationship to topic*
Goal	*Ans: To persuade the reader*
Motive	*Ans: Why this topic (and persuading reader) is important*
Conflicts and problems	*Ans: Erroneous beliefs (ignorance) of the reader*
Risk and danger	*Ans: To the author and to the reader if the author fails to persuade*
Struggles	*Ans: Arguments and information author uses to persuade reader*
Details	*Ans: Details of the characters, settings, actions, and objects*

*** There is one other option for the main character, discussed in the following section.

Let's look at the answers. Some explanation of the wording in the righthand column will be helpful as you discuss these elements with your class.

Students may find this chart conceptually difficult. Still, it is worth having them ponder and struggle with two important questions this chart uncovers:

1. Are essays and stories structurally the same?
2. What do readers of a persuasive essay really need?

Give students several minutes to complete the chart. Whether they successfully complete it or not, the chart will serve as a valuable springboard to the follow-up discussion of each element.

1. **Main character?** The main character is the one readers will follow, the one through whose eyes they will view the world. There are two choices for the identity of this character in a persuasive essay—choices that dictate the structure of the rest of the writing.

    Student writers could choose to designate one individual about whom they are writing as the main character (a sperm whale, a child in Afghanistan, an aphid, a Little League baseball player, or an elementary school student). The writer must select a specific individual to become the main character of their writing and will organize the writing as a nonfiction story. The writer will write a story following the principles laid out in Chapters 1, 2, and 3. Through that story, student writers reveal the reasoning and arguments they hope will persuade readers to adopt a new belief about the subject group.

    The piece will look like, and be developed like, any other story: character, goal, motive, conflicts, and so on. The writer will follow this main character over a period of time, presenting the desired information through the eyes and actions of this character. Every school library has many nonfiction books written for this purpose and in this style. Ask your school librarian to help you find examples.

The other option for the main character is far more common for persuasive essays: student writers become their main characters. As a persuasive essay writer, you want to present your own viewpoint, your own arguments, your own perspective, and your own ideas. That's much easier to do if you are the main character. The rest of this discussion as well as the rest of the activities on expository writing to persuade, will assume that the writer is the main character.

2. **Character traits.** Selected character traits make the main character vivid, real, and interesting to readers. Another key word is *relevant*. While writing a story, you wouldn't present *everything* you created about the main character. You would use only those traits that are relevant to the story. The same is true for an essay.

   Which character traits are relevant for a persuasive essay? Those that describe the main character's relationship to, knowledge of, or history with the assigned essay topic. Those are the character traits writers should use to make the main character interesting in an essay.

3. **Goal.** A goal is what the main character is after. What is the author (the main character) after in a persuasive essay? What does the author want? To persuade the reader to accept and believe the arguments presented in the essay. That's why we call them *persuasive* essays. The goal of the main character is always to persuade.

4. **Motive.** Motive explains why a goal is important. Because the goal is to persuade about something (the essay's topic), persuasive essay writers must show why that topic is important—both important to the main character and vitally important to the reader. Convincing readers to believe arguments and reasoning, in part, depends on convincing them that it is important for them to consider the topic at all.

5. **Obstacles.** Obstacles block characters from goals. In an essay, then, obstacles keep the author from persuading the reader to adopt the writer's beliefs and view. What does that? The current beliefs of the reader (misbeliefs, misconceptions, and ignorance—from the author's viewpoint). In an essay, writers struggle to overcome those misconceptions.

6. **Risk and danger.** In stories, risk and danger represent what could happen to the main character if he or she fails to successfully overcome the obstacles. Risk and danger serve the same function here. Risk and danger describe what will happen to the author (and the community) if the author fails to convince the reader to believe the author's position. Risk and danger are often portrayed as the worst-case scenario.

   Often motive is lumped together with risk and danger in the writing of a persuasive essay. Why should readers care about the topic (motive)? Because of what could happen (risk and danger) if they don't adopt the correct belief and act on it.

7. **Struggles.** Struggles are what the main character *does*. What does an author do in an essay to overcome the ignorance of the reader? The writer provides reasons, beliefs, arguments, ideas, sentiments, and emotional pleas as well as factual information. That is how readers are convinced, essay obstacles are overcome, and goals are met. Reasoned arguments form the plot line of an essay.

8. **Details.** Readers must be able to visualize key essay images in their minds. It is as important for an essay as it is for a story. Details are still what creates those images.

Activity Review

An essay is built on the same structural elements as a story. Those elements serve the same purpose, function, and relationship in an essay that they do in a story. We see in the next activity that they can (and should) be created in the same way and in the sane order that they are created in a story.

Activity 64: Theme versus Goal _____

What Students Will Learn:

Students will learn the meaning and purpose of **theme** in narratives and will learn how to differentiate theme from goal.

Time Estimate: 15 minutes for Part 1; out-of-class work and 20 minutes for in-class discussion for Part 2

Directions:

This activity is divided into two parts. You should begin with a general class discussion of the term *theme* and its relationship to goal and motive.

We did not deal with theme while learning stories because theme is an advanced concept for student creative writers, one that they grow into over time. However, theme is a central element for structuring other expository writing forms. Theme is the students' assigned topic for persuasive pieces and for personal narratives.

But what is a theme? What does it do? *Pinocchio* is about honesty. Pinocchio doesn't think that. He just wants to fit in and be a real boy. But we readers know that his lying (dishonesty) is what gets him into trouble. Honesty is the theme. Being a real boy is the goal. *Snow White* is about jealousy. The queen is so jealous that it turns her into a wicked witch who dies in the end. *Peter Rabbit* is about disobedience. *Goldilocks* is about curiosity. Stories are written about selfishness, self-confidence, faith, perseverance, friendship, greed, laziness, and so on. Those are themes. But the story characters don't think about themes; they think about goals.

Theme *n.* The matter with which a story or essay is chiefly concerned. A narrative's theme is the topic and viewpoint the writer wants the reader to consider. A goal is what the characters inside the narrative focus on and consider.

The goal of the main character is what every story is about *for story characters.* Goal defines where a story will end and the purpose of every scene and story event. What is theme? Theme is what the story is about *for readers.* Theme exists for readers. It makes the story relevant to readers. Theme is what the writer wants to say to readers, what he or she wants readers to ponder while they read.

Writers pick a main character, a goal for that character, obstacles, and struggles that will allow them to explore and write about their chosen theme.

In the expository essays your students write, theme is the assigned topic they are going to write about. Theme may be treated like another writing element for expository writing.

Part 1. Let's begin with a quick review of the difference between theme and goal and with a look at the purpose of theme. Readers understand that goal creates internal story structure. But readers also know to ponder a story's theme and to view the story events in light of the theme.

Have students read these three versions of the same situation and answer the questions that follow on their worksheet. Each uses the same character and goal but presents a different theme by changing the motives, actions, and attitude of the main character.

Version #1

Twelve-year-old Maya wanted some ice cream. In fact, she wanted all the ice cream, and she wanted it now, now, NOW! Why should anyone else get any ice cream until Maya had eaten all she wanted? Which she never would. So everyone else had just better keep their paws off cause Maya really wanted that ice cream!

Who is the main character? *Ans: Maya*

What is her goal? *Ans: To get ice cream*

What is the theme? *Ans: Selfishness*

What do you want to have happen in this story? *Ans: Most readers will want Maya to get her ice cream only if she gives up her selfish ways.*

Version #2

Twelve-year-old Maya wanted some ice cream. But she was sprawled on the couch watching TV and didn't want to have to walk twenty whole feet into the kitchen and miss part of her show to get it. "Mom, get me some ice cream!" But her mother was next door. What a hassle to have to actually get up, dig the container out of the freezer, and scoop it out herself. Someone should get it for her, so she wouldn't have to move. But Maya really wanted that ice cream right now!

Who is the main character? *Ans: Maya*

What is her goal? *Ans: To get ice cream*

What is the theme? *Ans: Laziness*

What do you want to have happen in this story? *Ans: Most readers won't want Maya to get her ice cream until she is forced to overcome her laziness.*

Version #3

Twelve-year-old Maya wanted some ice cream. But every time she had $2.50 saved up to buy a sundae, she'd have to walk past the homeless shelter to reach the ice cream shop. The kids stuck there didn't even have a house or a yard to play in. How could Maya feel right about getting ice cream while they sat in the gutter and watched? So she always gave them the money. But she really wanted that ice cream!

Who is the main character? *Ans: Maya*

What is her goal? *Ans: To get ice cream*

What is the theme? *Ans: Generosity (possibly excessive generosity)*

What do you want to have happen in this story? *Ans: Most readers will want Maya to get her ice cream and some reward or recognition for her efforts to help the homeless children.*

The worksheet then asks students to compare the three versions. How do you feel about Maya and her goal in each version?

Discuss your students' answers as a class. In that discussion, emphasize an understanding of what a theme is, of its relationship to goal, and of the effect of theme on readers.

Part 2. Have students reread two stories they have recently read and enjoyed. They are to identify the main character, that character's goal, and the story's theme for each and write that information on the provided spaces on their student worksheet.

Discuss and compare students' answers. Ensure that your students clearly see the difference between theme and goal. Looking at their combined answers, do the themes fit into categories or types of information? Are they about values? Human beliefs? Hopes? Dreams? Fears?

Activity Review

Theme for an essay is the assigned topic, what your students are told to write about. In a story, theme is something the writer creates for the reader, something the writer wants the reader to ponder. Story themes usually relate to the human condition, to human values, beliefs, and idiosyncrasies. However, theme is an advanced concept for story writing, one your students will grow into as they mature.

Activity 65: Hidden Pieces

What Students Will Learn:

Students will learn to recognize story elements in a persuasive essay and to understand the role and purpose of each.

Time Estimate: 30 minutes

Directions:

Have students read the following persuasive essay and answer the seven questions that follow before conducting a class review and discussion. This essay was written by a sixth-grade girl in California about a proposed city law. I use it here with her permission, having only condensed the narrative of her arguments.

My name is Jordan Fielder and I am a sixth grader at Jefferson Elementary School. I've skateboarded all my life. I even built my own skateboard. My skateboard is much more important to me than my father's bike was to him when he was a boy. It's the only way I have to get around.

Twice in the past month, sidewalk collisions have happened between skateboarders and elderly women. This is a big problem. We have to make our streets safe for everyone.

I want to convince you that skateboarders should be given priority in using the city sidewalks. This problem affects everyone. Our city is responsible for accidents that happen on city property (the sidewalks). Even worse, this situation creates bad feelings and distrust among different groups of residents. And it's bound to happen again and again until we fix it.

You probably believe that sidewalks are for walkers and that the elderly should get preference. You might think that kids don't really need to get around on their own. These beliefs are all wrong.

My best friend was involved in one of the recent collisions. The woman she hit is okay. But my friend broke her wrist in her fall and still has nightmares. All us kids are afraid of what will happen next if the city doesn't make the sidewalks safe.

Here are my six reasons why skateboards should have priority use of the sidewalks.

1. It's easier for pedestrians to step aside and dodge a skateboard than vice versa.

2. Elderly women can take cabs. Kids can't.

3. Modern kids have more hectic schedules (school, after school activities, music, sports, church activities, etc.) than our parents did.

4. Elderly women can take buses to shopping centers. But city buses don't go where I need to go (school, music lessons, church choir practice, soccer practice, etc.).

5. The city has set aside lanes in streets for bikes and needs to do the same for skateboards on the sidewalks.

6. It's not safe for skateboards in the street. They have to ride on the sidewalks and the city needs to create a lane for them where it's safe.

I'm sure you now agree that we must create safe sidewalks for skateboarders and I hope you will join me at the next city council meeting to demand that they do. You'll feel a lot better and safer if you do.

1. Who is the main character? *Ans: Jordon Fielder (from the first line)*

2. What is the essay's theme? *Ans: The obvious, assigned theme for this essay was public use of city sidewalks. But other themes emerge from this essay, including the rights of individuals, public safety, and public acceptance of skateboards as a legitimate mode of transportation.*

3. What is the main character's goal in this essay? *Ans: To persuade readers that skateboarders should be given priority use of the sidewalks*

4. Evaluate this essay: What do you think is good about its structure and writing? What needs improvement? How do you react to it? *Ans: This is a well-written essay. All elements are present. Good sprinkling of details in key moments and images. Relevant character traits are presented. Motive and risk and danger are forcefully presented. The following needs improvement: Jordon's arguments (struggles) drift some and could be more tightly focused and worded to stay on the single topic at hand and to directly address the obstacles she listed in her essay.*

Con•vince *vt.* To persuade by argument or proof. *Convince* and *persuade* may be used interchangeably in a persuasive essay.

5. Five specific lines from this essay are repeated below. Decide which writing element each line represents.

   A. *I've skateboarded all my life. I even built my own skateboard. My skateboard is much more important to me than my father's bike was to him when he was a boy. It's the only way I have to get around.*

   Is this:

   1. Conflict
   2. Motive
   3. Character traits

   Ans: 3. Character traits

   B. *You probably believe that sidewalks are for walkers and that the elderly should get preference. You might think that kids don't really need to get around on their own. These beliefs are all wrong.*

   Is this:

   1. Risk and danger
   2. Conflict
   3. Struggle

   Ans: 2. Conflict. Jordon is stating the readers' beliefs that she thinks block her from reaching her goal.

   C. *This problem affects everyone. Our city is responsible for accidents that happen on city property (the sidewalks). Even worse, this situation creates bad feelings and distrust among different groups of residents. And it's bound to happen again and again until we fix it.*

   Is this:

   1. Motive
   2. Risk and danger
   3. Character traits

   Ans: 1. Motive. Jordon is saying why this topic is important to herself and to the reader.

   D. *I want to convince you that skateboarders should be given priority in using the city sidewalks.*

   Is this:

   1. Motive
   2. Goal

3. Theme

Ans: 2. Goal. This is what Jordon wants to do.

E. *Twice in the past month sidewalk collisions have happened between skateboarders and elderly women. This is a big problem. We have to make our streets safe for everyone.*

Is this:

1. Conflict

2. Theme

3. Struggle

Ans: 2. Theme. Jordon is telling us what she is going to write about.

6. What is the last paragraph? *Ans: The resolution of the main character's goal—she assumes that she has convinced the reader ("I'm sure you now agree that we must create . . .") and a final sequel ("You'll feel a lot better . . ."). These are the same elements we find in a successful story resolution.*

7. Jordon listed six arguments in favor of her position. What element do they represent? *Ans: Struggles. They are the plot, her attempt to overcome the obstacles she has acknowledged are in her way and to gain her goal.*

Review and discuss the answers to all seven questions. All but Question 4 are factual questions asking students to extract specific information from the essay and to match that information with the *Get It Write!* Eight Essential Elements. Question 4 allows students some latitude in their evaluation, assessment, and opinion of the essay. Allow students to voice their opinion and to defend their view with story material and the *Get It Write!* concepts. Do not allow your students to digress into a debate on the topic Jordon wrote about. Keep the class's focus on the effectiveness of her essay.

Activity Review

Persuasive essays depend on the same Eight Essential Elements used in stories to engage and captivate a reader. Just as plot-based stories are less effective than character-based stories, so, too, plot-based (information) essays are less effective in holding and swaying readers than are character-based essays. Develop character and a few relevant traits first; motive to support the persuasive goal, second; and reasons, arguments, and information, third.

Is this the only successful model for expository writing? No, of course not. However, this particular structure takes advantage of the natural allure and power of stories in a way other models don't. Using the *Get It Write!* model changes (enhances) the way readers relate to the material and to the writing. It naturally draws readers in and creates important purpose for every element included in the writing.

Students can study and master the Eight Essential Elements while developing their writing skills with stories (fiction or nonfiction) and then be ready to create powerful and successful expository pieces. It's an easy, specific writing guide that has shown itself to be consistently successful, and it makes sense to students struggling to master narrative writing.

Activity 66: Preventing Persuasive Planning Pitfalls _____

What Students Will Learn:

Students will learn the advantages and disadvantages of alternate choices when composing persuasive essays.

Time Estimate: 10 minutes for Part 1; 30 minutes for Part 2

Directions:

This activity is divided into two parts. Part 1 allows students to experience both of the most common expository writing traps—most will create plot first and will write before they fully create their essay. Having demonstrated those two big pitfalls in action, Part 2 guides students through a better approach to creating a persuasive essay—one that uses the *Get It Write!* Eight Essential Elements.

Part 1. Here is a theme, or topic, for a persuasive essay: Children should be paid $8.00 per hour to do homework. Do you agree or disagree and why?

Tell your students that they get one minute to write as much of this essay as they can in that short amount of time. Certainly, they won't finish, but they should write as much of their essay as they can. Space is provided on the student worksheet for this writing.

After one minute, have students look at the *kind* of information they wrote. The student worksheet offers five choices:

Es·say *n.* A writing dealing with a particular subject. Essays are a form of narrative writing. They may be written to persuade, to inform, to amuse, to inflame, to shock, and so on.

A. I provided arguments in favor of my position.

B. I introduced a character and goal.

C. I provided rich sensory details to paint an initial image in the minds of readers.

D. I established the importance of the topic to readers.

E. I never got to write anything because it took almost the whole minute to plan my essay.

Your students most likely answered **A.** But that's the *plot* of their essay. Just as we naturally think first of story plots (and thereby make the writing as hard as possible), so, too, we naturally want to start with the plot of an essay. That approach will result in the same disastrously boring product that results from starting a story by planning plot first.

Also point out that few if any of your students paused to plan before they began writing (create first; write second) and that few (if any) thought first of establishing an interesting character before launching into their arguments.

Just as with stories, student writers have to consciously develop the habits of thinking of character first and of creating before they write.

Part 2. Let's work through the development of a persuasive expository essay. We'll use the same assigned topic: Children should be paid $8.00 per hour to do homework. Do you agree or disagree and why?

Have students pause after each question for class discussion and agreement before continuing to the next question. Use the paragraphs that follow each question to direct the discussion.

1. Who will be the main character?

   A. The school principal

   B. A parent of a student at the school

C. You, the student writer

D. The president of The United States

Ans: C. You, the student

Any of the four provided choices could work. However, A, B, and D would be much harder for a student to write about. The writer would have to conduct interviews and research to be able to view the topic through the eyes of their new main character and to present the views, opinions, arguments, beliefs, and attitudes of the main character. That is doable, but not within the severe time constraints of a timed writing assessment.

C is a far better choice. The writer already knows everything he or she needs to know about the main character and can proceed directly to planning the essay.

2. Which of the following should we use in this essay to make this character interesting? Circle all those that could appropriately be used.

Tell students not to worry about whether or not each statement actually applies to them. They should pick those that fit with the role of relevant character traits.

A. You get good grades and do lots of homework.

B. Your family is poor. You *have* to work. But having homework every day keeps you from being able to get a good job.

C. You like money and want more.

D. You want to buy a twenty-horsepower, chrome-plated power skateboard.

E. You like to have a full hour to get dressed in the morning.

F. You want to be rich.

G. Because of homework, you can't work after school, so you have to work every weekend and every holiday.

Ans: A, B, and G

C, D, E, and F *are* traits about the main character. D and E are even interesting. However, none of these four is either relevant to the topic or supportive of the main character for this essay. The character traits included in an essay should make readers feel interested in and supportive of the main character.

A, B, and G are traits relevant to the assigned topic and will make readers sympathetic to what the main character will have to say.

3. Write what you want to be the goal of the main character in this persuasive essay. *Ans: To persuade readers to believe the writer's viewpoint*

The goal of a persuasive essay is always to persuade the reader to believe and accept the position of the writer.

4. Which of the following should we include in the essay to make the theme and goal seem important to readers? Again, don't worry about whether or not each actually applies to you.

A. Homework is easy.

B. I think it would be cool to get paid to study.

C. We need to improve the state educational system.

D. The educational system is failing its basic purpose and nothing else has worked.

Ans: C and D

A seems to argue against the position that students should be paid. If it's easy, students shouldn't get paid to do it.

B may be true but doesn't make the topic important to readers.

C and D (assume for the sake of this essay that they are true in your state) make the topic important to everyone and should be circled.

The student worksheet asks students to create one additional motive, or reason that the topic is important to readers. Allow various students to read their creation. Discuss each as a class and decide if it fulfills the basic function of a motive—it must make the topic seem important and relevant to both writer and reader.

5. In general terms, what obstacles will the main character face?

Ans: The beliefs of the reader, which is always true in a persuasive essay

6. Which of the following beliefs would make good obstacles to address in this essay?

   A. Kids don't need money.

   B. Homework is just part of life and school. You shouldn't get paid for it.

   C. School days are shorter than they used to be.

   D. The state and district have no money to pay students to do homework.

   E. Children should do more chores around the house.

   F. Kids should cook dinner and clean up afterward.

   G. Kids already get allowances.

Ans: A, B, D, and G make good obstacles. Writers will use the ones they think they can argue against the best.

Obstacles in an essay are the reader's beliefs, values, and attitudes that block the writer from persuading the reader and that the writer hopes to overcome in the essay. A, B, D, and G serve that function; C, E, and F do not. The obstacles to list in an essay are the ones you think you can argue against. Make a list of all the major obstacles. Make a list of all of your reasons and arguments. See which obstacles you can argue against and list those in the essay.

7. Now it's time to plan the plot, time for your students to list their arguments. They are instructed to write four strong arguments they could use to support their position. Here are seven arguments students could use. (These are not listed on the student worksheet.) See how many others they create. If the class questions the value of any argument offered by another student, the student who wrote it should identify the specific obstacles his or her argument is designed to overcome and how it supports the stated goal.

   A. Getting paid for homework will motivate students to learn more and will make learning more important.

   B. A better educated community is a better community for everyone.

   C. The program will eventually pay for itself since better educated students will get higher paying jobs and pay more taxes.

   D. The real goal is to educate America's children. This will help do it.

   E. Kids face far greater demands for money (lunch money, sports, entertainment, clothes, etc.) than did their parents when they were kids.

   F. This is an easy way to monitor homework efforts to see if students study efficiently.

   G. Homework is important. Paying kids for doing it will reinforce its importance in adults' minds.

The basic information to form a successful essay has now been created. The student writer has two more tasks before writing:

1. Decide on the most effective order for presenting their information (This is like laying out the plot sequence in a story.)

2. Decide which images, statements, and scenes need the rich details that will make them real, vivid, and memorable to readers

We know the ending—the writer will assume that he or she has achieved their goal and has convinced the reader and will so state. There are, however, real choices for how to start. In Activity 56, you learned four effective kinds of openings for a story that immediately hook readers. Those same options exist for an essay. You will have a chance to work with them in Activity 68.

Having made these simple plotting decisions, your students should be ready to write. Even if students spend three minutes planning these elements, available writing time will not be seriously reduced and the writing will be far easier and more effective.

Activity Review

Students fall into the same writing traps with an essay that plague student story writing. These pitfalls should be corrected for essays using the same strategies and techniques learned for story writing.

First, pause to plan an essay before writing—even if available time is tightly limited. Second, plan the character, traits, and motive before thinking of obstacles and persuasive arguments.

Working through the elements each time they write is a habit all students can develop. It just takes a little practice.

Activity 67: What's Wrong with *That?* _____

What Students Will Learn:

Students will learn to evaluate and correct persuasive essays.

Time Estimate: 20 minutes for each essay

Directions:

This activity involves two short persuasive essays. Students are asked to read and evaluate each and to then decide how best to improve the essay. Pause to discuss the first essay before allowing students to venture on to the second. That way students can apply to the second essay both what they learned while editing the first essay and what they learned from the class review and discussion.

Essay #1. Read the following short essay and answer the following questions. The assigned theme is **the most important part of a good education.**

I'm a fifth grader and go to a school that doesn't have any sports equipment. But on weekends I go to the high school track and can already high jump as well as anyone on the high school track team. I love to high jump. It feels like I escape gravity, like I can fly. I want to persuade you to agree that elementary school students should be allowed to take electives. We don't get any choices at our school. We all have to go to music and to computer lab. But I'd rather study ancient history and archeology.

Auth•or *n.* A person whose profession is writing. The writer of a published work.

Writ•er *n.* Someone who forms letters on paper with pen, pencil, or other writing instrument.

Writer is a general term for anyone who writes. The term *author* specifically refers to a professional writer who has written published works.

1. What are the strengths of this essay? *Ans: An interesting character is presented (even though the provided traits aren't relevant to the theme). A goal is clearly stated (even though it doesn't relate to the assigned theme).*

2. What writing elements are included in this essay segment? *Ans: Character traits, goal ("persuade you to agree . . ."), and conflicts ("We don't get any choice . . ." and "all have to go to music")*

3. What problems do you find with it? *Ans: Neither the essay nor the stated goal relate to the assigned theme. Information provided to make the main character interesting doesn't relate to the theme or goal. No motive is provided to make the theme important to the writer or readers. No real arguments are provided in favor of electives (the stated goal) or that relate to the assigned theme. There is no resolution to the essay.*

4. If you were the writer of this essay, what would you do to improve it? *Ans: Change character traits and goal to match the assigned theme. Provide a motive to make this topic important and identify obstacles that can be argued against. Create meaningful arguments to use in favor of the goal and topic. Finally, create a short resolution paragraph.*

Essay #2. Read the following short essay and answer the questions below. The assigned theme is children should be allowed to vote.

It's dumb that kids have to live here but can't vote. Adults just want to hold all the power. Parents rarely let kids in on important family decisions. It's the same for voting. Adults are afraid to let kids help make important community and national decisions—decisions that affect us as much as them. Kids could probably do better than adults. After all, kids' decisions didn't mess up the environment or get the country into debt.

1. What are the strengths of this essay? *Ans: Identifies obstacles, implies a goal, and provides some arguments to overcome the stated obstacles*

2. What writing elements are included in this essay segment? *Ans: Conflicts ("Adults want to hold...," "Parents rarely let...," and "Adults are afraid to let..."), struggles ("Kids could probably do much better"), and risk and danger ("mess up the environmnet.")*

3. What problems do you find with it? *Ans: No character is identified. No character traits are provided. No goal is stated. Nothing is provided to make either the goal or the theme important. Arguments are weak and ineffective. Tone is antagonistic, which will never persuade anyone.*

4. If you were the writer of this essay, what would you do to improve it? *Ans: Clearly identify a character, relevant traits, and motive to make the issue important and to tell readers who is talking. Change the tone to be more positive. Specify obstacles and create strong arguments to overcome those obstacles. Create a resolution sentence.*

Have students pick one of these two themes and write their own persuasive essay ensuring that their effort avoids each of the problems they identified. Space is not provided on the student worksheet for this writing assignment.

Activity Review

Essays depend on the same Eight Essential Elements that define and structure creative writing. Students can learn to identify each in an essay and to reword and improve those that fail to do their job in the essay. Have students review their own previous writing and evaluate and repair it as they have done for the two brief essays in this activity.

Activity 68: The Way to Begin _____

What Students Will Learn:

Students will learn the three most effective beginnings to a persuasive essay and the strengths of each.

Time Estimate: 30 to 40 minutes for Part 1; 40 minutes for Part 2

Directions:

This activity is divided into two parts. Part 1 allows students to compare an opening they create for a persuasive essay with two provided openings. Part 2 helps students explore effective alternatives for essay openings.

Part 1. Students are given this theme: **Kids should be allowed to talk as much and as loudly as they want in the cafeteria at lunch.** They are asked to write the first four sentences of their essay on this topic. This should be completed without preliminary discussion.

Sen·tence *n.* A group of words that states or asks something. A sentence commonly contains both a subject (noun or pronoun) and a predicate (verb).

Note how many students take time to plan before they rush into writing and how many don't. Mention and discuss this aspect of their essay writing after they have completed their first four sentences.

Their worksheet next asks them to evaluate two provided openings on the same theme (shown here) and to compare their opening sentences to these openings. Allow students to complete their worksheet and then discuss their answers.

Opening #1

I'm a sixth grader and am bussed to school from across town. I don't make friends easily, and the ones I have are very important to me. We can't hang out together after school because the busses leave right away, so the only times we get to see each other are between classes and at lunch. I think students should be allowed to talk in the cafeteria during lunch because it's important to spend time with friends and to share with, talk to, and learn about each other.

1. Evaluate this essay opening. Which essential elements are here? *Ans: Character, character traits (details), goal, motive, obstacles, and several arguments in support of the goal*
2. Does it draw your interest? Why? *Ans: Yes, this opening creates sympathy with the main character by introducing a character and providing relevant traits. It provides a clear goal and has started to list arguments in favor of that goal.*

Opening #2

What right do teachers have to tell us we can't talk at lunch? We have to be quiet in class, quiet at PE, and now we have to be quiet in the cafeteria, too. We gotta get to talk sometime and lunchtime is that time. We're supposed to be relaxing, and this isn't some military school where we have to sit at attention all day.

3. Evaluate this essay opening. Which essential elements are here? *Ans: Two arguments, an implied goal (get to talk at lunch), and a conflict (teachers tell us we can't)*

4. Does it draw your interest? Why? *Ans: Not as much as the first. Readers need to know who's talking and the goal and topic need to be made important (motive and risk and danger)*

The student worksheet allows students to compare these two openings with their own by completing the following questions:

5. Which writing elements did I include in my opening?
6. Does my own opening draw my interest and make me want to read more? Why?
7. Which of the three openings (mine and the two provided on the worksheet) do I like best? Why?

There is some room for personal opinion and discussion on why an opening either does or does not draw a particular reader's interest (Questions 2 and 4). Focus the final discussion on which of the three openings students like best and why (Question 7). Encourage them to be specific in explaining why they liked their favorite opening. They should be able to articulate their answer in terms of the *Get It Write!* Eight Essential Elements.

Part 2. We are now ready to look at the effectiveness of other kinds of narrative openings. First, review Activity 56 with your class. That activity looked at alternative effective openings for a story and identified four types of story openings that are consistently effective:

1. Present the first five (or six) writing elements right away to bring the reader into the heart of the story.
2. Focus the opening scene on making the main character interesting by showing both the character doing something interesting and characteristics of the character's personality and attitudes (provide interesting character traits).
3. Establish risk and danger by introducing the antagonist being cruel and powerful.
4. Show an event that makes the main character's eventual goal important (create motive).

Do those same types of openings work as well in persuasive essays? Let's see. Four openings are shown below. Each is an opening for a persuasive essay on this theme: **Should students wear uniforms to school?**

Have students read and evaluate each four-sentence opening and answer the questions that follow.

Opening #1

> *Sports teams wear uniforms. Military people wear uniforms. Police and firemen wear uniforms. In some restaurants waiters wear uniforms. But prisoners wear uniforms, too. So did people forced to live in World War II internment camps and concentration camps.*

Evaluate this opening using the following questions:

1. Which essential elements are included? *Ans: Probably plot or argument. Right now, it is only information without a purpose or point. But without a statement of theme and goal, readers can't be sure.*
2. Does this opening match one of the four types of effective openings listed previously? If so, which one? *Ans: No*
3. Do you find any problems with this opening? *Ans: Readers need to know what the point is, what the essay is about.*

4. Does it draw your interest? Why? *Ans: Only a little. Readers don't have a reason to listen or to pay attention.*

5. What do you need to know next? What questions are on your mind about this essay? *Ans: Who's talking (character) and what are they trying to tell us (goal)?*

Opening #2

I know a family with four school-age children. The children act like robots, forced to dress like every other child, act like every other child, think like every other child. Their individuality, their uniqueness, has been squashed by the school's effort to require uniforms and make everyone the same. Worse, the parents can't afford the hundreds of dollars each semester for school uniforms and have to choose between uniforms and food for the family. The children go to school hungry and undernourished in their crisp school uniforms. This could be the bleak reality many families in our own community face if students are forced to wear school uniforms everyday.

Evaluate this opening using the following questions:

1. Which essential elements are included? *Ans: Risk and danger—the worst-case image of what could happen if we don't act—and theme (teachers' pay), details*

2. Does this opening match one of the four types of effective openings listed previously? If so, which one? *Ans: Yes, this opening matches Type C by establishing risk and danger first.*

3. Do you find any problems with this opening? *Ans: No, it is an effective opening, though it may be overstated and melodramatic in its presentation.*

4. Does it draw your interest? Why? *Ans: Yes, the image is vivid and the topic is important to everybody.*

5. What do you need to know next? What questions are on your mind about this essay? *Ans: Who's talking (character) and what are they trying to tell us (goal)?*

Opening #3

Imagine a school and community where prejudice and snobbery do not exist, a school where no child is picked on by classmates, where peer pressure doesn't force families to waste countless dollars on the latest fad and fashion. Imagine a school where all children walk in equal, where status is based on accomplishment, not on buying power, where dollars count less than hard work and intelligence. It may sound like utopia, but it is really much closer than you might think. The first step is to adopt school uniforms.

Evaluate this opening using the following questions:

1. Which essential elements are included? *Ans: Motive, goal, theme, and details*

2. Does this opening match one of the four types of effective openings listed previously? If so, which one? *Ans: Yes, it matches Type D by presenting motive first (establishing the importance of the goal and theme).*

3. Do you find any problems with this opening? *Ans: No, it is an effective opening.*

4. Does it draw your interest? Why? *Ans: Yes, it paints a vivid and interesting image and makes readers curious to read more.*

5. What do you need to know next? What questions are on your mind about this essay? *Ans: Who's talking (character) and what are they trying to tell us (goal)?*

Opening #4

> *Wearing uniforms could be bad for lots of kids, and not fair to some. Some might be hurt by it, and most don't like the idea.*

Evaluate this opening using the following questions:

1. Which essential elements are included? *Ans: It's hard to tell because readers don't know what the essay is about yet. Probably arguments (struggles), but they are very vague, general, and unsupported.*

2. Does this opening match one of the four types of effective openings listed previously? If so, which one? *Ans: No, starting with arguments is always a weaker start than starting with character, goal, and motive.*

3. Do you find any problems with this opening? *Ans: A severe lack of details makes it hard to visualize the images, so the arguments don't interest the reader.*

4. Does it draw your interest? Why? *Ans: No, neither details nor essential essay elements (character, traits, goal, motive) are provided.*

5. What do you need to know next? What questions are on your mind about this essay? *Ans: Who's talking (character) and what are they talking about?*

Review your class's answers and compare these four openings.

> **Openings #1 and #4** present plot (arguments) only and fail to grab readers' attention—just as plot-based stories typically fail to grab readers.
>
> **Opening #3** starts by establishing motive (why the topic of teacher pay is important to consider). By including sufficient strong details to paint vivid images in the readers' minds, this opening draws readers' interest and makes them curious to read on.
>
> **Opening #2** establishes risk and danger to hook the reader. That opening provides enough details to create vivid, interesting images.

Draw students' attention to their answer to the last question after each opening. What readers need most after each of these openings is to establish character, character traits to make the character interesting, goal, and motive—the first four *Get It Write!* story elements. Remind students that that information is exactly what readers needed in a story.

> All the writer has done in each opening is to change the order in which the *Get It Write!* Eight Essential Elements have been presented. In Opening #3, the writer began with Element #4 (motive) and then needed to backtrack and present Elements #1, #2, and #3 before presenting the arguments that would persuade readers. Establishing the importance of the goal and topic (motive) is the same as a story opening that first shows an event that makes the main character's goal important.

In Opening #2 the writer first established risk and danger (Element #6). This is like opening a story by introducing the antagonist, and it can be an extremely interesting and effective opening.

Activity Review

Many student writers want to open with a more dramatic hook than the classic opening that presents the story elements in order. This is simple to do. Just invert the order in which several of the key elements are presented. For added drama, begin by describing the theme and its importance to the reader (Opening #3). Paint a picture of the world as the writer wants it to be (and as the writer wants to persuade readers to want it to be). Show how wonderful readers' lives could be if everyone adopted the correct views and beliefs.

Alternatively, show how dismal and unacceptable life will be if readers don't correct their thinking (Opening #2 and #4). This opening begins by establishing risk and danger—like opening a story by showing the antagonist in action. Either establishes the relevance and importance of the theme to the reader. Now jump back and introduce the main character and his or her relationship with this subject theme. The student is off and running with a powerful, dramatic opening and a solid structure to back it up.

How do the concepts presented in Activities 64 through 69 prepare your students for greater success on standardized writing assessments? Here are four important ways:

1. By creating and presenting the *Get It Write!* Eight Essential Elements (augmented by including theme) in order, students are given an effective outline for quickly identifying and creating the information that will make their essay shine.

2. Students are given virtually a sentence-by-sentence outline for writing their essay by following, in order, the Eight Essential Elements.

3. They are given powerful alternative openings to consider by inverting the order in which they present the *Get It Write!* elements. These will make their essays stand out for additional recognition and merit by reviewers.

4. They have a checklist (the Eight Essential Elements) that ensures they create and present the information in assessment rubrics that reviewers use.

   • Students must write with clear and interesting language. They do this by developing and presenting rich details for character, traits, obstacles, motives, risk and danger, and struggles.

   • Students must stick to the assigned topic. They do this by clearly stating goal, theme, and resolution.

   • Students must develop the assigned topic. They do this by clearly articulating goal, motive, obstacles, and struggles.

- Students should write with a clear, definite voice (present a sense of the writer). They do this by developing and including character, traits, and details.
- Students should present a clear and logical flow to the essay. They do this by creating and clearly presenting the Eight Essential Elements.

Activity 69: A Persuasive Approach _____

What Students Will Learn:

Students will reinforce their understanding of effective essay structure and of the process of creating a persuasive essay.

Time Estimate: 20 minutes for Part 1; 20 minutes for Part 2

Directions:

This activity is divided into two parts. Part 1 takes students through the process of planning (creating) a persuasive essay. Part 2 gives them a chance to write one. Discuss Part 1 with students before allowing them to begin to write in Part 2.

Students' assigned theme is **what my town needs most.**

Part 1. The student worksheet instructs students to show their step-by-step planning for this persuasive essay before they begin to write. In order, as they plan (create) each new writing element of essay information, they are told to write the type of information they are gong to create and to then write a brief summary of what they are going to say in the essay for that element. (They don't need to use eight planning steps. Tell them to use as many as they need.)

Give students no more than ten minutes to complete Part 1. Five minutes may be a more realistic time limit. When faced with a persuasive essay on a standardized writing assessment,

---

Create first; write second

- When you *create,* create the Eight Essential Elements.
- When you *write,* write the details.

---

they will only be able to devote a few minutes to planning if they are to be able to complete their writing within the allotted time limit. A good rule of thumb is for them to plan on using 15% of their available time on planning and 85% on writing and editing.

Review and discuss your students' answers. First, review the order in which they created information and the type of information they chose to create. Did they create *Get It Write!* Eight Essential Elements? Did they create them in order, beginning with identification of the main character?

It is not essential for students to start with character and character traits when planning a persuasive essay because the identity of the main character is always the writer and is already known. Students might want to define their theme and goal first (what they think their town needs most) and then backtrack to character and traits. They might want to jump next to outlining their arguments or their motive (why their topic and goal are important to readers). However, it is important for them to have considered and outlined each of the *Get It Write!* Eight Essential Elements during this planning period.

Next, have students read what they wrote as they summarized each element. Did they identify strong details (information that is specific, unique, and vivid), or did they write in vague generalities that will not spark readers' interest?

Give them a few minutes to revise and improve the detailed information they have created.

Part 2. Allow students to now write the essay they have outlined. Give them a time limit generally equal to about 85% of the time they would be given during a writing assessment (assume that the planning process consumed 15% of their total available time).

As time permits, allow students to share their essays. As an optional add-on activity have several students read their essays to the entire class and have the class critique the work, focusing on how each of the elements was developed and presented.

Activity Review

Expository writing to persuade relies on the same elements that students learned and mastered when working with stories. If students develop the habit of creating and presenting in their writing those same Eight Essential Elements when they write to persuade, their essays will develop a depth and interest that will set them well ahead of other students' essays.

SECTION B: PERSONAL NARRATIVES

A *narrative* is something written in prose style. *Personal* means of or pertaining to a specific person. Combine them together and you have a short essay written to tell something about a specific person. That person is usually—but not necessarily—the essay's author.

Is there any difference between a personal narrative and a persuasive essay? Activity 71 examines that question. Activities 72 through 74 then examine the structure of, and process of building, successful personal narratives.

Activity 70: Personal versus Persuasive _____

What Students Will Learn:

Students will explore the requirements of a personal narrative and see if the same elements that define stories and persuasive essays also apply to personal narratives.

Time Estimate: 10 minutes for each part

Directions:

This activity is divided into two parts. Part 1 allows students to decide if the elements they need to create for a personal narrative are the same as those they have created for stories and persuasive essays. Part 2 focuses on themes for personal narratives.

Part 1. Should students use the same Eight Essential Elements for a personal narrative that they used for a persuasive essay? Are there any differences in how students will create each element for this new expository writing form? Are there any of the Eight Essential Elements personal narrative writers don't need to create and include in their writing? Are there any new elements that personal narrative writers need to consider that story and persuasive essay writers don't?

Per·son·al *adj.* Of or pertaining to a specific person. Personal essays are normally about the writer and present that person's experiences, feelings, and views or about the experiences, feelings, and views of other persons important to the writer.

These are the questions students are asked to ponder and answer on the student worksheet. Give them only a few minutes to complete this part of the activity before you lead a review and discussion of their answers.

1. Should you use the same Eight Essential Elements for a personal narrative that you used for a persuasive essay? *Ans: Yes, personal narratives are stories.*
2. Should you create any of these Eight Essential Elements differently for a personal narrative than you would for a persuasive essay? *Ans. Yes, personal narrative writers view goal, motive, and struggle as they would when writing a story than when writing a persuasive essay.*
3. Are there any of the Eight Essential Elements personal narrative writers don't need to create and include in their writing? *Ans: No, all narrative writing uses the same Eight Essential Elements.*
4. Are there any new elements that personal narrative writers need to consider that story and persuasive essay writers don't? *Ans: No*

Use the following paragraphs as a guide for your class discussion about these four answers.

The central theme of this discussion is personal narratives are the same as stories—they are stories—and should be viewed as such by student writers. Their writing will be more successful if they search for each of the Eight Essential Elements and incorporate them into their personal narrative writing.

Only Question 2's answer requires some examination and explanation. Each element of a personal narrative much more closely resembles a story than was true of persuasive essays.

Character. The main character is the person being written about. Most often, that person is the student writer (it *is* a personal narrative). But it need not be. The main character could be a grandparent, parent, sibling, pet, or friend—anyone with whom the writer is connected and about whom the writer could write from personal knowledge.

Character traits. The tight focus of a persuasive essay forced student writers to limit themselves to using only information relevant to the theme in making themselves interesting to readers. This is not the case in personal narratives. As is true for stories, personal narrative writers are free to use whatever traits fit with their story.

Goal. The main character's goal in a persuasive essay is always to persuade *the reader*. The writer (main character) talks directly to the reader. This is not so in a story and not so in a personal narrative. In a personal narrative—as in a story—the goal of the main character is whatever that character needs to do or get in this narrative and could be anything that meets the writer's needs and the assigned theme.

Motive. The motive in a personal narrative is exactly the same as in a story. Motive explains why the main character wants the goal—why it is so important to that character.

Conflicts and problems. Obstacles have not changed. They block the main character from reaching the goal and create risk and danger for the main character.

Struggle. In a persuasive essay, the main character provides reasoned arguments to persuade the reader and achieve the goal. In a personal narrative—just as in a story—the main character will *act*, do things, in his or her attempts to reach the goal. The struggles in a personal narrative are not information provided to convince but the actions and events undertaken by the main character.

Details. Details are unchanged. The details about characters, settings, events, and objects make the narrative vivid and interesting.

Part 2. It is valuable for students to glance at an assigned theme and recognize the narrative style they will have to write. It will help them organize their thinking and planning and will speed the process of successfully developing each element.

The student worksheet offers the following seven possible essay themes and asks students to identify which are themes for a personal narrative. Give students only a minute or two to complete this part of their worksheet before reviewing and discussing their answers.

1. What is your favorite color and why?
2. Tell about a time you were scared.
3. What's the most important thing about a free society?
4. Tell about your best birthday.
5. Write something about your favorite relative.
6. Write everything you know about sharks.
7. Should the police be allowed to listen in on anybody's telephone conversation?

Ans: 1, 2, 4, and 5 are personal narrative themes.

Let's look at the possible choices.

Numbers 3 and 7 are persuasive essay themes. The writer's assigned goal is to state a belief and persuade readers to believe it also.

Number 6 is the subject of an informative expository essay. It asks the writer to gather information and prepare a report to inform the reader.

Numbers 1, 2, 4, and 5 ask the writer to express something personal. Information about sharks is not personal to the writer. The writer will not try to persuade the reader to also believe that the writer's favorite color or best birthday should also be the reader's favorite and best. Each reader has his or her own favorites. The essay will share something about the writer (the person) by explaining why one color is the writer's favorite. That makes it a personal narrative.

Activity Review

Personal narratives are structured and developed identically to stories. Using the assigned theme as a prompt, student writers should develop the Eight Essential Elements for a personal narrative just as they would for a story. The same major strategies apply: create first; write second. Create the Eight Essential Elements but write the details.

Planning, however, is even more important for a personal narrative than it is for a story. Without adequate preplanning, student writers tend not to include enough relevant character information and character reaction to engage readers. They also tend to omit critical scenic and character details that readers need.

Activity 71: The Personal Elements _____

What Students Will Learn:

Students will learn to recognize the Eight Essential Elements in a personal narrative.

Time Estimate: 25 minutes

Directions:

The following personal narrative is included on the student worksheet. Have students read this narrative and answer the questions that follow. Have students complete their worksheet before reviewing the answers as a class.

The assigned theme is to **tell about a time you were scared.**

Per•spec•tive *n.* Evaluation of events according to a particular way of looking at them.

View•point *n.* A vantage point, a place from which to view events.

Common writing perspectives include first person, third person, and omniscient. Personal essays are most commonly written in first person. Viewpoint identifies the character readers will most closely follow and through whose eyes they will view the events of the writing. For personal essays this is usually the writer.

> *Sunny Saturday afternoon is not the sort of time you'd expect to get scared—well, certainly not me, anyway. I was out behind the garage with a wire brush cleaning rust off my bike chain. I heard our cat hiss and screech and saw him bolt down the driveway. I heard our dog whimper and saw her scurry across the backyard with her tail between her legs.*
>
> *I dropped my cleaning rag and ran to the back door, but it was closed and locked. I pounded on the door and yelled, "Mom!?" No one answered.*
>
> *Just that fast I was scared. Really scared. Something awful must be happening. But I didn't know what. It was the not knowing that really scared me. I had to find out, and I knew I'd be scared until I did.*
>
> *I ran around to the front door. It was unlocked, and I slipped inside, heart pounding. My mother and sister stood plastered against one corner of the dining room wall. Their eyes were wide with terror as they stared at the floor.*
>
> *There a huge poisonous snake was curled, staring back at them, its triangular head swaying on its long neck, its tongue flicking at the air. It was eight-feet long, easy.*
>
> *Heck, snakes don't scare me. I grabbed a pillow and walked over jiggling the pillow to make the snake strike at that. When it did, I grabbed its neck, hauled it outside, and stuffed it in a big ice chest until animal control came to take it away.*
>
> *Being scared is a funny thing. The snake terrified my mother, sister, dog, and cat. But not me. I was just as scared, but I was only scared of the unknown.*

1. Is this a personal narrative? *Ans: Yes, it tells readers about an event, a moment, in one person's life. It is not a factual report about big snakes or about the writer's house. It doesn't try to persuade readers to agree with anything. It simply tells about a personal incident.*

2. Who is the main character? *Ans: The writer, but not enough character traits are included to tell us who that is.*

3. What character traits are included? *Ans: The writer owns a bike, apparently takes care of it, isn't afraid of snakes, doesn't expect to get scared on a Saturday afternoon, but does get afraid of the unknown.*

4. Several individual lines from this narrative are repeated here. Decide which writing element (or elements) are included in that line and circle the correct answer. Several important parts of a

narrative in addition to the Eight Essential Elements may be listed for you to consider (resolution, sequel, opening, etc).

A. *I heard our cat hiss and screech and saw him bolt down the driveway. I heard our dog whimper and saw her scurry across the backyard with her tail between her legs.*

1. Character traits
2. Resolution
3. Motive
4. Goal

Ans: 3. Motive. This helps explain why the main character was scared and, thus, needed to find out what was happening.

B. *I grabbed a pillow and walked over jiggling the pillow to make the snake strike at that. When it did, I grabbed its neck, hauled it outside, and stuffed it in a big ice chest until animal control came to take it away.*

1. Humor
2. Struggles
3. Risk and danger
4. Goal

Ans: 2. Struggles. This is what the main character does, an action.

C. *I had to find out, and I knew I'd be scared until I did.*

1. Character traits and motive
2. Conflict and problem and risk and danger
3. Goal
4. Goal and motive

Ans: 4. Goal and motive. "I had to find out" is a statement of this character's goal. "I knew I'd be scared until I did" explains why that goal is important to the character and is therefore a motive.

D. *There a huge poisonous snake was curled, staring back at them, its triangular head swaying on its long neck, its tongue flicking at the air. It was eight-feet long, easy.*

1. Risk and danger
2. Character
3. Struggles
4. Details

Ans: 1. Risk and danger. A poisonous snake is a danger to the characters. However, Number 4, Details, is also correct since details about the snake are being used to establish risk and danger.

E. *I dropped my cleaning rag and ran to the back door, but it was closed and locked. I pounded on the door and yelled, "Mom!?" No one answered.*

1. Opening hook
2. Struggles
3. Character traits
4. Risk and danger

Ans: 2. Struggles. This describes a series of actions, things that the character does.

F. *Just that fast I was scared. Really scared. Something awful must be happening. But I didn't know what. It was not knowing that really scared me.*

   1. Struggles
   2. Goal
   3. Conflicts and problems
   4. Sequel and character traits

   Ans: 4. Sequel and character trait. "Just that fast I was scared. Really scared," is a pause to check in with how the main character is thinking and feeling after an action or event. That is a sequel. The last sentence tells readers about the character's fears. That is a character trait.

G. *Sunny Saturday afternoon is not the sort of time you'd expect to get scared—well, certainly not me, anyway.*

   1. Details about the setting and a character trait
   2. Struggles
   3. Goal
   4. Motive and risk and danger

   Ans: 1. Setting detail (Sunny Saturday afternoon) describes the day and time—part of the setting. The rest of the sentence tells readers about one aspect of the character's personality (a character trait).

5. What is the last paragraph of this narrative? *Ans: A final sequel, a check-in with what the main character feels and thinks after the event is over*

6. Think of two ways you could make this narrative stronger. List them below. *Ans: The two best ways to quickly improve this narrative are to, first, include more character traits (name, age, sex, physical characteristics, etc.) so readers can better see and empathize with the main character and, second, expand the description of the risk and danger for the main character. The narrative simply states that the writer was scared because he or she didn't know what was happening. Why and how did that scare this person? What did the character think was happening? What did the character fear might be happening? Other improvements are possible, but those are the two that will have the biggest impact on readers.*

   Discuss the answers to each question with your class and allow students to voice (and try to support) their opinions. This is especially true for Question 6, which allows more room for student creativity and individual ideas.

Activity Review

Personal narratives are ministories. They usually tell about one particular event or moment. However, they are still stories and should be developed as such. Readers care most about the characters and the conflicts, not about the plotting events. Student writers must plan their narratives if they are to include enough character information to successfully engage readers.

Activity 72: The Personal Planning Process _____

What Students Will Learn:

Students will learn the most common problems student writers face when writing personal narratives and the steps essential to planning and structuring a successful personal narrative.

Time Estimate: 50 minutes

Directions:

Personal narratives would seem easier to write than fictional stories because the writer already knows the characters and events. The writer *is* one of the characters and *was there* for the events of the narrative. That knowledge, however, is actually what makes writing personal narratives difficult.

That sounds backwards. But student writers know *everything* about the narrative's characters and they know *everything* about the narrative's events. It's often hard to decide what should be included and what should be left out of the writing.

Student writers tend to leave out too much character information and present only an abbreviated plot summary in their personal narratives. It is important for students to be more methodical, more careful, in their approach to planning a personal narrative than when planning a story. When student writers create a fictional story, they more naturally pause to plan each element. Students tend, however, not to pause and plan their personal narratives because they think they already know what they are going to write.

The Eight Essential Elements
Character
Character traits
Goal
Motive
Conflicts and problems
Risk and danger
Struggles
Details

This activity takes your students through the process of planning a personal narrative. If they develop the habit of considering each of the story elements whenever they write, no matter what they write, they'll find that their writing more consistently delivers an interesting, enjoyable experience for readers.

While students plan the Eight Essential Elements in order, it is not necessary for them to present the resultant information in that order.

For this activity, we'll use the theme **the biggest surprise I ever got was . . .**

As a demonstration of the process, I'll work through each of the steps for a surprise I got when I turned eleven. This demonstration is not on the student worksheet. Use it as a reference for yourself or share it with students before they begin their work on this activity.

Who is this narrative going to be about? This is where pausing to plan really pays off. There is a real choice here. There are usually two choices for the main character I'll have to consider for this type of theme: myself, the writer, and the person who surprised me. To see which will be easiest to write, I'll have to determine which of the Eight Essential Elements I can most clearly and easily present for these two different viewpoints.

To demonstrate, I'll work through the planning steps of this essay twice—first with me as the main character and then with my grandfather (the one who surprised me) as the main character. The following is an example with me as the main character:

1. Character: Who is this narrative going to be about? *Ans: Me, the author*

2. Character traits: What about this character will be important or interesting to include in this narrative? *Ans: My image of and beliefs about Disneyland and my lingering hope for a bike*

3. Goal: What is this character after in this narrative? What is the character trying to do or get? *Ans: Get a new bike for my birthday*

4. Motive: Why is that goal important to this person? *Ans: I don't recall why I wanted that bike, so I won't put that in—or will have to say that I don't remember.*

5. Obstacles: What conflicts and problems are keeping this character from reaching the goal? *Ans: My parents lacked the money to pay for a new bike.*

6. Risk and danger: Is there any risk or danger to the main character if he or she doesn't reach the goal? *Ans. The only risk I can remember is the disappointment of not getting a cherished wish. In the narrative, I'll have to emphasize that one risk.*

7. Struggles: What does the main character do to try to reach the goal? How does the surprise fit in? *Ans: I didn't do much of anything—other than whine and plead for a new bike for a month before my birthday. The events I want to write about were done to me. That's what made it a total surprise. However, if the main character doesn't struggle, he can't face the risk and danger, and the essay will not be very exciting.*

8. Details: What details will you have to include about the scenes, actions and objects in this story to make it vivid? *Ans: I want to include details about my image of Disneyland and our distance from it; about the bike; about the hotel lobby; and about the fireworks.*

Now the same process with my grandfather as the main character.

1. Character: Who is this narrative going to be about? *Ans: My grandfather, Wooch*

2. Character traits: What about this character will be important or interesting to include in this narrative? *Ans: His name, that he lived in Hawaii, and that he was a magician. He loved to do things in real life that seemed magic, to make normal life seem magic. Finally, he is the one for whom I was named.*

3. Goal: What is this character after in this narrative? What is the character trying to do or get? *Ans: Unclear because I (the author) was not privy to the thoughts of main character. It is implied—but only implied— that he wanted to create a magic birthday for me. This could be trouble. Without an identifiable goal for the main character, the story could fall apart.*

4. Motive: Why is that goal important to this person? *Ans: He loved magic and liked the reputation for being the magic man who made magic happen everywhere he went. He also loved his grandson.*

5. Conflicts and problems: What obstacles keep this character from reaching the goal? *Ans: Unclear since it was all a surprise to me. Presumably he spent considerable time and effort to set the whole thing up, but I'm not sure and can't put that in my story. Without clear obstacles, the story will be weaker and less exciting for readers.*

6. Risk and danger: Is there any risk or danger to the main character if he or she doesn't reach the goal? *Ans: Again, unclear since it was all a surprise to me. This, again, is a potential red flag for this version of the narrative. I'll have to tell it from my point of view to gloss over these elements I do not know.*

7. Struggles: What does the main character do to try to reach the goal? How does the surprise fit in?
Ans: Again, unclear. I'll have to focus on the final event and effect and let the reader imagine all he had to do to set it up.

8. Details: What details will I have to include about the scenes, actions and objects in this story to make it vivid? *Ans: I want to include details about Wooch, his clothes, his magic, his gestures and actions; about my reactions and impressions; about the hotel lobby; and about the bike. I won't provide many details about Disneyland since I want to keep the focus on Wooch.*

Conclusion: I don't know enough about what my grandfather wanted, thought, planned, and did to make him the main character. Thus, I will have to be the main character. To try to increase excitement and interest, I'll have to emphasize the wonder of the moment and the sense of being swept away by my grandfather's actions. That will let suspense ("What is the grandfather going to do?") build excitement to make up for a lack of struggles by the main character.

The following is the resulting narrative:

Two months before my eleventh birthday, we moved from Salt Lake City to southern California. I told all my friends that I was going to live next door to Disneyland and go there every afternoon after school. I said I'd be able to see Tomorrowland's Matterhorn Mountain from my bedroom window. We actually moved into a community fifty miles away from the Magic Kingdom and hadn't made one trip since we moved. I was crushed.

For my eleventh birthday I was hoping for a new bike. Bikes with shifter gears were new, and I was hoping to upgrade from my clunker one-speed to a new three-speed. But southern California was expensive compared to Salt Lake City, and my parents had told us to expect thin birthdays. My sister's birthday (in July) consisted of just a couple of small dolls.

So, in September, I braced myself for disappointment but could not extinguish my glimmer of hope. I wished and hoped and told the smog-covered stars above about the new three-speed, delux, Glide-o-matic Schwinn every evening and whined to my parents that I needed that bike each morning.

On the morning of my birthday, my parents told me to get in car. They drove me down a maze of freeways to a hotel and dropped me off at a side door. They told me to wait by the front desk. I heard a loud call, "Moo-ki-wa-hee!!" (It was a greeting call my grandfather made up.) I turned and saw my grandparents from Hawaii sweep into the lobby. Wooch—that was my grandfather's nickname—wore yellow pants and a bright Hawaiian shirt. Wooch was here!

Wooch was a main-stage magician. He could do tricks that dazzled everybody. When he came to visit, all the kids flocked to our house for his magic shows. Wooch loved to make life, itself, seem magic. Every moment was a chance for a show (the bigger the better), and it was hard to tell where life ended and his magic shows began.

Like magic, at Wooch's slightest gesture, the hotel front doors opened, and— bammo!—Disneyland appeared across the street—like magic! Deep down, I knew it had probably been there all along. But at that moment it felt like he had conjured it up with a twitch of his fingers. I swear I didn't remember seeing it as my parents drove me to the hotel.

We hit every ride in the park and many of them more than once. That night, Wooch checked his watch and announced it was time to leave and dragged me quickly back down Disneyland's Main Street. Wooch gestured and fireworks exploded over the castle and over the train station. As the last starburst faded, Mickey Mouse himself stood near the Disneyland firehouse holding a Schwinn three-speed. While everyone watched, he gave it to me. That was the grand surprise I glowed about all winter.

It doesn't get any better than that—my first trip to Disneyland, my grandparents, and a new bike all in same day. Now, forty-five years later, I still remember that day and my grandparents but can't picture the bike anymore. It's odd how what's surprising and important changes over the years.

Have your students work through the same process with the same theme, **the biggest surprise I ever got was . . .**

You should give your students a time limit for both planning and writing this narrative. They will always face time limits on standardized writing assessments.

They should complete their answers to these questions on their worksheet in the allotted time but should not begin writing the narrative, itself, until you signal everyone to do so.

1. Character: Who is this narrative going to be about?
2. Character traits: What about this character will be important or interesting to include in this narrative?
3. Goal: What is this character after in this narrative? What is he or she trying to do or get?
4. Motive: Why is that goal important to this person?
5. Conflicts and problems: What obstacles keep this character from reaching the goal?
6. Risk and danger: Is there any risk or danger to the main character if he or she doesn't reach the goal?
7. Struggles: What does the main character do to try to reach the goal? How does the surprise fit in?
8. Details: What details will I have to include about the scenes, actions, and objects in this story to make it vivid?

Have several students read their answers to each of the eight questions and then their final essay. The class should listen to make sure that the narrative both springs from and is consistent with the information identified in each answer. The author should be asked to explain any discrepancies. Certainly it is permissible—even common—for a narrative to change, to adjust, to grow, as it is being written. However, the author should be able to explain those redirections.

Activity Review

The sequence of questions presented in this activity matches that presented in earlier chapters for creating stories and also that presented earlier in Chapter 4 for creating persuasive essays. Narratives are most effective when developed using the progressions and strategies developed both here and in the book *Write Right!* for creating and developing stories. All narratives depend on the same Eight Essential Elements and on the same relationships between those elements for their success.

SECTION C: EXPOSITORY WRITING TO INFORM

Expository means descriptive or explanatory. *Inform* means to communicate information—news, knowledge, or fact. Thus, an expository writing to inform is a short essay whose purpose is to communicate factual information to the reader.

Most students face informative writing in the form of school reports. That's what reports are—writing to inform.

What's the difference between writing to inform and the other expository forms—writing to persuade and personal narratives? That question is the topic of Activity 73. In Activity 74 students have the chance to locate the Eight Essential Elements in a short informative essay. Activity 75 focuses on a most important decision for informative writers—picking the best main character. Activity 76 looks at potential problems with informative pieces, and Activity 77 takes students through the process of creating, building, and forming an expository essay to inform.

Activity 73: What's New?

What Students Will Learn:

Students will learn the differences and similarities between expository writing to inform and the other expository forms—writing to persuade and personal narratives.

Time Estimate: 30 minutes

Directions:

This introductory activity is divided into two parts. Without preliminary discussion, have your students complete the three questions of Part 1 on their worksheet. Use the answers printed here as a guide to review and discuss their answers before continuing with Part 2.

Part 1

1. What are the differences between writing to inform and the other two expository forms—writing to persuade and personal narratives? *Ans: There are four significant differences that are summarized on the following chart.*

2. Are there any of the Eight Essential Elements that informative essay writers need not develop and present? *Ans: No*

3. Are there any new elements that informative essay writers need to create that persuasive essay writers did not need to create? *Ans: No*

In•form *vt.* To communicate information, news, knowledge, or fact.

In•for•ma•tion *n.* News, knowledge, fact, etc told or communicated.

Comparison of Expository Writing Differences

Area	Persuasive Essay	Informative Essay	Personal Narrative
Struggles (information content)	Rely on reason, using opinions, beliefs, emotional appeal, and fact	Rely on factual information using findings, facts, and research	Character that allows the writer to reveal their research
Theme	Assigned topic	Usually selected by the writer within the more general assigned topic	Assigned topic
Main character	The writer	Any character that allows the writer to present research	*Usually* the writer, but could be another person the writer knows well
Goal	To persuade	To inform, but the main character will have his or her own goal, picked to allow the writer to present their information	Picked for the main character to allow the writer to develop the narrative on the assigned theme

It is valuable to demonstrate what is meant by several of those chart entries.

Struggles (content): Informative writing is research and fact based. Persuasive writing is opinion and reason based.

Theme: While the assigned topic for a persuasive essay usually specifically defines the essay's theme ("School students should wear uniforms. Do you agree, and why?"), assigned topics for an informative essay usually leave room for the student to select a specific theme. For example, if the assigned topic were volcanoes, a student could select either "the distribution of volcanoes around the world" or "the physical shape of the three types of volcanoes" or "underseas volcanoes" or "volcanic ash and gasses" as a specific focus and theme. If the assigned topic were "the history of your family," a student could decide to write about one particular ancestor or about his or her grandparents or about all of the relatives who lived in a particular state.

Part 2

Have students read the ten possible essay themes on their worksheets (also shown in the following list) and decide whether each is a theme that calls for an informative essay or not. If they believe that the stated theme calls for something other than an informative essay, they should write in the blank space which kind of essay that particular theme requires.

1. Tell us the history of your family. *Ans: Yes*
2. Who is your favorite relative and why? *Ans: No. This calls for a personal narrative.*
3. Tell about a day at your school. *Ans: Yes*
4. What do you think the duties of being a citizen should be? *Ans: No. This calls for a persuasive essay.*
5. Write about life in a tide pool. *Ans: Yes*
6. Write about your best birthday. *Ans: No. This calls for a personal narrative.*
7. Explain why you like being an American citizen. *Ans: No. This calls for a personal narrative.*
8. Explain the legal duties of being an American citizen. *Ans: Yes*
9. Write a report on sharks *Ans: Yes*
10. Why do you think we all should like being Americans? *Ans: No. This calls for a persuasive essay.*

Numbers 2, 6, and 7 direct the writer to tell something personal about his or her own beliefs, values, feelings, or attitudes. The writer is not asked to persuade the reader of anything or to provide information of a general nature that will provide knowledge to the reader. Thus, these prompts call for a personal narrative.

Numbers 4 and 10 direct the writer to persuade the reader to adopt a specific view or attitude. Thus, they are persuasive essay prompts.

The remaining five numbers (1, 3, 5, 8, and 9) ask the writer to provide information for the benefit of the reader and are thus prompts calling for informative essays.

Notice how similar numbers 4, 7, 8, and 10 are. The student worksheet asks why and how these four themes are different. *Ans: These four themes address the same topic but ask for different types of information. That makes them, and the essays they call for, different. Numbers 4 and 10 ask the writer to persuade readers to agree with the writer's assessment and, thus, call for persuasive essays. Number 7 asks the writer to communicate personal feelings and opinions. That makes it a personal narrative. Number 8 asks the writer to relay factual information only and is thus an informative essay.*

Activity Review

Informative essays rely on the same elements as do persuasive essays, personal narratives, and stories. Each of these narrative forms is best created and developed using the same strategies and progression. The differences between expository forms lies in what information may be used to fulfill several of the writing elements. However, those differences are minor. The more important lesson is the similarity of each of these expository forms. They all depend on, and are created from, the same Eight Essential Elements we identified as the core structure of stories.

Activity 74: Picking Out the Pieces

What Students Will Learn:

Students will learn to recognize the Eight Essential Elements in an informative essay.

Time Estimate: 25 minutes

Directions:

The student worksheet presents part of an informative essay (shown in the following paragraphs). Have students read this essay and answer the structural questions that follow. After students have completed their work, review and discuss their answers.

An unstoppable sea of sixty million ants flowed like a dense, moving carpet of hungry, meat-eating carnivores through the Peruvian rain forests of South America. Towering trees rose 150 feet to create a lush canopy high overhead. The size of eight football fields, this moving carpet of ants marched at a rate of several hundred feet an hour and scoured the forest floor for food and a new site for their home nest. Even if each ant daily ate only $\frac{1}{100th}$ of an ounce of food, this army would gobble up 37,000 pounds of food each day. In less than a month, this vast horde could strip bare six square miles of the forest.

Every living creature either fled in terror before this great army or died. A lizard mistakenly popped its head out of a hole. It tried to retreat but was instantly swarmed. It tried to eat the ants. But for every one it ate, fifty raced onto its head and body, biting, tearing, stinging. A massively thick cluster of thousands of ants swarmed over the lizard.

Beetles, centipedes, and worms were caught and devoured. A tree squirrel slipped and fell from the safety of overhead branches. Before it could rise to its feet it was covered black with ants. Unable to see, it ran in circles for a few moments before collapsing. In less than two minutes every part of the squirrel was cut up for ant food. Only bones were left. And still it wasn't enough. The colony needed more food.

Effective Details Must Be:

Accurate
Specific

Effective Details Should Be:

Unique
Unusual
Vivid

1. Which of the Eight Essential Elements are included in this essay segment?

   Ans: All eight are stated or strongly implied. Motive is the only implied element. If they don't find more food (their goal) the colony will starve (implied motive).

2. Who is the main character of this essay?

   Ans: The ant colony. Rather than selecting one particular ant for the main character, this essay treats the entire sixty million ants in the colony as a single character to show their cohesive unity.

3. What, in this essay, is the main character's goal?

   Ans: Find a new nest site and more food

4. Are any conflicts or problems mentioned? If so, what are they?

   Ans: Several are mentioned. There is not enough food in the nearby forest. Most animals flee from the ants and can run faster than the ants. The lizard does kill a few ants and is thus a minor conflict.

5. Several individual lines from this essay are repeated below. Choose the writing element (or elements) that best identifies what each is. In addition to the Eight Essential Elements, other important parts of a narrative may be included from which you may select (resolution, sequel, opening, etc.).

A. *The size of eight football fields, this moving carpet of ants marched at a rate of several hundred feet an hour and scoured the forest floor for food and a new site for their home nest.*

   • Character traits

   • Struggles

   • Goal

   • Resolution and final sequel

   Ans: Character traits

B. *Even if each ant daily ate only 1/100th of an ounce of food, this army would gobble up 37,000 pounds of food each day. In less than a month, this vast horde could strip bare six square miles of the forest.*

   • Risk and danger

   • Struggles

   • Goal

   • Conflicts and problems

   Ans: Problem ("strip bare six . . .") and struggles ("Even if each ant daily ate . . .")

C. *. . . this mass of ants scoured the forest for food and a new site for their home nest.*

   • Character traits

   • Struggles

   • Goal

   • Conflict and problems

   Ans: Goal

D. *Every living creature either fled in terror before this great army or died.*

   • Details

   • Struggles

   • Conflicts and problems

   • Motive

   Ans: Problem. This is a part of why the ants need to hunt for food.

E. *In less than two minutes every part of the squirrel was cut up for ant food. Only bones were left. And still it wasn't enough. The colony needed more food.*

   • Motive and goal

   • Struggles and conflict and problem

   • Goal and conflict and problem

   • Conflict and problem and risk and danger

   Ans: Conflict and problem ("It still wasn't enough. The colony . . .") and struggles ("In less than two minutes . . ."). This describes what the ants did and then restates their main problem—a lack of food.

F. *A lizard mistakenly popped its head out of a hole. It tried to retreat but was instantly swarmed. It tried to eat the ants. But for every one it ate, fifty raced onto its head and body, biting, tearing, stinging. A massively thick cluster of thousands of ants swarmed over the lizard.*

- Conflict and problem
- Struggles
- Risk and danger
- Details

Ans: All of the above. Details are provided that describe a conflict (with the lizard), risk and danger (the lizard eats ants), and struggles (what the ants do).

Activity Review

The same Eight Essential Elements that make a story gripping and engaging also serve the same function for informative writing. Those Eight Essential Elements should be created in the same way and in the same order. Each writing element serves the same purpose and function in an informative piece that it does in a story. Expository writing to inform is best thought of as nonfiction stories.

Activity 75: The Main Role

What Students Will Learn:

Students will learn the options for a main character in an informative essay and also the structural implications of their choice.

Time Estimate: 25 minutes

Directions:

An important decision to make when writing an informative essay is the selection of a main character. More options exist for this key element in an informative essay than for a persuasive essay or for a personal narrative. For this activity, we use the following assigned topic: **great white sharks.**

The worksheet tells students to assume that they have information in the following key areas that they want to include in their writing:

Top·ic *n.* The subject of discussion or writing. *Topic* and *theme* are often used interchangeably. However, a topic is assigned for student writing. An essay theme either is the topic or is a more specific subset of the topic.

- The shark's sensory system (sharks have the most advanced sensory system in the world)
- The shark's diet
- The shark's territory (where this shark lives and prowls)
- The shark's life span
- A physical description of great white sharks
- The great white's rows of shark teeth
- How great white sharks attack

Students are told to identify four possible main characters for this essay and to fill in the chart on their worksheet for each of these possible main characters. There are many possible choices for the main character. Eight of the most logical choices are shown in the following list, along with goals and conflicts that will allow the writer to easily include the areas of information listed previously. Certainly, other possible characters and goals are possible.

1. Main character: *Ans: The writer*

   Goal: *Ans: Inform the reader about a day in the life of a shark*

   Motive: *Ans: Grade depends on it*

   Conflicts: *Ans: The writer really faces no conflicts unless he is afraid of sharks or worried about a bad grade.*

   Risk and danger: *Ans: Again, the writer faces no real risk and danger.*

2. Main character: *Ans: A baby shark*

   Goal: *Ans: Grow to adulthood*

   Motive: *Ans: All beings want to survive.*

   Conflicts: *Ans: Other sharks, some whales, and several species of large fish feed on baby sharks.*

   Risk and danger: *Ans: Death—either being eaten while still small, being caught by human fishermen, or starving.*

3. Main character: *Ans: A female adult great white shark*

   Goal: *Ans: Successfully give birth to and rear baby*

Motive: *Ans: Maternal drive*

Conflicts: *Ans: Birthing and nursing take attention away from hunting and make the shark susceptible to attack. Baby sharks have many enemies.*

Risk and danger: *Ans: Loss of food and loss of her baby if she doesn't protect it*

4. Main character: *Ans: A human shark fisherman*

    Goal: *Ans: Catch the biggest great white*

    Motive: *Ans: He who catches the biggest is the best. The biggest shark will bring the best price at the fish market.*

    Conflicts: *Ans: The shark. Shark fishing is always a fight to the finish.*

    Risk and danger: *Ans: The shark could win. That is, the fisherman will fail to catch his shark.*

5. Main character: *Ans: A human marine biologist researcher*

    Goal: *Ans: Learn about life habits and life cycle of the great white shark*

    Motive: *Ans: Save the species from extinction*

    Conflicts: *Ans: Fishermen, pollution, government regulators and legislators, the great white sharks that want to eat the biologist*

    Risk and danger: *Ans: Scientist could fail to protect this species or could die while studying shark behavior up close.*

6. Main character: *Ans: A leopard seal (prime prey for the shark)*

    Goal: *Ans: Avoid being attacked by a great white*

    Motive: *Ans: Survival*

    Conflicts: *Ans: Great whites. Leopard seals are a favorite food of the great white.*

    Risk and danger: *Ans: Great whites are the most efficient hunters in the sea.*

7. Main character: *Ans: A human surfer (who has been bitten by a shark)*

    Goal: *Ans: Board surf without being bitten again*

    Motive: *Ans: Has 137 stitches and spent three months in the hospital after the last attack*

    Conflicts: *Ans: Two are possible: an internal conflict, love of ocean surfing versus a fear of being attacked by a shark, and an external conflict, the shark who wants to attack him.*

    Risk and danger: *Ans: Great whites often mistake the sound and look of a surfer on a board for a large seal.*

8. Main character: *Ans: A pilot fish that swims with the shark*

    Goal: *Ans: Learn to anticipate the actions of the great white*

    Motive: *Ans: Wants to stay close enough to eat the scraps without getting eaten itself*

    Conflicts: *Ans: With this and other sharks and with other pilot fish who might want to follow the same shark*

    Risk and danger: *Ans: A shark will eat a pilot fish if the fish gets too close to the shark's mouth.*

The worksheet then asks students to compare their four choices by answering the following three questions:

1. List the advantages and disadvantages of each of these characters as your main character for this essay.
2. With which character as the main character will the story be easiest for you to write? Why?
3. With which character as the main character will you be best able to include all of the information you are pretending that you have amassed? Why?

Allow several students to read their four potential main characters and to explain which one they would use if they were going to write the essay.

Lead a class discussion on these student answers and decide on appropriateness of each student nomination for main character. What determines appropriateness? Focus the discussion on their final evaluation of each of their possible main characters. Emphasize the variety of possible characters and how the choice of main character determines essay structure and what and how the writer will be able to insert the information he or she have collected.

Activity Review

The selection of a main character is an important decision for informative essay writers. Readers will identify and sympathize with this character. The writer must present the information they have gathered through the eyes and actions of this character. The choice of a main character will, in large part, dictate the shape and content of an informative essay or report.

In general, a student writer has six choices of character for an informative essay—the student writer him- or herself; an individual of the species being studied and reported on; an individual higher up on the ecological, social, or economic ladder (a predator or superior, such as the king or company president); an individual lower on the ecological, social, or economic ladder (a prey species, an employee, or a lower social class); an outside observer; or a scientific researcher who is studying the species the writer is reporting on.

Activity 76: What's Wrong?

What Students Will Learn:

Students will learn to identify typical weaknesses and flaws in family informative essays and strategies for fixing those shortcomings.

Time Estimate: 40 minutes

Directions:

The student worksheet shows four shortened versions of informative expository essays on the theme **the history of my family**. Each is only part of a complete essay.

Without preliminary discussion, students should read the first partial essay and complete the questions that follow. Review and discuss the answers to those questions and students' rewrites of that essay before allowing students to proceed to the other three essays. As a time-saving option, you can have students omit the rewrites of one or more of the last three essays and only answer Questions 1 through 5.

Essay #1

> *Like everybody else, I have sixteen great-great-grandparents. But I only know where four of them were born. One great-great-grandfather and one great-great-grandmother on my mother's side were born in Georgia. One of my father's great-grandfathers was born in New Hampshire. Another was born in upstate New York.*
>
> *I know where seven of my eight great-grandparents were born: two in Georgia, two in California, one in Vermont, one in Michigan, and one in Maryland. Two of my grandparents were born in California and two in Georgia.*

Answer the following follow-up questions:

1. What writing elements are included in this essay? *Ans: A main character is introduced (the writer) and some character history (birthplaces of great-great-grandparents, great-grandparents, and grandparents) is given.*

2. What's wrong with this informative essay? *Ans: The essay provides only historic facts (plot) and omits character traits, goal, motive, obstacles, risk and danger, and most of the necessary details (ancestral birth states are a form of detail). There is no point or purpose to this information (no goal is presented).*

3. What are the strengths of this essay? *Ans: It provides some facts but has no strong qualities and fails to produce reader interest.*

4. What are the weaknesses of this essay? *Ans: It lacks virtually all of the Eight Essential Elements.*

5. What would you do to improve it? *Ans: The writer must state a goal and motive so that the reader will care where these ancestors were born. Readers need more information about the main character and some sense of conflict and risk and danger. Finally, readers need details to visualize the moments and events of this essay—once that essay is created.*

6. The worksheet instructs students to rewrite just the part of this informative essay shown previously using their answers to these questions as a guide to correct its weaknesses while holding on to the strengths. Space is not provided on the worksheet for this writing assignment. Students will need a separate sheet of paper. *Ans: Any rewrite that solves the problems and weaknesses will do. The following is provided as one plausible example:*

When I look in the mirror, I see more than a face. I see history—my family's history. I see places and people who have come before me. To understand my face, I want to know who my ancestors were and where they came from.

Like everybody else, I have sixteen great-great-grandparents. But I only know where four of them were born. One great-great-grandfather and one great-great-grandmother on my mother's side were born in Georgia. One of my father's great-grandfathers was born in New Hampshire. Another was born in upstate New York.

I know where seven of my eight great-grandparents were born: two in Georgia, two in California, one in Vermont, one in Michigan, and one in Maryland. Two of my grandparents were born in California and two in Georgia. So when I look in the mirror, I see America—lots of Georgia and California with a dash of New England.

Essay #2

My great-grandfather, Harvey Butler, went to law school at UC Berkeley, but he wanted to grow corn. So he bought a farm in Antioch, California, and grew corn. He lived there for almost forty years until he died. He never became a lawyer, but he sure must have grown a lot of corn in almost forty years on a farm!

Answer the following follow-up questions:

1. What elements are included in this essay? *Ans: Character, a few character traits, goal (grow corn), and character actions*

2. What's wrong with this informative essay? *Ans: There are no obstacles or conflicts for the main character to contend with and struggle against. There is no risk and danger for the main character. Readers also need motive for the main character's goal and more character information to make Harry Butler interesting.*

3. What are the strengths of this essay? *Ans: In this short paragraph several relevant character traits are presented. That could make the main character interesting if relevant obstacles and struggles were developed.*

4. What are the weaknesses of this essay? *Ans: No motive, no conflict, no risk and danger, no struggles, insufficient details*

5. What would you do to improve it? *Ans: Present motive, conflicts, risks, and struggles surrounding the process of getting and running his corn farm. If none exist, then this may not be a suitable topic for an essay about a family's history. Search elsewhere for an essay topic.*

6. The worksheet instructs students to rewrite just the part of this informative essay shown previously using their answers to the questions as a guide to correct its weaknesses while holding on to the strengths. Space is not provided on the worksheet for this writing assignment. Students will need a separate sheet of paper. *Ans: Any rewrite that solves the problems and weaknesses will do. The following is provided as one plausible example:*

My great-grandfather, Harvey Butler, went to law school at UC Berkeley in 1898 because both his father and grandfather were lawyers. But Harvey wanted to grow corn. He loved to work his hands into dirt and wanted to spend his time producing something worthwhile (rather than arguing law points in court).

One year shy of graduation, he dropped out of school. His parents were furious. His father threatened to disown him. Still, Harvey bought a farm in Antioch, California, and started growing corn. He had always lived in the city and didn't know farming. That first year his hands were covered with blisters, his back ached, and his first crop was wormy and poor. But Harvey was thrilled by every ear he grew.

He lived there for almost forty years until he died. Harvey's father finally visited the farm in 1916 and grudgingly admitted that Harvey grew good corn. Harvey Butler never became a lawyer, but he sure must have grown a lot of corn in almost forty years on a farm!

Essay #3

My grandfather is a magician. He was an army general, but now he does magic shows. He is really good at magic. He wears loud Hawaiian shirts because he lives in Hawaii. He is old because he has already retired from the army and has been a magician for as long as I can remember. I like it when he does his magic tricks for us. He has never made a house or an airplane disappear, but he is really good with cards, ropes, and metal rings.

Answer the following follow-up questions:

1. What elements are included in this essay? *Ans: Character and character traits*

2. What's wrong with this informative essay? *Ans: It lacks details. No scene or event can be vividly pictured by readers. It also fails to clearly identify the main character and includes no goal, motive, obstacles, or struggles.*

3. What are the strengths of this essay? *Ans: It presents the makings of an interesting character.*

4. What are the weaknesses of this essay? *Ans: Main character is not clearly identified (could be either the grandfather or the writer). There is no stated or implied goal or motive, conflicts, risk and danger, or struggles. The piece desperately lacks details of all kinds.*

5. What would you do to improve it? *Ans: Specify the main character, state a goal and motive, and create obstacles, risks, and struggles. Then vivid details would be added that would make the images and scenes come alive for a reader.*

6. The worksheet instructs students to rewrite just the part of this informative essay shown previously using their answers to the questions as a guide to correct its weaknesses while holding on to the strengths. Space is not provided on the worksheet for this writing assignment. Students will need a separate sheet of paper. *Ans: Any rewrite that solves the problems and weaknesses will do. The following is provided as one plausible example:*

My grandfather is a magician. He was an army general, but now he does magic shows. He is really good at magic. He wears loud Hawaiian shirts because he lives in Hawaii. He is old and has already retired from the army and has been a magician for as long as I can remember. I like it when he does his magic tricks for us. He has never made a house or an airplane disappear, but he is really good with cards, ropes, and metal rings.

Every time he visits I hound him to put on a big show and perform some new amazing trick that's never been seen before. Mostly he just laughs and says, "I'd like to see that, myself."

But this one year he said, "All right. I'll try to saw someone in half. I've never done it before, but I might as well give it a try." We roared our approval. And then he picked me as his victim.

My eyes grew big and I began to shake. He made me lie down in a box and he nailed the lid on so just my head and feet stuck out. I whimpered, "This is just a trick, right? This is just a trick, right?"

Then he pulled out a chain saw and fired it up, saying that a lot of magicians used hand saws but that looked like too much work to him. I screamed and cried, and they tell me I fainted dead away. . . . And I never did find out if he sawed me in half or not.

Essay #4

> *My family used to go camping every summer for our vacation. My mother always hated it and called the campground bathrooms Fort Repulsive. Our dog, Shep, always loved it and said that the smells in the mountains were much better than down in smoggy Los Angeles.*
>
> *One year my sister, Cathy, decided to bring her pet parakeet camping with us. Shep said that, since he was out in the wilds and in the mountain air, he felt like catching his own dinner and said, "I'm going to eat that noisy bird tonight!"*

Answer the following follow-up questions:

1. What elements are included in this essay? *Ans: Good character first impression for mother and dog, goal and motive for the dog, implied risk and danger (eating a person's pet is bound to cause trouble)*

2. What's wrong with this informative essay? *Ans: Informative essays are supposed to present factual, truthful information. In reality, dogs do not say things nor do they clearly express their feelings and desires.*

3. What are the strengths of this essay? *Ans: It presents interesting characters and an interesting situation.*

4. What are the weaknesses of this essay? *Ans: It's not factual or real. Dogs don't talk in nonfiction writing.*

5. What would you do to improve it? *Ans: Remove the quote and paraphrases for the dog. Replace them with the writer's impressions of the intent and desire of the dog. Let the writer say what the dog seemed to want to do from the writer's viewpoint.*

6. The worksheet instructs students to rewrite just the part of this informative essay shown previously using their answers to the questions as a guide to correct its weaknesses while holding on to the strengths. Space is not provided on the worksheet for this writing assignment. Students will need a separate sheet of paper. *Ans: Any rewrite that solves the problems and weaknesses will do. The following is provided as one plausible example:*

> *My family used to go camping every summer for our vacation. My mother always hated it ands called the campground bathrooms Fort Repulsive. Our dog, Shep, loved the mountains and especially the mountain air. He'd stand still on top of some big rock with his nose held high and savor the smells, as if he found mountain air much better than air down in smoggy Los Angeles.*
>
> *One year my sister, Cathy, decided to bring her pet parakeet camping with us. In hindsight, I think it must have been the fresh, wild mountain air that got to Shep. Since he was now in the wild, breathing wild smells, it seemed that he figured he ought to act like a wild dog and hunt his own dinner. That's when he turned and stared at my sister's parakeet.*

Activity Review

The process for building successful informative essays is exactly the same as that for building effective stories or personal narratives. Each of these narrative forms depends on the same eight elements for its successful creation.

First identify the main character and develop the character traits that will make that character interesting to readers. Then, present that character's goal and motive and the obstacles and risk and danger that stand in the character's path. Then, lay out the events of the narrative you want to tell and find the details that will make key moments and scenes rich and vivid in readers' minds.

Activity 77: The Informed Process _____

What Students Will Learn:

Students will learn an effective process for creating and structuring informative essays.

Time Estimate: 10 minutes to plan, 30 minutes to write

Directions:

This activity will take students through the process of creating effective expository writing to inform. For this activity, we use the topic **a day in the life of my school.**

For timed writing assessments, students should allocate approximately 15% of the available time for their planning process. This allows students enough time to plan the essay and still leaves them plenty of time to write. After your students have worked through this process with this assigned topic, you might want to repeat the process with a different topic and give them a time limit for both their planning and for their writing, commensurate with the time they will be allotted on standardized assessments.

Create First; Write Second
- When you *create*, create the Eight Essential Elements.
- When you *write*, write the details.

Guide your class through the first two steps of this process. Then let them sketch out the next ten steps (Steps 3 through 12) on their own. Pause to review the process and clear up any questions before allowing students to actually write (Step 13). This need not be a lengthy process and is often accomplished in three or four minutes for a timed writing assessment.

1. Specify theme. What *specifically* do you want to write about? This theme should be in the form of a statement. Have students propose potential themes within the assigned general topic. Write them on the board and allow the class to briefly debate the appropriateness of each as well as the ease of writing about that particular theme.

Have the class vote for the two they think will be easiest to write. Keep track of the vote totals for each proposed theme and keep the top two vote-getters on the board, erasing all others. Tell your students that they will each write an informative essay using one of these two themes.

2. List blocks of information. Informative essays depend on factual information. Through class discussion, list on the board the major blocks of, and types of, information they want to include under each of the two finalist themes. The class should then debate which types of information will be easy or difficult to locate and write under each theme.

Students should now pick the theme that they think they can write about most easily and effectively. The student worksheet has spaces for them to include this information.

Students should now proceed on their own with their chosen theme. However, you may guide them through a demonstration of the planning process using the sample information provided in the following steps.

3. Define the main character. In Activity 75, we explored the process of evaluating alternative main characters for an informative essay. Each student should decide who their main character will be: the principal, a teacher, one of the school staff, a parent, themselves as a student at the school, or some other relevant individual.

Example:

For this example we will use the principal as the main character. We will also have to select a theme. Again, for this example, our theme will be "a day at my school is like a cattle stampede with the principal trying to manage students and staff as they thunder through the activities each day."

Information we will want to place in the essay includes the frantic pace of paper-work and scheduling in the office, the flow of supplies and food into the school through-out the day, the number of parents wanting to have conferences, the problems that crop up (air conditioning, refrigerator, and sound system breakdowns, discipline, etc.), and the variety of student activities during the day.

4. List important, relevant character traits. Students should now list several character traits about the main character that are relevant to topic and theme.

Example:

The principal is Mrs. Taylor, in her first year as principal. She used to teach creative writing at college before becoming a principal and thus has placed great emphasis on the school writing program.

5. Define the main character's goal. Student writers should now pick a goal for their main character that will allow them to easily include the major blocks of information they want to work into the essay.

Example:

Here are two possible goals for Mrs. Taylor on this day (many others are possible):

1. Go to the dentist to repair a chipped tooth

2. Restructure the school schedule to allow more time for student writing

Either would work well. If we picked the first, the constant flow of disruptions and de-mands on her time would keep her from ever getting to the dentist. She would leave school at night still with her toothache. If we picked the second, we would watch Mrs. Taylor struggle to free up her time and then struggle to create more writing time in the school schedule. Readers will thus understand the complexity of the daily school schedule.

6. Define motive. The stronger a character's defined motives are for achieving the goal, the better the final writing product will be and the easier the writing will be. It is always worthwhile to spend time understanding the motives of a main character.

Example:

For the first goal listed, her motive will be a severe toothache. Pain is always a strong motivator.

For the second goal, her motive might be that this school had low writing scores last year, and Mrs. Taylor was brought into this school specifically to raise writing scores.

7. List potential problems and conflicts. Characters need problems and conflicts to have a reason to act. What characters do will give the writer opportunities to include the desired information. Con-flicts give characters a reason to act, or do. Students should list as many as they can. They probably won't use all that they list, but it is far better to have too many conflicts and problems and to then pick the ones that best serve the writer's needs than to have too few.

Example:

If the first goal for Mrs. Taylor is used, her every moment will be filled with an endless string of demands for her immediate attention: bus duty, a missing computer, a parent complaint meeting, student discipline problems, a problem with the lunch supply deliv-ery, short staff because of staff sickness, lunch duty, a principals' phone conference, two state mandatory reports, a fire alarm test, a behavioral complaint from a school bus driver, lack of buses for a scheduled field trip, and so on.

If the second goal is used, these distractions would constantly pull her away from her planning time for the revised school schedule, which would prove to be far more difficult than she had imagined as she struggles to work around mandatory blocks of instruction and regular pullouts—PE, music, computer class, library, field trips, assemblies, and so on.

8. List the associated risk and danger. Problems have little impact on readers if readers don't clearly see that the characters face real risk or danger if they don't successfully resolve the problem. Dangers need not be physical. Emotional, social, financial, or mental dangers work just as well.

Example:

Mrs. Taylor is a new principal and needs the school to run smoothly. Lacking experience in her job, she must deal with each problem as it arises for fear that it will escalate into a major problem that will affect her performance rating.

9. Block out the events of the essay. Now it's time to sketch out the flow of events in this essay. Writers will pick events that allow them to present the factual information they have gathered while they develop their characters and conflicts.

Example:

It will be easier and more effective to organize this essay chronologically, tracking the principal's activities throughout the day. While she tries to take care of her chosen goal, we will have Mrs. Taylor deal with two absent bus drivers, one missing volunteer crossing guard, an administrative and support complaint from one team of teachers, the district computer support person who is late getting to the school, a missing school computer, several discipline problems, several parents who demand meetings with her about the appropriateness of several library books, a broken air conditioner in the multipurpose room, and two district reports that must be completed today.

10. Define the needed details. This will be a short essay. Not every scene and every character needs to be developed and presented to readers in rich and compelling detail. It is worthwhile for writers to list the moments, events, places, and characters that they want readers to picture most clearly and for whom they therefore want to develop vivid details.

Example:

Most of this essay will take place in the school office and in the principal's office. We'll need to make those places vividly clear to readers. We will also want to paint an image of the school's exterior at the beginning of the writing. Finally, we'll certainly need to describe Mrs. Taylor.

11. Pick a resolution. As is true for stories, informative essays need to end with resolution of the main character's goal. As is true for persuasive essays, informative essays also should end with the writer assuming that they have successfully achieved their goal of informing the reader.

Example:

Since this essay will follow chronologically through the day, we will end it at 8:00 P.M. as Mrs. Taylor struggles out to her car with an armful of books and papers to lug home. She's exhausted, and (if the first goal is picked) her chipped tooth still aches and is still untreated. If the second goal is picked, she will have only worked out two days of her new weekly schedule. The last line will be "It was just another average day at school," to reinforce the chosen theme and to show that this wasn't a uniquely bad day.

12. Choose an opening. Activities 56 and 68 presented alternative strategies for creating effective openings for stories and expository writing.

Example:

Because we decided to organize the essay chronologically, we will start with Mrs. Taylor arriving at school before sunrise and will immediately introduce her goal. Creating an early distraction will allow us to introduce the chosen theme. That will also give us a chance to describe the school.

13. Write it! The twelve previous steps will fix in the mind of the writer a solid and vivid image of what they want to say in this essay. The writing can now flow quickly and efficiently from these notes that form an effective essay outline.

Index

About the Author

The only West Point graduate to turn professional storyteller, Kendall Haven holds a doctorate in oceanography and has performed for 4 million people in forty-four states. He has published five audio tapes and twenty books, including more than 300 original stories, plus his breakthrough instructional books on narrative creation, writing, and telling. Haven has won more than twenty awards for his story writing and storytelling, has twice been designated an American Library Association "Notable Recording Artist," and is the only storyteller in the United States with three entries in the American Library Association's Best of the Best for Children.